Sacred Places and Profane Spaces

SACRED PLACES AND PROFANE SPACES

ESSAYS IN THE GEOGRAPHICS OF JUDAISM, CHRISTIANITY, AND ISLAM

EDITED BY

Jamie Scott & Paul Simpson-Housley

CONTRIBUTIONS TO THE STUDY OF RELIGION,
NUMBER 30
Henry Warner Bowden,
Series Editor

Greenwood Press
NEW YORK • WESTPORT, CONNECTICUT • LONDON

Library of Congress Cataloging-in-Publication Data

Sacred places and profane spaces : essays in the geographics of
   Judaism, Christianity, and Islam / edited by Jamie Scott and Paul
   Simpson-Housley.
        p.   cm. — (Contributions to the study of religion, ISSN
   0196-7053 : no. 30)
     Includes bibliographical references and index.
     ISBN 0–313–26329–9 (alk. paper)
     1. Sacred space—Comparative studies. 2. Judaism—Doctrines.
   3. Christianity. 4. Islam—Doctrines. I. Scott, Jamie S.
   II. Simpson-Housley, Paul. III. Series.
   BL580.S23   1991
   291.3′5—dc20   90–19896

British Library Cataloguing in Publication Data is available.

Library of Congress Catalog Card Number: 90–19896
ISBN: 0–313–26329–9

First published in 1991

Greenwood Press, 88 Post Road West, Westport, CT 06881
An imprint of Greenwood Publishing Group, Inc.

Printed in the United States of America

The paper used in this book complies with the
Permanent Paper Standard issued by the National
Information Standards Organization (Z39.48-1984).

10 9 8 7 6 5 4 3 2 1

Contents

Acknowledgments

The editors would like to thank the Faculty of Arts, York University, Canada, for financial assistance which made possible the preparation of this volume.

Series Foreword

There is no single method which scholars use to study religions. Some concentrate on textual analysis, while others focus on areas such as theology, worship, or institutional structures. Most studies of religion combine these topics, however, along with many others, and approaches to understanding them bring several methods to bear at the same time. This volume is an excellent example of how religion scholars are constantly alert to new ways of considering materials from interdisciplinary angles of vision. The authors of these essays range from specialists with international reputations to younger writers who have already begun to fulfill the promise others see in them. Their collective contribution presents an attractive synthesis of perspectives drawn from the history of religions, high-lighting the central concept of sacred space. The volume enhances and makes more sophisticated a tradition that traces its origins back to Mircea Eliade.

These essays are arranged to furnish balanced emphasis on Judaism, Christianity, and Islam. All three versions of "Religions of the Book" receive equal time, and each subdivision contains genuinely interesting topics. Some subjects have long been recognized as centrally important, while others bring new phenomena to light. Though individual topics are quite widespread, indicating a healthy diversity of interests among the authors, these essays center on broad considerations of religion and politics, with attention paid to the influence of shrines and holy places in that context. As readers will soon discover, these pieces of original research shed new light on themes like pilgrimages, temples, apocalyptic thought, differing religious experience among men and women, orientations in space and time, and the problems of trying to live up to religious principles in modern societies, whether these are dominated by a secular ideology or a conflicting set of confessional ones. These explorations of the dynamics between sacred centers and human religiosity are informative in their separate orientations and mutually supportive of continuing attempts to capitalize on interdisciplinary creativity. They will attract general readers, delight specialists, and have a strong impact on all students of human cultures.

Henry Warner Bowden
Series Editor

Introduction: The Geographics of Religion

Jamie S. Scott and Paul Simpson-Housley

Theologians and scholars of religion are used to discussing Judaism, Christianity, and Islam in terms of the temporal dimension. The God of the Hebrew Scriptures, the New Testament, and the Qur'an exercises his divine mercy and judgment in history. In fact, it has often been assumed that the historicity of the Religions of the Book is the crucial factor in differentiating them from Hindu, Buddhist, Taoist, Shinto, and other manifestations of *homo religiosus*. Perhaps because the study of religion seems in large part to be an invention of the Western, primarily Christian, academy, a God who acts definitively in history is often represented as distinctly preferable to, if not a notable evolutionary advance over, the mythical myriad of arbitrary divinities populating the Eastern religious landscape. This personal God lovingly works his creation towards some final purpose, while the impersonal karmic forces of the East subject not only humankind, but the gods themselves, to an endless round of suffering, life after life.

In recent years, however, the comparative study of religion, which in its early days served all too frequently as a means of establishing the superiority of Western monotheism, has begun to approach the study of Western traditions with the sort of scholarly objectivity brought so clinically to bear upon Eastern traditions. In terms both of matter and of method, this turn of events has led many scholars to moderate their preoccupation with the temporal dimension of the Religions of the Book. The spatial dimension of Judaism, Christianity, and Islam has become a more central object of critical inquiry. The God who acts in history occupies certain locales, works out his purpose in the effects of climatic phenomena upon the human environment, and inspires those who believe in his justice and mercy to visions of a world transformed at the end of time. Geography is the academic discipline which concerns itself with issues of spatial relations. As a major branch of geography, human geography addresses spatial phenomena having to do with human interactions with their environment. The human geographer has traditionally studied such topics as industrial locations, urban morphology, cultural landscapes, and economic, social, and political regions. The study of religion has not been a major domain of human geography, even though the manifestations of religious experience express themselves with spatial variety on the landscape.

Such considerations about the traditional identities of religious and geographical studies invite further reflection on the relationship between these disciplines. This book is thus an interdisciplinary project in the study of religion and geography. As a preliminary step, we may schematize this interdisciplinary study into three broad areas of inquiry. The first of these areas has to do with the literal role of particular places, regions, or geographical phenomena in the development of the religious self-understanding of Judaism, Christianity, or Islam, or of a particular community within one of these traditions. On the more literal plane, typical foci include the contrasting roles of such topoi as city and wilderness, river valley and mountain, in the life and thought of a religious community. In another vein, Jewish, Christian, and Moslem histories tell and retell the effects upon the community of such geographical phenomena as floods, earthquakes, whirlwinds, and famine. At the same time, an inquiry into any one of these geographical topics will involve the inquirer in more theoretical questions. Such questions might take a methodological turn, revolving around similarities and differences between a more theological and philosophical approach to the study of religion and geography, and a more social scientific approach. Alternatively, such questions might lead to the conclusion that the more literal study of the geographical dimensions of a religious tradition inevitably embroils the scholar in epistemological and ontological issues having to do with the kinds of truth claim made by the practitioners of that religion.

Second, therefore, we may speak of the symbolic role of particular places, regions, or geographical phenomena in the development of religious self-understanding. To give an obvious instance, the physical city of Jerusalem is a place of peculiar significance for Jews, Christians, and Muslims, but the practitioners of each of these faiths will give very different reasons for the special place Jerusalem holds in their hearts. These differences have to do with the distinct, if often overlapping and competing, histories of political engagement and theological interpretation which make Judaism, Christianity, and Islam separate yet related traditions. When we speak of a symbolic dimension of religion and geography, therefore, we are referring to the way the literal geographical dimension leads to, or even presumes, various sorts of interpretation.

In turn, this issue of interpretation leads us to a third area of inquiry of interest to the interdisciplinary scholar of religion and geography. This dimension has to do with the geography of prophetic and apocalyptic visions, and the role of the geographical imagination in the development of religious self-understanding. Here, we discover the more speculative dialectics between the geography of the prophetic and apocalyptic imagination and the geography of the natural and the historical. The eschatological world of this imagination is rich in geographical features. This world recapitulates the literal landscape in the vivid and sometimes terrifying colors of the end of time.

The nine chapters constituting the body of *Sacred Places and Profane Spaces* were solicited from established and rising scholars with this threefold schematization in mind. The first section of the book considers the geographical dimensions of Judaism. Yossi Katz shows how Jewish law has influenced the spatial layout and structure of the first Jewish quarters built outside the Old City of Jerusalem in the 1860s and 1870s. He also analyzes the impact of Jewish law on the first agricultural settlements established during the same period. By contrast, Roger Friedland and Richard Hecht examine the political and religious controversies surrounding access to the Temple Mount/*al-haram al-sharif* in Jerusalem. If traditional scholarship opposes Jewish and Palestinian interests, this chapter reveals the far more complex state of affairs which results from political and religious conflicts within the two communities. The third chapter in the section on Judaism addresses the visionary world of the Jewish geographical imagination. Martha Himmelfarb investigates some of the theological implications arising out of the association of the Garden of Eden with the Temple in the works of Ezekiel, the Book of the Watchers, and the Wisdom of ben Sira.

The second section of the book turns to Christianity. Ronald Bordessa considers Lutheranism the dominant social reality of Finland. The Lutheran stress on the importance of the individual, and the derogation of icons in Finnish Lutheranism, find expression in designed environments which preserve woodland and rock outcrops, thus allowing nature to articulate God's will directly to every individual soul. In a different vein, Ellen Ross illustrates the variety of ways in which women in the Christian tradition have used spatial discourse to express their faith. Ross advances six models as heuristic devices to explore how women draw upon geographical categories, both physical and metaphorical, to locate themselves in relationship to God. The third chapter in this section maps the apocalyptic world of the Revelation to St. John. Leonard Thompson argues that spatially oriented elements must be considered alongside temporal elements in the study of apocalyptic literature. An apocalypse envisages space insofar as a supernatural world is involved, whereas its temporal aspects find expression in terms of eschatological salvation.

Three chapters on the geographical dimensions of Islam round out the body of the book. Focusing on Iran, Michael Fischer considers Shi'ite Muslim feasting and pilgrimage circuits in relation to similar Zoroastrian religious activities. Fischer argues that on the Iranian plateau the intertwining of Muslim and Zoroastrian symbols and rituals serves to provide rural communities with their sacred identity. In the second chapter in the section on Islam, Juan Campo discusses aspects of Islamic pilgrimage in modern Egypt. Adopting a sociological stance, Campo identifies and analyzes the ways in which three distinct, yet politically interrelated social groups entertain three distinct attitudes to the Hajj. The final chapter in this section argues that although God is not restricted to a single place, certain locales are singled out for their religious significance. Annemarie Schimmel identifies ways in which Muslims assign special religious importance to certain geographical phenomena. In particular, Schimmel draws upon collections of mystical poetry to demonstrate how the geographical imagination venerates the sacred places of Islam.

Sacred Places and Profane Spaces closes with a constructive essay, "Afterword: The Geographics of Religion in a Postmodern Environment." We have coined the term "geographics" to describe the three distinct, yet interrelated spatial dimensions implicated in the study of religion. As we shall see, the chapters presented here fall broadly into these three areas. At the same time, however, it is important to realize that the literal and symbolic dimensions of inquiry we have schematized inevitably overlap. It is scarcely possible to discuss the literal function of geographical phenomena in Judaism, Christianity, and Islam without being drawn to certain interpretive conclusions, be they philosophical and theological, or social scientific. In fact, such interpretive syncretism may even embrace the third dimension of the geographical imagination. The themes and images of mystical and apocalyptic writings are almost always rooted in recognizable geographical realities, and couched within identifiable interpretive frameworks. It is also important to recognize that this sort of interpretive syncretism may make nonsense out of the simple opposition between the sacred and the profane traditionally advanced by scholars in the comparative study of religion. It is not unusual to hear the term "space" opposed to the term "place" in terms of a distinction between sacralized and secularized geography. With deliberate ambiguity, therefore, we prefer to speak of sacred places and profane spaces, rather than of sacred spaces and profane places. Bearing these caveats in mind, this volume offers one study devoted to each of the three dimensions in Judaism, Christianity, and Islam. Each chapter discusses the relationship between the discourse of the spatial and the discourse of the sacred, both in Scripture and in subsequent literary and theological reflection upon scriptural themes. The variety of topics and the variety of approaches adopted in these chapters reflect an unusual concern with the interpretive ambiguities which arise out of the economic, social, and political functions assigned to places of particular significance in the life and thought of a religious tradition or community.

PART I

JUDAISM

The Jewish Religion and Spatial and Communal Organization: The Implementation of Jewish Religious Law in the Building of Urban Neighborhoods and Jewish Agricultural Settlements in Palestine at the Close of the Nineteenth Century

Yossi Katz

Jewish religion has expressed itself spatially in manifold and varied spheres. A perusal of the Torah itself reveals a number of commandments with a distinctly spatial dimension. For example, one encounters the commandment to conquer the land of Israel and settle it with the Jewish people,[1] the commandment to erect the Temple at a site of God's choosing,[2] the Jewish obligation to reach the Temple at least three times a year,[3] and the commandments related to agricultural labor in the land of Israel, such as the prohibition on working the land during the sabbatical year (the commandment of *shmita*).[4]

The Jewish halakhic (religious-legal) literature, commencing with the Mishnah, and continuing with the Talmud, the decisions of Maimonides, the Codes of Jewish Law, and the Responsa literature cover many topics with a spatial bearing. This derives from the fact that halakhic literature addresses all spheres of life, since the Jewish religion which is governed by *Halakha* demands from its believers not only faith but concrete actions, including many actions with a spatial expression. Thus the *Halakha* addresses the subject of the boundaries of the land of Israel.[5] Other commandments which have a distinct geographic significance are those connected with Sabbath observance such as the prohibition on journeying or riding on the Sabbath or walking over a thousand meters outside a settled region in any direction.[6] The *Halakha* also defines what is a city and a village according to its conception, for there are commandments which specifically apply either to the city or to the village.[7] The *Halakha* determines the distances governing land usage if such usage occasions a disturbance to city residents (tanneries, cemeteries, for example) and deals with relations between neighbors, property rights, and so on.[8]

One can justifiably contend that an Orthodox Jewish community which conducts its life according to the Jewish *Halakha* will adhere, even in the modern era, to the religious commands with a spatial import. Such a community will of course take account of the differences over time as decreed by the authorized rabbinical authorities. Relying on this premise, the research whose findings are detailed below will attempt to examine how Jewish religious law influenced the contours of the spatial and organizational structure of the first Jewish neighborhoods erected during the 1860s and 1870s outside the walls of the Old City of Jerusalem. Similarly it will explore the influence of Jewish religious law upon the shaping of the spatial and organizational structure of the Jewish agricultural settlements which were also established during this period. The Jewish communities engaged in the building of these neighborhoods and the establishment of the settlements were homogeneously Orthodox in the full sense of the word.[9] It was therefore almost plausible that on all relevant matters concerning the construction of neighborhoods and settlements and their organization there would be proper regard for the Jewish *Halakha* in those instances where the *Halakha* could be brought to bear on the issue.

THE HISTORICAL BACKGROUND BEHIND THE ESTABLISHMENT OF THE NEIGHBORHOODS AND SETTLEMENTS

During the course of the first half of the nineteenth century, a tremendous increase occurred in the size of the Jewish population in old Jerusalem because of a huge surge of immigration to Palestine from Eastern Europe. The fact that the steamships began at that time to call on the Mediterranean ports, enabled the Jews in the Orthodox centers of Eastern Europe to fulfill their dream and the religious commandment to emigrate to the land of Israel with greater facility. The vast majority of the immigrants settled in Jerusalem with its concentration of Jewish holy places including the centerpiece, the Western Wall—the sole remnant of the second Temple. A second source for the increased Jewish population was provided by the migration of Jews from the cities of Safad and Tiberias in the Galilee, following the earthquake which struck the Galilee in 1837 and caused vast devastation. In the year 1860, the Jewish population of Jerusalem reached about 8,000 out of a total population of 18,000, in comparison with the year 1800, in which their number totaled only 2,000 out of a population of 8,750. Almost the entire Jewish population was concentrated in the Jewish Quarter of the Old City, whose total area did not exceed 850 dunams. The growth in the

Jewish population led to a huge increase in the population density of the Quarter, with all the negative repercussions tied to overcrowding such as deficient sanitary conditions and diseases. This hope of alleviating the conditions of overcrowding was one of the primary motivations which fueled the aspirations of the Jewish population to build new Jewish neighborhoods outside the walls of the Old City, and move into an area that prior to the middle of the nineteenth century was totally desolate. Construction of these neighborhoods began in the 1860s and 1870s, and they constituted the nucleus for Jerusalem outside the ancient city walls. The primary initiative for the building came, as stated, from the inhabitants of Jerusalem. Nonetheless, there were also initiatives from Jewish philanthropic bodies abroad who wished to assist the Jewish community in Jerusalem. Neighborhoods were 100 percent Jewish. Some of the neighborhoods were mixed in that they encompassed different Jewish communities; some were confined to specific communities. A few were even organized according to the population of the country of origin. What they all had in common, at least until the 1890s, was that their population was homogeneously Orthodox in every sense.[10]

The first Jewish agricultural settlements were established at the end of the 1870s and the start of the 1880s. Some were started by Ashkenazic Jews from Jerusalem and Safad, with a view towards expanding the Jewish sources of income and existence and providing substance to the ideological aspiration for productivization. Hitherto, the Jews who belonged to the Ashkenazic communities in Jerusalem and the Galilee had subsisted on the contributions from their brethren who had remained abroad. They were engaged for most of the day in Torah study. For the Jewish community in Palestine, this created a condition of dependency on Jews residing abroad which influenced all spheres of life. During the 1870s, the Jewish community was expected to manage its own affairs without outside interference and to concern itself with, among other things, earning its own way. This was the background behind the decision of the Jews of Jerusalem and the Galilee to turn towards agricultural work. But there was an additional reason explaining the vocational penchant of Jerusalem's Jews for agricultural work, and it was directly connected with our topic. They were inspired by the religious aspiration of fulfilling the religious commandments connected with the land of Israel. These commandments could be fulfilled and religious completion was obtainable only if one worked the soil of the land of Israel. Among other things, these commandments entailed the law obliging a person to leave part of the crop in the field for the poor, and a commandment to set aside or destroy a percentage of the crop before it would be permissible to eat the remainder (at the time when the Temple existed, this quantity was given over to the Priests, the Levites, and the poor). Similarly another commandment proclaimed that one had to abstain from working the land one year out of seven.[11]

Another segment of Jewish agricultural settlement was established by Zionist immigrants who began arriving in the country at the start of the 1880s. The backdrop to their arrival was the pogroms against the Jews of Eastern Europe and the concomitant awakening of National Zionism. The aspiration of these immigrants, who were also strictly Orthodox, was to establish agricultural settlements and engage in farming, thus fulfilling the Zionist ideology of returning to the land and inverting the Jewish occupational structure from trade and finance to agriculture.

Settlements were established near the city of Jaffa, south of Haifa, and in the Upper Galilee. In the period under discussion, each settlement (*moshava*) comprised some tens of families and was conducted by an elected *moshava* committee that also dealt with public matters. The settlements received large-scale assistance from Baron Rothschild, who enlisted himself in their assistance after they had fallen into a severe economic crisis shortly following their establishment—a crisis which jeopardized their very existence. Towards the end of the nineteenth century and at the start of the twentieth, a nonreligious population began to penetrate the settlements, which of course influenced the life-style and character of the settlements.[12]

JEWISH RELIGIOUS LAW AND THE CONSTRUCTION OF THE JEWISH NEIGHBORHOODS IN JERUSALEM

Jewish religious law found expression in a number of spheres, both in the construction and the organization of the neighborhood. First of all, there were the public edifices designed to service communal commandments prescribed by Jewish religious law: a synagogue and a ritual bath. The ritual bath primarily served women who had completed their menstrual cycle. According to Jewish religious law, every woman must immerse herself in the ritual bath a week after the conclusion of her monthly menstrual cycle. If she has not immersed herself, she cannot have sexual relations with her husband.[13] Additionally the ritual bath served as a place for immersion of men. Although, according to Jewish religious law, after the destruction of the Temple there was no obligation upon men to immerse themselves in the bath, Jewish custom called for immersing and purifying oneself at least before Sabbaths and festivals. Many religious Jews were accustomed to immerse themselves in the ritual bath every day.

Jewish religious law was embodied not only in the physical construction of the building requisite to the provision of these neighborhood religious functions. It found expression even in the building details such as the location of the houses, the house plans, and ecological and environmental issues, and we will immediately cite examples to corroborate this. The location of a synagogue in a neighborhood was determined according to Jewish religious law, which stipulates that "one may build a synagogue only at the summit of a city."[14] The concept "summit of a city" is not clearly defined in the original, and we are left with ambiguity as to whether Jewish religious law intended that a synagogue should be built in the highest place in the city or that the synagogue should be the highest structure in the city. Most of the commentators do not accept either of these possible explanations and explain the concept "the summit of the city" as the central location of the city from a functional standpoint. In other words, the location of the synagogue should be in the functional, not the geometric, center of the city neighborhood or community.[15] This was justified not only by the symbolic aspect but by the functional aspect as well. This vindicated the implicit assumption that a synagogue would most conveniently serve a maximum population if it were situated in the functional center. Indeed, the application of this law can be discerned in neighborhood construction, for the synagogues were placed in the functional center of the neighborhood (and not in the highest place in the neighborhood) and the synagogue was not even the tallest structure in the neighborhood. This center encompassed the three primary public functions of the neighborhood: the ritual bath, the stove and the water cistern which adjoined each other, and the synagogue. The public bath implements were connected to the ritual bath, for the houses contained no indoor plumbing and washing facilities. The water cistern where rainwater was gathered served as the neighborhood's source of water for both drinking and bathing. Water was drawn by the inhabitants of the neighborhood directly from the water pits. The baking stove was also central to all inhabitants of the neighborhood because household stoves were uncommon.[16]

Another religious law which found expression in the planning of a house was the commandment prohibiting the building of a window in one of the walls of the house, if through it a member of the household could gaze directly into the house of a neighbor, or even into his courtyard. If the window did not face the private property of the neighbor, one could build a window. Likewise, if there was an intervening public domain (for example, a street) between the two private domains, one could build a window even if he could look out from it onto the courtyard or house of his neighbor. These commandments stem from another fundamental commandment which deals with the concept of "visual damage," that is, damage in every sense of the word, which one is therefore enjoined from committing. Such damage is incurred when a person can gaze into the house or courtyard of another.[17] The damage that is caused does not express itself solely as an infringement upon privacy, but also by the possibility that it effectively contacts the areas of the affected house. The owner must presumably concentrate his activities, or at least some of them, in that portion of the house which escapes scrutiny from his neighbor's house. If in any case one can gaze into the private domain from the public domain, then the neighbor is allowed to build a window facing that same private domain from the public domain. The neighbor is allowed to build a window facing that same private domain, since the owner is in no wise injured by the public domain, and this is therefore not considered visual damage.[18] It emerges that these commandments were also fully implemented in the construction of the neighborhoods and the windows were simply not built in a way that one could look out from one private domain onto another but only through a window that faced the public domain.[19]

Ecological subjects which are addressed in Jewish law also found their expression in the building process. For example, it was prohibited to make noise even in one's own house, if this was a deviant noise which could bother the neighbors.[20] Likewise, it was prohibited to cause smoke in any manner that could harm the other inhabitants. One could not open up a barn in a house or courtyard because of the foreseeable ecological damage. The positioning of building materials in the public domain as well as any other tenant requirement was prohibited as a potential public nuisance. These matters were explicitly dealt with by Jewish religious law, which determined that even if the nearest neighbors consented to the existence of this ecological blight, this was in no wise tantamount to permitting or allowing the existence of such a blight.[21] Together with the aforesaid, it was explicitly determined in the bylaws of the neighborhoods that noise caused by the study of the Torah, whether it emanated from a school or from a private house, could not be deemed a blight.[22]

The inhabitants were obligated to maintain not only the cleanliness of their house, but the cleanliness of that part of the public domain adjacent to their houses as well as the cleanliness of the common public facilities.[23] These matters were also based on the injunction of the Torah, "And your camp shall be holy."[24] Another environmental subject was the planning of gardens within the center of the neighborhood. Indeed, Jewish religious law does not mandate the planting of gardens in a place of residence, but with regard to Jerusalem there is an explicit commandment that prohibits the planting of gardens in Jerusalem because of the city's holiness. The founders of the new Jerusalem neighborhoods, and those heading them, were aware of this law and of the problematic situation which it created. The prospects for planting gardens in the neighborhood and thus enhancing the quality of neighborhood life while creating conditions that were the very opposite to those which had existed within the walls of the Old City appeared jeopardized. In the end, the community leaders relied on a different religious law, which determined that the prohibition on planting, as well as the prohibition on raising chickens, for reasons of holiness, had been valid only at the time when the Temple existed.[25]

Regarding matters of organization, Jewish religious law is expressed in various ways. First of all, each neighborhood had a committee that dealt with all public affairs and enjoyed broad authority and sweeping powers. Among other things the community could evict people who did not meet their payments for the construction of their houses or who caused disputes between other neighbors. Let us emphasize that it was possible to evict people even thought they already had made some of the payments.[26] The authority was also derived from Jewish religious law, a fact which one can deduce from the compendia of neighborhood laws, which among other things determined the laws of behavior in the neighborhood and governed relations between the inhabitants. With regard to the source of a neighborhood council's authority, local ordinances referred to the rabbinic decree which rules that if members of the city had accepted upon themselves a group of people to head and lead them, then those people, with a view towards preserving order and the well-regulated city, had the right to inflict even a monetary loss upon one of the city's members.[27] An additional ordinance decreed that a dispute or suit by one of the tenants had to be adjudicated before a Jewish court and the tenant or the neighborhood council was enjoined from turning to a secular court (the Turkish court).[28] This ordinance was also rooted in Jewish law, which prohibited a Jew from addressing a secular court and permitted him to petition a Jewish court, for only the latter court adjudicated on the basis of the laws of the Torah.[29]

As religiously observant people, the founders and leaders of the neighborhoods decided that, in addition to the synagogue and ritual bath which were mandatory for the observance of basic commandments, other communal institutions which also emanated from a religious life-style should be constructed in the neighborhood. These institutions included a Talmud Torah, a school for elementary education which taught exclusively religious subjects; *Bikur Cholim* (visiting the sick), an organ whose purpose was to assist the infirm and their families in all that was needed; a free loan fund for the needy and their families; and the building of houses to be set aside especially for hospitality. The study of the Torah, aiding the sick, and hospitality are commandments to which Judaism attaches special importance, and therefore it was self-evident that the communal institutions associated with them had to be in place from the time the neighborhood was populated.[30]

Another organizational matter which was determined by Jewish religious law dealt with the order of settling in the neighborhood. This was performed in two stages. During the first stage, a lottery was conducted among all the future tenants for the houses whose construction was to be completed during that year. The winners of the lottery lived in houses which they obtained on a temporary basis until the construction of all the houses in the neighborhood was completed. Upon completion of construction of all the houses, an additional lottery took place which determined the permanent house of each tenant. Until the conduct of the second lottery and the determination of the permanent homes, those living in the apartment were prohibited from making any alterations or additions to the apartment whereas these were permitted after the second lottery.[31] The source for the prohibition to make changes after the first lottery is found in the Laws of Partnership in Jewish law which determine that, in the event of a partnership, no partner is permitted to do anything to partnership property without the knowledge of the second partner. This prohibition also applied if one of the partners performed something unknown to his fellow partner, and when subsequently the fact became known to his partner, the latter remained silent and seemingly gave tacit consent to the action of the first. Even in such a case the actions of the first partner are null and void and he must restore the status quo ante.[32] According to Jewish law, the legal status of a person living in an apartment after the first lottery has the status of a partner together with all the other persons who have not yet received apartments. Therefore it is prohibited to make any changes or additions to the house. In contradistinction, after the second lottery, the tenant resides in a house which is exclusively his own and therefore he can make alterations and additions as he deems fit.[33]

From the 1890s onwards, a less observant population began penetrating the neighborhood and the centrality of Jewish law to neighborhood life diminished. In contradistinction, beginning in the 1960s we can observe a renewed and accelerated process of neighborhood construction, where the neighborhoods are populated exclusively by the ultra-Orthodox. Some of the subjects raised above, and especially the erection of public and communal institutions which are required by a Jewish life-style, also characterized these neighborhoods. One can recognize in these neighborhoods an effort to ensconce Jewish religious law in daily life (such as the prohibition on vehicular traffic in the neighborhood on the Sabbath, obligating visitors from outside the neighborhood to walk about in modest dress, and other sundry examples). However, this topic exceeds the scope of our discussion.

RELIGION AND THE OBSERVANCES OF JEWISH RELIGIOUS LAW IN THE AGRICULTURAL SETTLEMENTS

Upon their establishment and in the initial period following their inception the entire population of the agricultural settlements was, as mentioned, a religious population. Therefore religion occupied a central place in the lives of these settlements. The very mode of agricultural settlement was predicated on nuclear settlements and not upon separate family farms, and this choice was partially due to religious reasons. Consider, for example, the combined religious obligation to pray in a synagogue with a quorum of no less than ten males over the age of thirteen, the prohibition of riding on the Sabbath, the prohibition of venturing outside a settled area on the Sabbath beyond one thousand meters, the need to seek rabbinic counsel on various matters, decisions rooted in religious law regarding religious questions, and the woman's obligation to immerse herself. All these factors, taken together with the fact that we are dealing with the pre-motor age in Palestine, mitigated against a framework based on separate farms and dictated frameworks based on nuclear settlements, that is, villages. Indeed in the period of our discussion (and in fact afterwards as well), one cannot find any Jewish farms in Palestine, and the isolated attempts to establish farms ended in failure.

As was the case with urban neighborhoods, the settlements were established and managed according to a set of laws legislated by those who initiated the establishment of the settlements. One of the first and most fundamental of the ordinances determined that the settlements had to be conducted according to the laws of the Torah, and the farmers were commanded to observe all commandments of the Torah in their day-to-day life.[34] Indeed, this ordinance determined that one should appoint a rabbi for the settlement who would handle all religious affairs.[35] An additional ordinance determined that one should appoint a rabbi for the settlement who would handle all religious affairs.[36] This ordinance was also observed in its entirety. However, it emerges that even in subsequent periods, when the entire population of the settlement was no longer Orthodox, the post of settlement rabbi remained. Generally, the rabbi served as the ritual slaughterer too, as well as the circumciser, and this was his *raison-d'être* in the *moshava* even in periods subsequent to the era of our discussion, when the settlements had already experienced processes of secularization. In the settlements, the requisite religious institutions, such as the synagogue and ritual bath, communal functions which a religious life-style mandated, were established. In addition, among other things, a religious school for children and a hospitality house were erected, and according to the ordinances, settlers were permitted to sue a Jew only before a Jewish religious court, not in a civil court.[37]

Like neighborhoods, settlements were managed by a committee which derived its power and authority from Jewish religious law. By virtue of this authority, as in the case of the neighborhood committees, this committee could evict a settler from the settlement if he behaved in defiance of the ordinances. Eviction procedures could be carried out even in the event that they would inflict severe economic damage on the settler.[38] Land use that would constitute an ecological blight for the *moshava* in its entirety or to the adjacent neighborhoods was prohibited, even if such use took place on private property. This ordinance too is based on Jewish religious law.[39]

THE OBSERVANCE OF COMMANDMENTS DEPENDENT ON THE LAND IN THE MOSHAVOT: THE PROBLEM OF THE SABBATICAL YEAR

It is therefore possible to discern a great deal of similarity between the place occupied by Jewish religious law in the construction of urban neighborhoods and the analogous place of Jewish religious law in the establishment and development of the rural settlements. However, one topic was unique to the agricultural *moshavot* and should be dealt with in detail. The subject concerns the observances of religious commandments connected with agriculture and which are termed in halakhic literature "commandments on the land." The commandments were mandatory primarily within the boundaries of Israel, not outside it. The desire to observe the commandments "dependent on the land" and to reach religious completion was, as we have seen, one of the actual reasons for the shift towards agricultural settlement. In the settlement ordinances, it was specifically noted that "the members of the settlement were obligated to observe all the commandments dependent on the land."[40]

There are five groups of commandments connected to agricultural labor, and the area of applicability and obligation is basically limited to the land of Israel. These groups are: *shmita* (the sabbatical year), tithes and offerings, gifts to the poor, laws of hybrids, and *orla* (immature trees). The laws concerning the sabbatical year postulate that once in seven years a Jew is prohibited from working the land for an entire year. All forms of work are prohibited, including care for existing vegetation, sowing, planting, irrigation, and fertilizing. Those species which grow spontaneously during that year are not considered the property of the field owner, and anyone interested can enter the field and eat them. Tithes and offerings are a set percentage of the agricultural yield which at the time of the Temple were given over directly by the field owner to the Priests, Levites, and the poor people. According to religious law, it is prohibited to eat from the crop before tithes and offerings have been set aside. In contradistinction to many laws that lapsed with the destruction of the Temple, the obligation to set aside tithes and offerings continued to exist even after its destruction. Indeed even today, according to Jewish religious law, there is an obligation to set aside a specific amount of each species before one can eat the crop. The quantity set aside is destroyed. Gifts to the poor entail a series of commandments that obligate the field owner to set aside in his field a part of the crop for poor people. The poor are invited to the field to take for themselves what has been set aside from the crop. Likewise, the field owner has to leave one-sixtieth of the crop during the reaping or picking so that the poor people can take it. He has to leave wheat or fruit that fall from the scythe during reaping, or from the hand during picking. Likewise, the field owner is prohibited from returning and gathering grain or fruit which he has forgotten to remove from the field. He must leave it in the field for the poor. Another commandment determines that crops that grow separately and not in clusters must also be left for the poor. Hybrid law constitutes a prohibition to sow together two different species of seeds (wheat with barley, for example), or to graft two types of trees (an almond and a plumb, for example). The *orla* commandment determines that a Jew cannot eat the fruit of trees during the initial three years of the planting. In the fourth year, at the time when the Temple existed, an additional commandment was observed. The owner would bring the fruit of the tree to Jerusalem and eat it there in a state of holiness. After the destruction of the Temple, the Jew must redeem the fruits of the fourth year monetarily (they are considered sacred) for a certain sum, and this money must be destroyed. Let us note that whereas the commandments of the sabbatical year, offerings and tithes, hybridization of seeds, and the redemption of the fourth year are applicable only in the land of Israel, gifts to the poor, hybridization of trees, and the prohibition on eating fruit before the fourth year are applicable outside Israel as well.[41]

All the commandments connected with agricultural labor were obligatory upon the Jews in the agricultural settlements (in Israel's religious kibbutzim and *moshavot*, these laws are observed to this day). While the observance of most of these agriculturally related commandments did not occasion any special difficulties, the same could not be said regarding observance of the sabbatical year. This observance encountered more severe obstacles because it involved the total cessation of every form of work on the land for the period of an entire year, with all its huge implicit economic damage. This was especially true if we consider that the agricultural areas were quite young, and failure to cultivate them for a year could produce irreversible damage. This problem led to a clear clash not only between religious law and economics, but between religious law and the national vision of agricultural labor. Observance of the sabbatical year command would have led inevitably to an abandonment of the land by a farmer not only during the sabbatical year, but even during the following year, given the inability to rehabilitate the damages from the sabbatical year. The rabbis in Palestine and in the Diaspora were requested by the farmers in the settlements to furnish a legal opinion. Did one have to observe all the strictures of the sabbatical year command, or could one find at least a temporary solution within the framework of religious law which would permit cultivation during the sabbatical year? The rabbis were divided in their opinions. Some decided unambiguously that one had to observe the sabbatical year with all its strictures, without any compromises and without any considerations for the economic results or the repercussions on the Jewish settlement project in Palestine. Their principal contention was that the sabbatical year was a clear and explicit commandment in the Torah for which one could not grant any easements. They suggested the organization of special monetary appeals in order to solve the economic problem of the farmers during the sabbatical year.[42] Other rabbis sought to find various permits which would allow cultivation under certain conditions. All these permits, which in any case were given only on a temporary basis, and were never considered a permit in principle, rested on a common base: the fictitious sale of the land to non-Jews (generally to Arabs). In such a manner, the land was not in practice under Jewish ownership, and the obligation of maintaining the sabbatical year did not apply. However, additional conditions were imposed on the farmers. They had to sell the crops to non-Jews (in a fictitious sale), and to perform only certain tasks, while employing non-Jews for agricultural labor. The sale had to be fixed for a determined time so that it would be a limited sale (a quasi-tenancy).[43] The last condition was required in order to get around another item of religious law that prohibited the sale of real estate, and anything tied to that real estate, to a non-Jew in the land of Israel.[44] In practice, this posed a difficult question for those seeking to grant a permit. On the one hand, one could not permit labor on the land during the sabbatical year without selling to a non-Jew. On the other hand, the sale of land to a non-Jew in the land of Israel was also prohibited by the Torah. The sole solution discovered was to sell land for a limited time. In other words, land was put under tenancy or rented, even though this too was quite problematic, because religious law also prohibited the renting of land to a non-Jew in the land of Israel.[45] The problem of renting to a non-Jew was not explicitly stated in the Torah, but was merely a decree of the Talmudic sages, who feared that a person renting his land would in the end sell it. This provided a legal opening for rabbis to issue the permit and to assent thereby to the working of the land during the sabbatical year.[46] Farmers were divided among themselves between those who relied on this permit and those who accepted the decision of the stricter rabbis and totally refrained from working their land during the sabbatical year.[47]

JEWISH RELIGIOUS AND SPATIAL AND COMMUNAL ORGANIZATION IN PALESTINE FROM THE BEGINNING OF THE TWENTIETH CENTURY UNTIL THE PRESENT

Although this study makes no pretense of venturing beyond the nineteenth century, it emerges nonetheless that the influence of Jewish religious law upon spatial and communal organization, in both the urban as well as in the agricultural settlement setting, was not a passing phenomenon. The influence exerted by Jewish religious law persists to this day in those neighborhoods or agricultural settlements whose entire population is Orthodox and particularly ultra-Orthodox. It must be emphasized, however, that observance of Jewish religious law in urban neighborhoods or agricultural settlements was considered the natural order of things, as the entire Jewish population was Orthodox. The present situation is different. Due to the fact that since the close of the nineteenth century the majority of the Jewish population is non-Orthodox and totally nonobservant, the religious neighborhoods and the religious agricultural settlements now afford the possibility for maintaining a robust religious framework and a life-style which will not be molested by the nonreligious surroundings.[48] Let us briefly sketch the influence of religious law on the spatial and communal organization of town and countryside during the last generations.

During the period of the British Mandatory Government in Palestine (1918–48), a number of associations were founded in Jerusalem whose membership was Orthodox and which endeavored to "establish a Hebrew neighborhood in the environs of Jerusalem which would be governed by the oral and written law."[49] These associations stipulated, inter alia, in their ordinances that each resident of the neighborhood would be legally bound to a clause that "a member may not rent or transfer his apartment to someone who does not comport himself according to the written and oral law."[50] In other words, private and communal life would be regulated by Jewish religious law. The residents had to obey the neighborhood committees, who drew their authority from various Jewish religious laws connected with governing a community. The committees were obliged to construct the entire range of religious institutions in the neighborhood.[51]

Following the establishment of the State of Israel, and especially during the past twenty to twenty-five years, many neighborhoods in Jerusalem and elsewhere have been established containing thousands of homes whose population is homogeneously ultra-Orthodox. Due to their size, these neighborhoods have been termed townlets (*krayot*). They are governed by committees which exercise sweeping authority derived from Jewish religious law. The committees are entrusted with drawing up special ordinances for their neighborhoods. (This was in contrast to the nonreligious neighborhoods which arose at the same time, where neither neighborhood committees nor ordinances existed, and residents were solely obliged to observe the laws of the municipality.) The ordinances governing neighborhoods arising in recent decades stipulate that "the right of residence in the neighborhood is restricted to someone who personally observes Torah and the religious commandments."[52] Other ordinances enjoin the neighborhood's residents to adhere strictly to the laws of modesty, to be diligent about setting aside time for Torah study, and to assist one another. All these are fundamental commandments of Jewish religious law. One way of providing concrete expression to the ordinance on mutual assistance has been establishment in these neighborhoods of voluntary associations which engage in providing interest-free loans and lend out various items gratis. Both the items and the basic capital of the loan funds are gathered from the neighborhood's residents. Prominent features of the aforesaid neighborhoods are the numerous synagogues and other religious institutions, such as yeshivas, Talmud Torahs, and religious schools and kindergartens. The siting and size of the synagogues is most noticeable. On the Sabbath, when travel is prohibited by Jewish religious law, the neighborhood is closed to vehicular traffic.

Proposals have been raised in recent years to base the ordinances of the religious communal settlements in Judea and Samaria (which are to all practical purposes suburbs), upon Jewish religious law also.[53] This has not been put into effect, and the ordinances are still based on the general law. However, the acceptance committees of these settlements will only accept religious residents, and the latter obligate themselves not to sell or rent their houses to someone who is not religious.

The influence of Jewish religious law on the spatial and communal organizations of religious agricultural settlement is apparent in many spheres. The avowed purpose of the religious agricultural settlements (kibbutzim and *moshavot*) which were established in Palestine from the 1920s onwards was to create "a new type of life-style in The Land, a rejuvenated and verdant life of Torah, a life befitting a laboring people, rooted to the soil of its homeland—in short, the creation of a society of religious workers in Israel," predicated on "the imposition of a Torah regime and a sound social order throughout the land."[54]

The religious settlements sought to establish themselves adjacent to each other because of the inability of a solitary settlement to shoulder the burden of the cultural and educational institutions unique to a religious community. There was an explicitly stated apprehension that an isolated religious settlement submerged in a sea of nonreligious settlements could not survive spiritually in its secular surroundings. This led to the formation of a unique settlement model—blocs of religious settlements, which survive to this day.[55]

The "commandments dependant on the land" which we noted above are observed in the religious agricultural settlements, and this applies to the sabbatical year as well. Most of the settlements have solved the problem of work during the sabbatical year by a fictitious sale of the land to non-Jews.[56] Nevertheless a small portion of the religious settlements have not adopted this solution, and they do not work their lands at all during the sabbatical year. Growing hydroponic species and employing the settlement population in recreational enterprises during that year offer a partial solution to the income problem during the sabbatical year.[57]

From time to time the religious settlements encounter difficulties in operating an agricultural farm according to Jewish religious law. The rabbis generally manage to find a solution within the framework of Jewish religious law. A thorny problem, which was only partially resolved at the beginning, was that of milking on the Sabbath. In principle, milking on the Sabbath should be prohibited by Jewish religious law, since it constitutes labor and the Jew is forbidden to labor on the Sabbath. The problem was resolved in the 1950s with the introduction of electronic milking machines. The machines are turned on prior to the Sabbath and operate automatically (rather than manually), which is permissible according to Jewish religious law.[58]

SUMMARY AND CONCLUSIONS

Jewish religious law was a central factor in the establishment and development of neighborhoods in Jerusalem and Jewish agricultural settlements towards the close of the nineteenth century. The Orthodox religious character of the populations in both the neighborhoods and the settlements underscored the obligation to implement relevant Jewish law that dealt with the construction of residential areas, and the management and organization of the community that dwelt there. Likewise, a deeply perceived commitment existed to fulfill the commandments connected with agricultural labor in the land of Israel to which Jewish religious law addresses itself extensively. It seems that in the period of our discussion, the religious laws dealing with various geographic settlement matters were implemented for the first time in many generations. Over many generations the Jewish people had not of its own initiative engaged in either building living quarters or in agricultural labor in the land of Israel. The Jewish religious law rooted in the Pentateuch, the Mishnah, and Talmud, while addressing itself to the new contemporary conditions, expresses the fundamental values of Jewish culture. These are enunciated in the various spheres of life which encompass the Orthodox Jew's mode of life, and they found concrete expression in the realm of spatial organization during the process of constructing neighborhoods in Jerusalem and the early settlements. A distinctive Jewish settlement organizational setting was created, which differed from what the Moslem or Christian communities produced, and from the subsequent creations of non-Orthodox Jewish communities whose life-style was not colored in the main by an obligation towards religious law. The Jewish settlement organizational setting created in Palestine towards the end of the nineteenth century was not a passing episode, and one can still encounter it, especially in ultra-Orthodox communities (particularly in Jerusalem) and in religious settlements in the State of Israel.

NOTES

1. See, for example, The Book of Numbers 33:50–55.
2. See, for example, The Book of Exodus 24:8.
3. Exodus 23:17.
4. See, for example, The Book of Leviticus 25:1–7.

5. Chaim Bar Daroma, *V'Zeh Gvul Ha-Aretz* [*These Are the Boundaries of the Land*] (Jerusalem: Beer Publications, 1958), which deals extensively with the subject.

6. See, for example, Yehoshua Neuwirt, *Shmirat Shabbat K'Hilchata* [*Sabbath Observance According to All its Laws*] (Jerusalem: Beth Medrash Halakha Moriah, 1979), especially pp. 189, 339, 373, 377.

7. *The Mishnah: Tractate Megillah* I:1–3. See also the entry on city (Ir) in *The Talmudic Encyclopedia.*

8. *The Mishnah: Tractate Baba Batra* II:1–5, 7–12.

9. Yehoshua Ben-Arieh, "Legislative and Cultural Factors in the Development of Jerusalem 1800–1914," in D. H. K. Amiram and Y. Ben-Arieh, eds., *Geography in Israel* (Jerusalem: n.p., 1976), pp. 90–105.

10. The growth of the Jewish community within the city walls, the factors leading to the establishment of the Jewish neighborhoods outside the wall, and the process of their development are summarized extensively in Yehoshua Ben-Arieh, *Jerusalem in the 19th Century—the Old City* (Jerusalem: n.p., 1984), and *Jerusalem in the 19th Century— Emergence of the New City* (Jerusalem: n.p., 1986).

11. Mordechai Eliav, *Eretz Ysrael v'Yishuva b'Meah Ha-Tsha Esreh* [*The Land of Israel and Its Settlement in the 19th Century*] (Jerusalem: n.p., 1978), pp. 92–139, 167–178; Chaim Peles, "The Attitude of the Old Community to Settlements in the Land of Israel during the 19th Century," *Zion* 41:3 (1976): 148–58; Yisrael Bartel, "Settlement Plans from the Second Voyage of Montefiore to the Land of Israel, 1939," *Shalem* 2 (1976): 231–96; and Yehoshua Kaniel, "The Controversy Between Petal-Tiqva and Rishon Lezion Concerning Primacy of Settlement and its Historical Significance," *Cathedra* 9 (1978): 26–53, especially 42–45.

12. Kaniel, "The Controversy," ibid.; Ron Aaronsohn, "Stages in the Development of the Settlements of the First Aliyah," in Mordechai Eliav, ed., *Sefer Aliyah Rishona* [*The First Aliyah*] (Jerusalem: n.p., 1989), 1:25–84.

13. See the entries on menstrual cycle (*Nida*) and ritual bath (*Mikveh*) in *The Talmudic Encyclopedia; Code of Jewish Law, Yoreh Deah*, Part II, "Laws concerning Menstruation" and "Laws of Ritual Baths," chs. 183–99, 200–1.

14. *Code of Jewish Law, Orach Chaim, Laws of Synagogues*, ch. 150, par. 1; and Moses Maimonides, *Laws of Prayer*, ch. 2, par. 2.

15. Y. Gotthold, *Veshahanti Btoham* [*I Shall Dwell in Them*] (Jerusalem: n.p., 1977), p. 20; Yosef Shillhav, "Principles for the Location of Synagogues: Symbolism and Functionalism in a Spatial Context," *Professional Geographer* 35 (1983): 324–29.

16. Yossi Katz, "Principles in the Construction of Jewish Neighborhoods Outside the Old City of Jerusalem in the Years 1860–1914," in *Mehkarim Bageografiyah Yishivit-Historit Shel Erets Ysrael* [*Studies in the Settlements Historical Geography of Palestine*], 2 vols. (Jerusalem: n.p., 1991).

17. *Code of Jewish Law, Hoshen Mishpat*, "Laws Concerning Damages to Neighbors," ch. 154, par. 3.

18. Ibid.

19. Katz, "Principles of Construction," ibid.; *Code for the Meah Shearim Neighborhood* (Jerusalem: n.p., 1889), ch. 5, par. 3. The Meah Shearim neighborhood was the fifth to be built outside the walls of the Old City, and its founders worked up detailed codes to govern ways of life in the neighborhood and its management. These codes, which were copied by other neighborhoods, are based in their totality on sources of Jewish religious law.

20. *Meah Shearim Code*, ch. 4, par. 1.

21. Ibid., pars. 1, 3.

22. Ibid., par. 4.

23. Ibid., par. 6, pars. 2, 3, 4.

24. The Book of Deuteronomy 23:15.

25. *Meah Shearim Code*, ch. 1, par. 3, n. 2.

26. Ibid., ch. 1, pars. 5, 6.

27. *Code of Jewish Law, Hoshen Mishpat*, "Laws of Judges," ch. 2, par. 1, especially the comments by Moses Isserlish and the "Turei Zahav."

28. *Meah Shearim Code*, ch. 6, par. 8.

29. *Code of Jewish Law, Hoshen Mishpat*, "Laws of Judges," ch. 26.

30. *Meah Shearim Code*, chs. 8, 9, 10, 11, 12.

31. See the *Code Book for the Neighborhood "Even Yisrael" and "Mishkenot Yisrael"* in the Jerusalem Municipal Archives.

32. *Code of Jewish Law, Hoshen Mishpat*, "Laws of Partnerships," chs. 176–82.

33. *Code Book for the Neighborhood "Even Yisrael" and "Miskenot Yisrael"*.

34. See, for example, *Codes of Jewish Law for the Settlement of Rishon Lezion*, in Eliav, ed., *First Aliyah*, 2:35–38.

35. Yehoshua Kaniel, "The Old Community and the New Settlement," and Yosef Salmon, "The Bilu Movement," in Eliav, ed., *First Aliyah*, 1:269–88, 136–37.

36. *Code for Rishon Lezion*, in Aharon Freiman, *Sefer Hayovel Lkorot HaMoshava Rishon Letsion* (Jerusalem: n.p., 1907), pp. 3)–9, and especially Ordinance #37.

37. Ibid.

38. Ibid., Ordinance #44.

39. Ibid., Ordinance #33.

40. Ibid., Ordinance #36.

41. Regarding "Commandments Dependent on the Land," see Hayim Shevel, ed., *Sefer Hahinuh [The Book of Elucidation]* (Jerusalem: n.p., 1961); the entry on "Commandments Dependent on the Land" (*Mitsvot Hatluyot Baarets*) in *The Talmudic Encyclopedia*; Yehile Tukochinski, "An Abridgement of the Laws Governing the Land of Israel," in Shlomo Ganzfreid, *Kitsur Shulhan Aruh [The Abridged Code of Jewish Law]* (Jerusalem: n.p., 1977); and Kalman Kahana, *Mitzvot Haarets [Commandments of the Land]* (Tel-Aviv: n.p., 1979).

42. Yehoshua Kaniel, *Continuity and Change: Old Yishuv and New Yishuv During the First and Second Aliyah* (Jerusalem: n.p., 1981), pp. 129–34; Ben-Zion Dinburg, *Hibat Tsion* (Tel-Aviv: n.p., 1934), pp. 214–26; and Kaniel, *The Old Community*.

43. Yehiel Tukochinski, *Sefer Hashmita [The Book of the Sabbatical Year]* (Jerusalem: n.p., 1958), pp. 59–66.

44. *The Babylonian Talmud: Tractate Abodah Zarah*, par. 12b.

45. Tukochinski, *Sabbatical Year*, p. 61.

46. Ibid., pp. 60–61.

47. Ibid. See also note 42 above.

48. On this topic, see Y. Shillhav, "Religious Influence in Cultural Space: 'Haredi' Jerusalem," *City and Region* 19–20 (1989): 28–51.

49. "Ordinances of the 'Kyryat Shmuel' Neighborhood Association, Jerusalem 1930," in B. Kluger, *Yerushalayim Shehunot Savid Lah [Jerusalem Is Surrounded by Neighborhoods]* (Jerusalem: n.p., 1979), pp. 276–77.

50. Ibid.

51. Ibid., and "The Ordinances of the Bayit Vagan Association," in Kluger, *Yerushalayim*, p. 205; and M. Hazani, *Bain Ha-Ktzavut [Between the Extremes]* (Tel-Aviv: n.p., 1982), pp. 18–21.

52. See, for example, "Ordinances of Kiryat Sanz in Jerusalem," in Kluger, *Yerushalayim*, p. 77.

53. N. Tyler, "The Settlement's Secretariat and Its Practices," in *Tehumim: A Compendium of Jewish Religious Law, No. 9* (Jerusalem: Alon Shvut, 1988).

54. M. Hazani, "The Religious Settlement in the Land of Israel," in *BiNetiv Ha-Hagshama [On the Path to Fulfillment]* (Jerusalem: n.p., 1950), pp. 166–67.

55. The Hapoel Hamizrahi Organization in the Land of Israel, *The Executive Committee Report to the Eighth Congress* (Tel-Aviv: n.p., 1942), p. 124; *Sefer Yisrael Ha-Datit [Religious Israel]* (Tel-Aviv: n.p., 1954), p. 166.

56. For a copy of the formal deed of property sale, see *Tehumim: A Compendium of Jewish Religious Law, No. 7* (Jerusalem: Alon Shvut, 1986), p. 27.

57. *Religious Israel*, pp. 178–79. This practice has been adopted by Kibbutz Hafez Hayim, which belongs to the Poalei Agudat Yisrael Movement, as opposed to the kibbutzim of "Ha-Kibbutz Ha-Dati," which are affiliated with the Mizrahi Movement, and which rely on the rabbinical dispensation allowing for the fictitious sale of land during the sabbatical year.

58. H. J. Peles, *"The Religious Settlement Movement in Palestine in the 1920s–1930s,"* doctoral dissertation, Hebrew University, 1986, pp. 203–7.

2

The Politics of Sacred Place: Jerusalem's Temple Mount/*al-haram al-sharif*

Roger Friedland and Richard D. Hecht

Oct. 29, 1938: Arriving at the Wall this morning for the first time—after an intermission of two weeks—I discovered to my sorrow that the Wall was brutally desecrated. Bits of stone were chopped off. The marauders lit a fire and succeeded in blackening the face of the Wall with soot. The congregation was very upset. . . . Accompanied by the British sergeant and constable, I visited the rooms where we store the sacred vessels and discovered they have all been burned and destroyed: Torah scrolls, washbasin, bookshelves, more than two hundred prayerbooks and Psalms. . . .

Isaac Victor Orenstein,
Diary of the Western Wall (Jerusalem, 1951)[1]

. . . The active widespread propaganda undertaken by the Jews with a view to influencing the London Government and other powers as well as the League of Nations in order to take possession of the Western Wall of the Mosque at Aqsa, called al-Burak, or to raise claims over the place. . . . Having realized by bitter experience the unlimited greedy aspirations of the Jews in this respect, Moslems believe that the Jews' aim is to take possession of the Mosque of al-Aqsa gradually on the pretense that it is the temple, by starting with the Western Wall of this place, which is an inseparable part of the Mosque of al-Aqsa. . . .

Hajji Amin al-Husayni,
"Memorandum to the Shaw Commission 1930"[2]

These two texts reflect the claims and counterclaims of two religious traditions in the same sacred location in Jerusalem. The Jews refer to this wall and platform within the Old City of Jerusalem as the *kotel ha-ma'aravi,* "the Western Wall," and *har ha-hayit,* "the Temple Mount," while the Muslims call them *al-buraq,* referring to the Prophet's magical steed tethered to this wall, and *al-haram al-shariff,* "the Noble Sanctuary."

For Jews, the Temple Mount is the place where Abraham bound his son Isaac for sacrifice, where David and Solomon constructed the first Temple, where the second Temple was reconstructed after the Babylonian Exile, later expanded by Herod the Great, and finally destroyed by the Romans in 70 C.E. The sacrificial ritual of the Temple maintained the order of the cosmos and bound heaven and earth. Even though the Temple was destroyed and Jews were pushed from Jerusalem, they maintained mental citizenship in this city. They built its sanctity into the structure of their prayers, in the rituals marking life's transitions, in the architecture of their synagogues, in their vision of the messianic endtime, and eventually into the center of their nationalist movement.

For Muslims, the *haram al-sharif* was identified after the Muslim conquest of Palestine as the destination of Muhammad's *isra',* or "flight," from the Qur'an's *al-masjid al-haram* in Mecca to *al-masjid al-aqsa* (Sura 17:1). Still later perhaps, the traditions of the *mi'raj,* or "ladder" to heaven, were fused with the traditions of the *isra'* so that the Prophet was understood to have stopped in Jerusalem before ascending the ladder to the heavenly sphere. Some Muslim commentators in the early Middle Ages were revolted by the thought of judaizing Islam by making Jerusalem holy. They argued that Jerusalem is nothing for Islam and those who sought to sanctify Jerusalem were just copying the Jews. And some have speculated that it was really towards Mt. Sinai that Muhammad had been oriented; tradition evolved so that as R. J. Zwi Werblowsky has observed: "There are no direct flights from Mecca to heaven; you have to make a stop-over in Jerusalem."[3] The Muslims, too, built the sanctity of Jerusalem, but because they controlled the city for so many centuries they did it through the construction of vast structures on the *haram* like al-Aqsa mosque and the Dome of the Rock around the stone from which Muhammad was believed to have ascended to heaven, by building architecturally impressive walls around the city, complemented by hadith and poetry celebrating the virtues of *al-quds,* "the holy," and, of course through pilgrimage and their own speculation about the role of this city on the day of judgment.

The authors of the texts with which we began occupied very different positions within their respective communities. Rabbi Orenstein was a longtime resident of the Jewish Quarter and during the siege of Jerusalem from December 1947 to May 1948 was in charge of arrangements at the Western Wall.[4] He was killed along with his wife when a Jordanian artillery shell fell on their apartment shortly after the declaration of statehood in May 1948.[5] Throughout that period he kept a detailed account of events at the Western Wall attesting to the increased politicization of this sacred space in the conflict between Jewish and Palestinian nationalisms.

After World War I, Hajj Amin-Husayni, the Mufti of Jerusalem, became the preeminent leader of the Palestinian nationalist cause. As the highest Islamic cleric in Palestine, he mounted a campaign to protect the sanctity of the *haram al-sharif* which allowed him to mobilize the populace against the Jews and to lay claim to speak for all Palestinians, until he was forced to flee Palestine after the British put down the Arab Revolt of 1936–39. In 1948 the Mufti organized a small Palestinian army aimed at creating an independent Palestinian state. Yasser Arafat is a member of Husayni's extended family and received his initial political education at the Husaynis' home in exile in Cairo.[6]

Husayni's text was written in 1930 for the Shaw Commission convened by the British to determine the causes of the intercommunal rioting of August 1929 sparked by political conflict over the Western Wall. Orenstein's text was written for a private readership at the end of the 1930s. A half-century has gone by, yet the positions they reflect remain virtually unchanged.

The two texts illustrate an almost entirely overlooked element in the study of sacred places—their intimate connection with politics. The history of religions has understood sacred place to be the result of the sudden manifestation or eruption of the Sacred into the world. Because they undergird identities and ethical commitments, because they galvanize the deepest emotions and attachments, material and symbolic control over the most central sacred places are sources of enormous social power. Therefore these sites are periodically contested, states to be won in the struggle between different religious communities and between different groups who hold opposing worldviews within each community. These conflicts transform the meaning of the site, the doctrines which are ritualized there, and the identities of those who claim the site as their own. The history of religions has treated religious traditions as consensual and closed systems. Studies based on the "essentialist" interpretation tend to be apolitical, and thus necessarily consensual or at least nonconflictual, often textual and oriented to elite understandings of the normative tradition, and either completely ahistorical or reduced to a temporal sequence of ideas.

Control over the the organization and meaning of Jerusalem's Temple Mount/*al -haram al-sharif* has been repeatedly contested within and between the Jewish and Muslim communities. The degree and meaning of their sanctity to each community hinges historically upon their changing position in those intra- and intercommunal struggles. Just as the state stands as the ultimate guarantor of the "sanctity" of private property and the self-regulating market, so too the state stands at the profane perimeter of any sacred space as the guarantor of its sanctity. By implication, wherever there is political conflict over the organization of sacred space, it falls to the state to manage that organization. As we shall show, the state's role in the regulation of these sites is overwhelming.

In the case of the Temple Mount/*al-haram al-sharif*, the primary external conflict has been between the Israeli state on the one hand, and the Palestinian nationalist movement on the other. For Israelis and Palestinians, this site has been both a symbolic resource for political mobilization and a site for political struggle. In the 1920s and early 1930s the Western Wall was used by Revisionist Zionists to mobilize Jews to their standard within the Zionist community, as well as against the Palestinian nationalist movement. On the Palestinian side, clerical elites used the *haram al-sharif* to build Palestinian nationalism and advance their own leadership of the movement, and to struggle against Zionism. Ever since Jordan asserted sovereignty over Jerusalem in 1948, the site has been a battleground between the PLO, Jordan, and Islamic militants over the claim of the allegiances of the Palestinian people. And ever since Israel claimed sovereignty, the site has been a critical background between Israelis who are willing to achieve territorial compromise with the Arabs and those who are not, between those who seek to ground the legitimacy of the state in a secular democratic constitution and those who would ground it in the Torah and religious law.

AESTHETICS OR POLITICS OF SACRED SPACE

The social organization of space has long been "read" metaphorically to apprehend the divine world. This tradition can be traced back to the great urban civilizations of the ancient world.[7] The modern world has not gone far beyond poetic metaphors in its efforts to understand sacred and profane space. Gaston Bachelard was correct in alerting us to our own metaphorical reveries about space and other mysteries.[8] Scholars such as Otto von Simpson have read the cathedral and its light as metaphors for the medieval worldview, while John James understood it as a metaphor for the presence of God.[9] David Brodsly has interpreted the freeway as the metaphor for the experience of modernity.[10]

Naturally, the history of religions abounds with metaphorical descriptions of sacred space: Wensinck's *The Ideas of Western Semites Concerning the Navel of the Earth* (Amsterdam, 1917), Jeremias' *Golgotha* (Leipzig, 1926), and Mus' *Barabudur* (Hanoi, 1935). These three classical studies of sacred space develop metaphors to describe the cosmologies of holy space in the ancient Near East, where "navel" has a pan-Semitic root (*TBR*), in Judaism and early Christianity in late antiquity where Golgotha takes on the additional symbolism of the Greek *omphalos*, and at Barabudur where time and space are materialized in the structure of the Buddhist *stupa*.

Descriptive terms identified with the work of Mircea Eliade such as "center," *axis mundi, universalis columna*, "cosmic mountain," *imago mundi, templus et tempus*, or *terre pure* are more recent examples of this metaphorical treatment of space. Eliade's study of what he called "architectonic" symbolism[11] is part of a longer phenomenological tradition. For example, Gerardus van der Leeuw, in his *Phanomenologie der Religion* (1933), saw sacred space as "that locality that becomes a position by the effects of power repeating themselves there, or being repeated by man."[12] His evolutionary model began with its simplest form, the "natural shrine" where man adds nothing at all to a natural locale which is filled with an "awe-inspiring character"; moved to the house and temple where both are sacred by virtue of the power residing in them; to the city where man forms his settlement and converts the discovered possibilities of the locality into a new powerfulness; finally to the internationalization of sacred space where heart or soul becomes the holy of holies. In Muslim mystical tradition, van der Leeuw noted, the pilgrimage to Mecca might be undertaken "in one's room" or "by walking seven times around a sage: the real sanctuary is man."[13] Van der Leeuw, like Eliade, understood that sacred space was created by the presence of power, but van der Leeuw failed to tell us anything about the politics of that power. Their sacred space is devoid of real humans and their specific and divergent ideal and material interests.

Joachim Wach's sociology of religious experience pointed out that all such experiences are subject to far-reaching social forces acting upon them from outside.[14] Yet Wach's efforts to uncover the universals of religious experience forced him to separate both time and space from social forces. He wrote that the religious language which articulates religious experience is always metaphorical ("The way of negation, of analogy and eminence is used in all religious language"), and we must remember that the concepts of sacred time and sacred space are the frameworks "within which religious thought and religious acts enfold themselves."[15] Thus, while sacred space and time are social metaphors, their making and the evolutionary movement between them are not problematic. The human species somehow descends naturally into the sacrality of its individual members.

These approaches make sacred space into a static and substantive category. They simply assume the Durkheimian dichotomy of sacred and profane and ground it in Rudolf Otto's later attempt to secure the epistemology and ontology of the sacred. Consequently, under the tutelage of van der Leeuw, Wach, and Eliade, the history of religions has come to understand that the sacred manifests itself at a specific place, making it, for all intents and purposes, sacred for all time. The history of religion has then produced a marvelous tapestry of metaphors or aesthetic indices for space, but has not clarified how space is socially constructed, organized, and reproduced over time. Sacred space is stripped of politics and real history.

Students of religions, of course, now recognize that religious phenomena are multivalent, but they have a multiplicity of meanings, to use Eliade's terminology. But the meanings are chronologically arranged and never create conflict. Indeed, Eliade's real importance is his presentation of the multiplicity of meanings of religious phenomena, whether in chronological order or arranged structurally within his categories. So, when Eliade was forced to explain what he meant by "history" he wrote, "l'histoire des religions étant en grande partie l'histoire des dévalorisations et des revalorisations du processus de manifestation du sacré."[16] Kurt Rudolph recently commented that, for Eliade, "the history of religions is concerned not with historical processes in the context of political, economic, cultural, and social conditions, but with the 'history' of the transhistorical structures of religious meanings, of 'hierophanies,' or 'kratophanies,' we could also say of religious ideas."[17] Human beings, real actors, are apparently irrelevant to these transhistorical processes of the manifestation of the sacred.

Likewise in Eliade's approach, there are no conflictual meanings in religious phenomena. Everything always fits together. In his *Traité* Eliade provides us with the marvelous example of the crowd which comes to the Kalighat in Calcutta to worship Durga. For the great majority, Durga is an awesome goddess who must be appeased by bloody sacrifice. To the religious elite, Durga is a manifestation of cosmic life in constant and violent regeneration. To the crowd, the Siva *lingam* is the archetype of the generative organ, but for the initiates it is the symbol of the cycle of creation in which everything periodical returns to its primordial unity before being reborn again. He writes:

What is the true meaning of Durga and Siva—what is deciphered by the initiates, or what is taken up by the mass of the faithful? In this book I am trying to show that both are equally valuable; that the meaning given by the masses stands for as authentic a modality of the sacred manifested in Durga or Siva as the interpretation of the initiates. And I can show that the two hierophanies fit together—that the modalities of the sacred which they reveal are in no sense contradictory, but are complementary, are parts of a whole.[18]

While Eliade refuses to give primacy to any group's understanding, the mechanism by which the understandings of elites, initiates, and the populace "fit together" is not of theoretical concern. It is simply assumed.

More recent scholarship has also managed to recognize the multivalence of sacred space while retaining a consensual, apolitical understanding. In her magisterial work, Diana L. Eck interprets the city of Banaras as a "text" which continually acts to reinterpret the classical Sanskrit texts about the same city. In short, the relationship between the city text and canonical text is both complementary and contradictory. She writes in her preface:

The sacred geography of the city provides information the Sanskrit texts cannot provide. Some of the temples I sought out, which had clearly been important in the era of Sanskrit literature, no longer exist. Some such sites are now occupied by mosques. Others are marked only by tiny shrines or have been moved to new locations. Conversely, some temples barely mentioned in the Sanskrit texts have achieved great fame and popularity. Reading the text of the city's geography has often been difficult, for most of the city has changed in the past 700 years, with hardly a stone left upon stone. Parts of it, including many major temples, were destroyed by Muslims several times between the twelfth and seventeenth centuries, and in the eighteenth century whole new sectors of what is now the dense urban heart of the city were constructed. And yet, with all this change, most of the temples of the great Sanskrit tradition are still here, somewhere.[19]

Here, Eck understands the historical development of Banaras and the multivalence of its sacred geography (i.e., there are many Hindu and Muslim sites in the city) and even the conflict between the canonical texts and the urban text (i.e., those temples which are hardly mentioned in the canonical texts have great popularity). However, she pays little or no attention to the politics which formed the city in the classical Hindu period, the Muslim middle ages, or in the modern period with the renaissance of both traditions. The multiple meanings of sacred space may reflect both profound historical and contemporary conflicts. Unfortunately the historical relationship between the urban and canonical text is not theorized. It is not made into a problem in the original and so remains unexamined in the contemporary as well. The history of the city becomes a chronology of events without the political forces and the alternative readings which motivated them and have shaped the sacred spaces of contemporary Banaras.

More recent analysts have pointed out that sacred space is more a matter of interpretation, of setting boundaries, and of relationships than fixed categories which have universal consent and agreement among and between believers. Commenting on the work of Mary Douglas, Jonathan Z. Smith, for example, recalled an experience drawn from his youth working on a dairy farm in upstate New York. In the morning his boss would wash his hands, then go outside and rub them with dirt. When Smith asked about this curious series of actions, he was reminded by his host that folks from the city know little. Inside the house, he was told it's "dirt," outside it's "earth." You wash it off to be with your family inside and you put it on when you are with the animals outside. Smith uses this experience to argue against the essentialist or substantive tradition of sacred and profane within the history of religions. "There is nothing," he writes, "that is inherently or essentially clean or unclean, sacred or profane." Rather, Smith argues, there are situational or relational categories, "mobile boundaries which shift according to the map being employed."[20] At another point in his work, he reminds us of the similarity between attempts to fix canons and divinatory situations. He is struck by "the great variety of such canons and divinatory situations . . . by the differences in exegetical techniques and skills, by the variety of presuppositions. But the essential structure of limitation and closure along with exegetical ingenuity remains constant." The task of the history of religions, Smith argues, should be "an examination of the rules that govern the sharp debates between rival exegetes and exegetical systems in their efforts to manipulate the closed canon."[21] Sacred space must also be understood as a structure of limitation and closure, like the canon or the process of divination with a fixed and limited number of objects to be interpreted and understood. Sacred space then is a matter of context and relation with specific grammars which make them meaningful. Both the setting of relational boundaries and determining the grammars which regulate sacred space are political activities.

Indeed, the most rewarding studies of sacred space following from the critique of the history of religions' aesthetic interpretation are those which have focused on this political dimension or sacred topographies and landscapes. David Harvey has studied the social conflict between the contradictory sacralities of Paris' Basilica of the Sacred Heart and the Mur des Fédérés, where the surviving members of the Paris Commune were executed in 1871. Harvey demonstrates that the building of the Basilica concretized the ascendancy not only of a new national piety in the devotional cult of the Sacred Heart, but also the new ruling classes which emerged as a result of the civil war. The Basilica was sited on the exact location where the Commune had begun in order, as the National Assembly put it when it voted for its erection in 1873, to serve "in witness of repentance and as a symbol of hope." Not unlike the siting of early medieval churches on the sacred sanctuaries of pre-Christian Europe and the Islamic construction of mosques on top of Christian churches and Jewish synagogues, they appropriated the symbolic power of this site and imprinted it with their own understanding of the larger sacred territorial unit: France. Yet, the memory of the Commune did not die and was memorialized in the wall located in Père Lachaise Cemetery, creating an alternative sacred locale.[22] The Basilica and the wall are two sacred sites for the followers of conflicting worldviews of the meaning of the French nation. Today, both are pilgrimage sites for the right and left wings of France's political order. Each spring the National Front celebrates the feast day of Joan of Arc with huge bonfires on the hillside leading to the Basilica. Within view of Montmartre, the graves of almost all the major left-wing political elites as well as memorials to those deported to their deaths in the Nazi death camps are situated around the wall of the Paris Commune's martyrs.

Another seminal piece of work is that of David Carrasco, who has laid out the microeconomics of symbolic power which governed the relationship between the Aztec capital and its far-flung provinces, between center and periphery. He argues that the human sacrificial system which was acted out at the Templo Mayor was a system "to maintain Aztec dominance in the face of threats (rebellions) and fluctuations (droughts). . . . It was a religious strategy carried out to conserve the entire cosmogonic structure of the Aztec city-state."[23] More recently, using J. Z. Smith's interpretation of ritual as controlled space, he has argued that "just such a ritual substitution of spaces takes place in the Aztec sacrifice of warriors captured in battles fought in territories peripheral to the settlements of competing city-states. The accidents of variables of the battlefield are eliminated in the sacrificial ceremony, where the enemy warrior is under the total control of the sacrificer and the symbolism of the ceremonial center of the city. What was up for grabs in the periphery is completely under control in the center."[24] While the phenomena interpreted by Harvey and Carrasco are vastly different, their studies both demonstrate the relationship between the construction of sacred space and the social organization of power.

THE CONFLICT OVER THE WESTERN WALL FROM THE BRITISH MANDATE TO THE SIX-DAY WAR

The religious conflict over the sacred centers of Jerusalem must be understood with respect to the national conflict between Arab and Jew in Palestine. Islamic elites, centered in Jerusalem, used their control over its sacred sites to mold and to mobilize the Palestine people. Conflict over the city's sacred sites was a way both to establish a new Palestinian identity and to engage the enemy. The struggle over the platform and the wall surrounding it were linked to the struggle for the city in which both were interested.

Hajj Amin al-Husayni, the highest Islamic cleric in Palestine, built his nation and his own political base against the rival Nashishibni family by building the sanctity of Jerusalem. Before the British mandate, expressions of Muslim piety were regionally fragmented. Jerusalem's religious elites had long visited and made pilgrimage to the tomb of Moses, at least as Palestinian Islam understood it, on the road from Jerusalem to Jericho. Shortly after Salah al-Din conquered the city from the Crusaders, Palestinian Muslims located the burial place of Nebi Musa, or "the Prophet Moses" near Mt. Nevo. An elaborate multidomed mosque was constructed in the desert near Jericho marking that place.[25] Many visitors to the city in the nineteenth century already recognized that, unlike all other festivals in the Muslim religious calendar, this pilgrimage was correlated with the Orthodox Easter calendar in order to rival Easter celebrations.[26] The pilgrims traditionally arrived at the tomb of Moses on Monday of Holy Week and spent two days there. A whole local tradition of piety evolved in which Muslims from Jerusalem would walk in procession on the festival of Moses' burial to the desert shrine behind the large green banner of the Prophet Muhammad, one of the Dome of the Rock's most precious relics, which belonged to the Husayni family. The pilgrims would also bring their own family flags, which would be unfurled in the procession linking Palestinian families to the family of the Prophet. Amidst the feasting and flute and drum music, scores of young boys were circumcised there. Such a circumcision was believed to be particularly auspicious for the recipient. On Wednesday, all pilgrims returned in procession to Jerusalem, arriving there on Holy Thursday when the Orthodox Christians of the city reenact Jesus' washing of his disciples' feet. The Banner of the Prophet was carried at the head of the procession by Jerusalem's most influential Muslim families. On Friday, the *haram al-sharif* was crowded with pilgrims and the central ritual was the carrying of the Banner of the Prophet, along with all the other flags, from al-Aqsa mosque to the Dome of the Rock. At the al-Kas fountain directly between the two buildings, the procession would stop and point the banner toward an olive tree near the fountain. This olive tree was believed to become animated at this point; its trunk and branches would bend in recognition of the Prophet. The banner was then received at the Dome of the Rock and wrapped in silk and stored in the Dome until the following year.[27]

Before al-Husayni, the pilgrim to Nebi Musa might be joined by fellow pilgrims from Jericho and even Bedouin tribesmen from across the Jordan. But Muslims in the Galilee, on the coastal plain, or even nearby Hebron and Nablus were preoccupied with their own local saints whose tombs they visited on pilgrimage. Few came to Jerusalem for the festival of Nebi Musa.

In April 1920, Hajj Amin played an important role in violent demonstrations which broke out in Jerusalem in conjunction with the Nebi Musa pilgrimage.

That year the festivals of Passover, Easter, and Nebi Musa all took place at the same time in April. Earlier that year the Emir Faysal had been made king of Syria. Hajj Amin then wanted Palestine to become a part of Greater Syria under Hashemite leadership. When the procession winding its way up from the tomb of Moses arrived in Jerusalem, it circled the Old City and halted in front of the municipality building on Jaffa Road. There were a number of anti-Zionist speeches. When Hajj Amin rose to speak, he held up a portrait of Faysal and told the crowd, "This is your King!" The crowd roared back, "God save the King."

Jerusalem was not a stronghold for the dominant Labour Zionist movement. It was, however, a political center for the Revisionist Zionists, who would brook no compromise in the formation of a Jewish state that they hoped would include all of Mandatory Palestine. The Revisionists, led by Ze'ev Jabotinsky, had organized a counterdemonstration in the Jewish Quarter of the Old City. This apparently provoked the Muslim pilgrims, who rioted, killing three Jews and injuring scores. Jabotinsky's followers then attacked the Muslim rioters. When the British finally were able to separate the two groups, the death toll was five Jews and four Palestinians and there were nearly a hundred injured. The British dismissed the Palestinian mayor, Musa Kazim al-Husayni, who had addressed the group, and arrested Jabotinsky. Hajj Amin escaped the British dragnet and eventually fled across the Jordan River and was given a ten-year sentence in abstentia for his inflammatory speech to the crowd. Jabotinsky was sentenced to fifteen years, although this was quickly commuted to one year.[28] Hajj Amin was pardoned the following September and returned to Jerusalem. The Palin Commission, convened to determine the causes of the rioting, concluded the following year that the rioting appeared to be spontaneous, but that "firebrands" had exploited it for their own political purposes.[29] Throughout the 1920s Hajj Amin continued to press the prestige of the pilgrimage and even convinced the British that he did not wish the piligrimage to become another context for political violence. Indeed, the fact that there was no violence during the pilgrimage in 1921 was one of the factors which led Herbert Samuel, the High Commissioner of Palestine, to appoint Hajj Amin to the position of Mufti a month after the pilgrimage.[30]

Cemeteries provide powerful clues to social transformations. The cemetery surrounding the Nebi Musa mosque and hospice is filled with graves of prominent Jerusalemite families, indicating the prestige and power of internment there. Suddenly in the early 1920s people from all over Palestine were being buried in the cemetery at Nebi Musa near Jerusalem. Wealthy pilgrims who traveled from all over Palestine began to dedicate plaques in the mosque commemorating their pilgrimage. Each village, town, and city made its way separately to the shrine, behind its own flag, usually arriving and departing on its own appointed day. The Nebi Musa pilgrimage under the stewardship of Hajj Amin became a national pilgrimage. The pilgrims not only paid homage to Moses, but to Hajj Amin as well, whose organization largely financed the festival. Through the pilgrimage, he attempted to consolidate ritually a national community of Palestine, overcoming the fragmentation of clan and village, between cities and rural areas, and even the rivalries between prominent families of Jerusalem.

Almost immediately after his appointment to the position of Grand Mufti, he began an extensive restoration project on the *haram al-sharif*. Al-Aqsa mosque and many of the religious schools and foundations located near it had deteriorated under the Ottoman administration of the city and had been damaged as a result of earthquakes. In order to complete his project, he began to build a hotel for Muslim pilgrims and borrowed heavily from other Arab regimes. The project, completed in 1928, earned him the title of "Restorer of *al-Haram al-Sharif* and Defender of the Holy Places."

If the Mufti built his nation by building the sanctity of Jerusalem, he also engaged the enemy by politicizing access to the Western Wall. Muslims considered the Western Wall to be an inseparable part of the *haram al-sharif*, while the paved street below was part of a *waqf*[31] created by the Abu Madyan family in 1320 intended to provide housing and charity for Moroccan Muslim pilgrims.[32] A small Moroccan Muslim neighborhood developed around the original *waqf* property. Before the nineteenth century, Jews worshipped at other areas of the surviving Herodian walls surrounding the *haram* on the south and east. In the middle ages, there is some evidence that Muslims may even have allowed Jews to pray on the Temple Mount or the *haram* itself.[33] Muhammad Ali of Egypt had issued a decree or *firman* in 1849 granting Jews permission to visit the wall and to pray there. Muhammad Ali's decree became part of Jerusalem's complex code of rights and privileges to the holy places. Jews were permitted to worship there, but they were not allowed to bring chairs, reading tables, or screens to divide male and female worshippers as required by *Halakha* or religious law. They were not allowed to blow the *shofar* or the ram's horn which is normally a part of the Rosh ha-Shannah and Yom ha-Kippurim ritual.

In 1920, even before Hajj Amin became Mufti, there had been a serious conflict over the status of the wall. Minor repairs to the wall were initiated by the Muslim authorities of the *haram al-sharif*. These repairs included the removal of weeds on the top of the wall. The Jews objected and the matter was brought to the British military administration of Palestine. The arbitrators ruled that since the area cleaned was from the Ottoman period, well above the Herodian levels lower on the walls, the Muslims could clean the wall. But, since the wall was considered an antiquity, it must be cleaned or repaired under the supervision of the Department of Antiquities, and no work was to be done on either Friday or Saturday.

The British sought to manage the potential conflict between Jews and Muslims as well as between the diverse Christian communities of Jerusalem by retaining intact the entire series of Sultanic declarations awarding custody of the sacred places to one community or another. This body of *firmans* was widely known as the Status Quo in the holy places. The Muslims not only feared a Jewish homeland in Palestine, but also believed that the Jews were intent upon rebuilding their Temple on the *haram*.[34] Hajj Amin al-Husayni shared this fear from the very beginning. He believed that the Jews would not be content with only the

Western Wall, but desired the entire *haram* where they planned to construct the third Temple. He told a correspondent of *Le Journal* in September of 1929 that Lord Melchet had told him at the very beginning of the Mandate that "the day of rebuilding the temple has approached and I shall devote the rest of my life to building the temple on the spot of the Mosque of Aqsa."[35] Hajj Amin believed that the Jews were violating the Status Quo by bringing chairs and benches to the wall. On September 28, 1925, he wrote to the governor of Jerusalem saying that "you are undoubtedly aware of the fact that the Jews had on several occasions attempted to disregard the rules of the Wailing Wall by placing benches and wooden chairs [there]. . . . Recently the Jews renewed this attempt publicly [and hence] the Muslim community was greatly annoyed."[36] The Mufti made it increasingly more difficult for the Jews to worship at the Western Wall. The paved street used by the Jews, for example, was originally a dead-end alley. The Mufti ordered the closed end of the alley to be opened, converting the street to a public thoroughfare.

On September 23, 1928, the eve of Yom ha-Kuppurim, an Ashkenazic attendant at the Western Wall began making preparations for the religious services of the next day. He brought a larger than usual ark, spread mats, and set up lamps. But he also attached a dividing screen to the pavement. Apparently, this was brought to the attention of the *mutawalli* or guardian of the Abu Madyan *waqf*. He immediately notified the Mufti, who sent a formal complaint to Edward Keith-Roach, the Deputy District Commissioner of Jerusalem. The District Commissioner immediately ordered the screen removed and was assured that it would be gone by the following morning. However, when the District Commissioner visited the area the next day, the screen was still there. Again the District Commissioner ordered the screen taken down, but now the Orthodox Jews who were at prayer refused to desecrate Yom ha-Kippurim by performing what they considered an act of labor. The police were called and when they started to remove the screen, a fight began in which a number of Jews were injured.

Many have argued that the Mufti transformed this conflict over the Status Quo into a political struggle which allowed him to secure his position as the unrivaled defender of the *haram al-sharif's* sanctity and uncontested leader of the Palestinian nationalist movement. Indeed, both the Jews and Palestinians protested the conflict and both formed committees to defend the sanctity of either the *al-buraq al-sharif* or the Wailing Wall. The initial reaction of the British was in favor of the Mufti; the benches and chairs were ordered removed. But the strongest initial response came from the Yishuv and world Jewry. For the six days following the conflagration, Hajj Amin remained silent, and this has led one scholar to suggest that the Mufti did not consciously set out to transform the issue into a major political event, but was pushed to it by the strength of the Jewish protests of outrage and indignation. However, by the beginning of October his course of action was set.[37] In October the Mufti was prepared to write his memorandum to the newly convened Shaw Commission.[38]

The Mufti's diary entries from 1931 indicate that he considered the Jews' actions to take over the *haram al-sharif* and all Palestine so provocative that it might encourage other Westerners and Europeans to take over other Muslim countries, with the possible loss of even Mecca and Medina. Palestine would soon become a second Andulasia lost by the Muslims.[39]

In November 1928 he assembled a conference in Jerusalem to discuss the question of the Western Wall. Fearing the influence of the Jews in London, the Mufti suggested that if the Jews continued to violate the Status Quo, the Muslims would be compelled to initiative an uprising. Some of the delegates were from India, and the implied threat to the British was that if they did not restrain the Jews, the insurrections might even spread to India, then a British colony facing very severe communal conflict between Hindus and Muslims. This conference was the opening salvo of what became known as the *al-buraq* campaign in which Hajj Amin hoped to mobilize not only Palestinians, but all Muslims throughout the Arab world, around the issue. His campaign was designed to challenge the British government to adhere to the Status Quo, which they were beginning to see as a flashpoint for major political violence. The Mufti argued that Jewish rights at the Western Wall were only a favor which had been extended by the administrators of the Abu Madyan *waqf*. This ignored the fact that the Jews had established a customary right to the wall through centuries of usage and Muslim acquiescence, and the formal agreements which had been made between the religious Jews and the *waqf*. Hajj Amin was also well aware that the Jews had attempted to purchase sections of the wall immediately after World War I and again just two years before the conflict erupted. In 1918, Chaim Weizmann attempted to purchase the wall for 70,000 Palestine pounds as a way to stimulate enthusiasm for Zionism. The deal was only cancelled when Palestinian nationalists discovered that the *waqf*'s administrators had agreed to the transaction. In 1926 the Zionists raised the offer to 100,000 Palestine pounds for property in the Abu Madyan trusteeship. They were able to buy one large parcel only fifty meters from the Mughrabian Gate to the *haram* and were beginning to negotiate for property directly in front of the wall. Immediately after the disturbances in 1928, Weizmann offered 61,000 Palestine pounds for the wall itself, but Keith-Roach dissuaded him and suggested that he should postpone any further attempts to purchase Abu Madyan property until things had quietened down.[40] The whole affair of Jews attempting to purchase *al-buraq* and Palestinians wanting to sell it must have come as a great embarrassment to the Mufti, who resided in the same neighborhood.

But Hajj Amin also took a number of steps to make the Jewish situation at the Western Wall even more untenable. He ordered that a *mu'azzin* take a position on top of the roof of a house immediately adjacent from the wall to call Muslims to prayer. The house became a *zawiya* or a small mosque and hospice. Sufi Muslims would gather there for ritual *dhikr*, which would be accompanied by cymbals, gongs, and the shouting of "Allah akbar." While the cacophonous sounds that emerged from the *zawiya* interfered with Jewish prayer, in Hajj Amin's strategy it was to underscore the sanctity of *al-buraq* for Muslims. But just as the Muslims had appealed to the British that the Jews had violated the Status Quo, the Jews now turned to them and argued that the Mufti's actions were innovations not sanctioned by the Status Quo.[41]

The following year, Hajj Amin's activities to demonstrate that the Jews intended to use the Western Wall as a platform to regain the Temple Mount culminated in the rioting which spread from Jerusalem to Hebron. The Shaw Commission in 1930 would find that the Revisionist Zionist demonstrations on August 15, 1929, had set in motion the escalating politics of symbolic sacrilege. On that day, the Beta youth assembled at the wall, shouting, "The wall is ours," raised the national flag, and sang "Ha-Toqvah." The unsubstantiated rumor that they had attacked Muslim residents of the immediate area and had cursed the name of the Prophet Muhammad only fanned the flames. The following day, some 2,000 Muslims marched to the Western Wall and destroyed a Torah scroll and prayer books. While some argued that Hajj Amin attempted to manage the demonstration, the atmosphere was now so charged that there was no way to avert the explosion of violence which was unleashed a week later.[42]

The British ultimately took the issue of the Western Wall to the League of Nations, where they proposed that the League establish a commission to "study, define, and determine the rights and claims of the Jews, and Muslims . . . the Mufti protested and argued that decisions concerning the holy places of Muslims could only be established by Shari'a law and by no other authority. The British further attempted to move both Jews and Muslims toward some compromise, but the Mufti steadfastly refused to meet with the Jews, saying that "if he were to meet with the Jews, this would give them rights to the Wailing Wall."[43] The British quickly came to see the Mufti as the chief obstacle to any resolution between the contending parties at the Western Wall. For many Palestinian scholars who have attempted to exonerate Hajj Amin al-Husayni from any responsibility for the 1929 revolt, this was a turning point in the British attitude toward the Mufti. The British now recognized him as a distinct danger to the peaceful continuation of the Mandate. They determined to reduce his prestige and influence by stripping him of any control over the revenue of *waqf* property, declaring that all *waqf* land should be returned to the control of the Mandatory government as it had been under the Ottomans. Further, they expelled the Mufti from heading the Shari'a courts and the administration of *waqf* funds. For these scholars, the British also were instrumental in artificially intensifying the dispute between the Husaynis and the Nashishibnis.

The conflict over the Western Wall-Temple Mount and *al-haram al-sharif* continued to simmer throughout the 1930s and early 1940s. During the Palestinian revolt of 1936 through 1939, the *haram* was used to mobilize against both the British and the Zionists. In 1948 the most important Palestinian commander, Abdul Kader al-Husayni, who was also the Mufti's nephew, fell in battle and was buried on the *haram*. After the 1948 war which resulted in the division of Jerusalem and the annexation of the West Bank and the city by the Jordanians, both King Abdullah and then later King Hussein saw the *haram al-sharif* as the central mechanism to assert the legitimacy of their sovereignty in Jerusalem and the West Bank. Both the Hashemite Abdullah and the Mufti Husayni traced their line back to the Prophet and his followers. The Mufti, now in exile in Cairo, had opposed Jordanian annexation of any part of Palestine. Three years later the Mufti's network had King Abdullah assassinated as he made his way to pray on the *haram*. Thus the blood and bones of both Palestinian nationalists and Hashemite kings came to be buried on this sacred platform. Hussein tried to control the symbolic power of the *haram* by making the entire religious infrastructure of the West Bank and Jerusalem economically dependent on Amman as well as using the Muslim Brotherhood to undercut Palestinian nationalists, Communists, Baathists, and Nasserites.[44]

Despite the guarantees provided by Article 8 of the Armistice Agreement of 1949 allowing Jews daily passage to the Eastern sections of the city for purposes of prayer at the Western Wall, visitation of their cemetery on the Mount of Olives and the Tomb of Rachel, the Jordanian regime prohibited Jews and Israeli Muslims from crossing at the Mandelbaum Gate and tourists visiting the Jordanian Jerusalem were periodically required to show baptismal certificates when requesting tourist visas.[45] Gradually, the *haram* became one of the major centers of Jordanian power and influence on the West Bank. While Hussein relinquished sovereignty over the West Bank and Jerusalem in the summer of 1988, which included the termination of salaries for teachers and civil servants, he continued to fund the *waqf* of the *haram al-sharif* and to pay the salaries of its staff.[46]

THE THEOLOGICAL PROBLEMATIC OF THE SIX-DAY WAR

Immediately after the Six-Day War of 1967, the Israeli Knesset passed "The Law for the Protection of the Holy Places" which guaranteed free access to all holy places in Jerusalem, stipulated that the religious communities of each would administer them, and provided penalties for any violation of their sanctity. This law continued the language of Israel's Proclamation of Statehood stating that "the Holy Places shall be protected from desecration or any other harm, or anything which might affect the access of believers or their feelings for those places."[47] The Knesset's law failed to mention the Status Quo, which had regulated the holy places which had been used by General Allenby after the British conquered Jerusalem from the Turks in 1917. In 1931 the Mandatory government had sanctioned the Status Quo at the Western Wall with the King's Order in Council. The Status Quo discriminated against the Jews, prohibiting them from bringing benches, dividers, reading tables, and other basic ritual objects necessary for prayer at the Western Wall, and the blowing of the *shofar*. Suffice it to say that the Israeli government could not be expected to reconfirm the very system which had discriminated against the Jews and had been a major issue in the conflict between Jewish and Palestinian nationalists.

The Knesset's Law for the Protection of the Holy Places gave each of the non-Jewish religious communities of the newly united city exclusive control over its holy places. This created both administrative and theological problems for each religious tradition which was now subordinated to Israeli sovereignty.[48] The world's Christianities had long historical traditions which understood the dispersal of the Jews and the absence of Jewish sovereignty over Jerusalem as proof-texts that the Jews had been rejected by God or that their election had passed to the Christians as a result of their rejection of Jesus. Likewise, for the Muslim community of Jerusalem and the Middle East, Jewish sovereignty over the *haram al-sharif* also posed a theological problem. How could one of the subordinated minorities of traditional Muslim society now exercise political power and control over the Muslims?

For Christians, Jewish sovereignty in Jerusalem created a new problem; for the Muslims, it intensified an old one. Before 1967, the theological problem posed by Jewish sovereignty over Jerusalem for the Christians could be kept away. With the city's division after the 1948 war, Jewish western Jerusalem did not exercise political power over the four major Latin and Orthodox Christian holy places of the city, the Church of the Holy Sepulchre, the Tomb of the Virgin, the Church of the Ascension, and Bethlehem's Church of the Nativity, or even the Protestant alternative sacred space in the Garden Tomb. After 1967, the Christian holy places were subordinated to Jewish rule. For the Muslims, unlike the Christians, the creation of a modern Jewish state in the midst of the historic *umma* had already created a major theological issue which had been problematic before the unification of the city.[49] The capture of Jerusalem only intensified it.

But the unification of Jerusalem was equally problematic for the Jews. For one thing, sovereignty over all Jerusalem reinforced a profound shift in Jewish religious understanding of the movement of human history and their own role in bringing that history to its messianic end. In the late eighteenth and early nineteenth centuries, Jews had begun to shed their "passive messianism" which had been dominant ever since the disasters of the Jewish revolts of the first and second centuries. God's hand could be read in history. Redemption would not arrive by divine fiat; Jews, it was argued, would have to take an active role.

Elijah ben Solomon Zalman, the Gaon of Vilna (1720–97), at the end of the eighteenth century argued in his *Kol Ha-Tor* that it was possible during certain "favorable periods" to "awaken the above" by "awakening from below." The Gaon calculated that the next such "favorable period" would be the end of his century in the Hebrew calendar, 5600 or 1840. His messianic activism set in motion a groundswell of immigration to Palestine in the first decades of the nineteenth century which transformed the Jewish community there.[50]

In the mid-nineteenth century, Zevi Hirsch Kalischer, routinely described in the history of Zionism as a "proto-Zionist," had read the regime of Muhammad

Ali in Palestine, the move toward civic equality for Jews in Europe, and Christian interests in the Jewish return to the land of Israel (within their own messianic formulations) as indicators that redemption was near at hand. Kalischer believed that Jews should renew sacrificial offerings which would trigger God's compassion. God would then initiate the miraculous features of the Messianic Age. One recent commentator on Kalischer has written that he held sacrifice to be decisive in the mechanics of redemption because he "took to heart the rabbinic teachings that sacrificial offerings mediated between the divine and human realms and had the power to awaken God's compassion for humanity and bring the Redemption. Kalischer . . . felt that the absence of sacrificial worship left a profound gap in Jewish life, and he argued that only the sacrifices were powerful enough to convince God to bring the Redemption."[51]

When Israel captured the Temple Mount, these active messianic ideas suddenly became acutely relevant. Menachem Friedman, who has studied the anti-Zionist and non-Zionist Orthodox Jewish communities which constitute today the "Old Yishuv" of Jerusalem, has noted that

the boundaries delineated after the 1948 war severed the State of Israel not only from the Western Wall but also from the historic land of Israel, the Land of the Patriarchs, cherished as a living thing by generations upon generations of Bible-reading Jews. The State was bereft from many and perhaps most of the paths, lands and tombs of Jewish *Eretz Israel.* Jews had always expressed affinity for their homeland through direct contact with these sites. This situation—and especially severance from the site of the Temple—effectively "neutralized" the State of Israel from the more deeply religious and substantive dimension of the concept of "Redemption." It freed the various factions of the religious public from the need to cope with the religious, practical and concrete ramifications of Jewish sovereignty over the entire Land of Israel and especially the Temple Mount.[52]

As long as the sacred center of Judaism lay beyond Jewish sovereignty, anti-Zionist and non-Zionist Orthodox Jews could argue that indeed God had prevented the "evil Zionist" state from achieving control over the sources of symbolic power to legitimate itself. Israel was just a state like other states and did not necessarily contradict the messianic Jewish state that was still to come.

The Six-Day War undercut the passive messianism which had dominated Jewish messianic speculation. With the extension of Israeli sovereignty over Jerusalem and the Temple Mount, the anti-Zionist and non-Zionist Orthodox would have to find new strategies to delegitimize the Jewish state. Some of the most radical anti-Zionist Orthodox Jews sought to deny the event itself. For example, Moshe Hirsch, the self-styled Foreign Minister of the Nature-Karta, a small but aggressively anti-Zionist group, refuses to admit Jewish sovereignty. Only infrequently will he visit the Western Wall and when he does, he writes regularly to King Hussein for permission to travel to East Jerusalem. He regularly describes the Western Wall as the Golden Calf of Zionism which is leading an entire generation to false religion.

Jewish sovereignty over the sacred sites of Jerusalem has transformed Israel's political culture. The Western Wall now penetrated to the very core of the Israeli state's civil religion. Israel's elite military units are initiated in complex ritual ceremonies in the plaza in front of the wall and the state's new memorial festivals—Holocaust Memorial Day, the Memorial Day for Israel's soldiers who have fallen in war, Independence Day, and Jerusalem Day—all have important ritual ceremonies at the Western Wall. The Western Wall, argue Charles S. Liebman and Eliezer Don-Yehiya, "is the central shrine in the Israeli civil religion."[53] Some Israelis find this deeply upsetting. Yeshayahu Leibowitz, for example, argues that the Western Wall has been transformed into an idol. Leibowitz has consistently been critical of Israeli "civil religion" which imparts absolute meanings to the state. Only God is holy and only his commandments are absolute imperatives.[54]

Second, the extension of Israeli sovereignty to the eastern side of the city and conquest of the West Bank and Gaza triggered a move to redefine Zionism and a *Kulturkampf* over the basis of state legitimacy. It is beyond the scope of this discussion to explore this redefinition in great detail. However, a word or two are necessary. Palestine's first Ashkenazic Chief Rabbi, Avraham Yitzhak ha-Kohen Kuk (1865–1935), accomplished a major reinterpretation of the relationship of Zionism and Judaism, allowing for the possibility that secular Zionism established the foundations for the redemption of the Jews. His thought allowed religious Jews to participate in Zionist nation-building through the Mizrahi Movement and to make alliances with secular Zionist parties.[55] His son Rabbi Zvi Yehudah ha-Kohen Kuk exercised considerable influence over an entire generation of religious Zionists who were educated in his yeshivah, Yeshivat Mirkaz Ha-Rav in Jerusalem. The son translated his father's intellectual world into political action.[56] While the father spoke of the idealized state of Israel, the son spoke of the "real Israel" which was fully embodied in the state. In a collection of sermons and lectures published in 1969 he wrote that the "real Israel is the Israel which is redeemed; the kingdom of Israel and the army of Israel, a whole nation and not an exilic Diaspora."[57] The state's power had become sacred, its growth and territorial reach, an index of the Jews' relationship to God. It was the son's wielding of his father's ideas that lay behind the emergence of the Gush Emunim and the movement to settle the newly conquered biblical territories of Judea and Samaria shortly after the Six-Day War.[58] The members of the Gush Emunim believe that all of the events in the political history of Israel are divinely guided, that the growing power and territorial extent of state authority is nothing short of the realization of God's original promises to Abraham and his descendants. They view the Six-Day War as the stirrings of the messianic era and their settlement of the conquered lands of Judea, Samaria, and Gaza as the graduated movement toward the endtime.[59]

The Six-Day War and the Knesset's "Law for the Protection of the Holy Places" exposed the central contradiction of Zionism. The state had chosen to extend full sovereignty over the *haram* without allowing Jews, in whose name they claimed that sovereignty, to have access to the site which undergirds the very nature of that sovereignty. Within days of the cessation of fighting, this contradiction became clear in the debates within the rabbinate over the status of the Temple Mount. Does religious law or *Halakha* permit a Jew to enter the Temple Mount, regardless of its status within Israeli civil law? When the Israeli army's rabbinical staff loaded their staff car to follow the paratroopers to the Western Wall, they packed a Torah scroll, a *shofar*, and a bench to demonstrate that they would not abide by the Status Quo. When they arrived at the very narrow *al-buraq* alleyway, their first acts were to place the bench, hold up the Torah scroll, and blow the *shofar*. Rabbi Shlomo Goren, then Chief Rabbi of the Israeli army, was led by the rabbinical staff first across the *haram al-sharif* and then down to the Western Wall via the Mughrabian Gate. General Uzi Narkiss, who commanded the Israeli troops in the battle for Jerusalem, recalled meeting Rabbi Goren leading a column of paratroopers at the Lions' Gate with "a *sefer torah* under his arm, a *shofar* in his left hand, his beard bristling like the point of a spear . . . " Narkiss invited him to join him in his jeep, as they were going to the same place. They drove through the Gate of Tribes to the Temple Mount, where Goren got out of the jeep, prostrated himself in the direction of the Holy of Holies, and recited the ancient prayer of battle from Deuteronomy 20:3–4. At the Western Wall, Goren immediately donned his *tallit* and began to blow the *shofar*, roaring "Blessed be the Lord God, Comforter of Zion and Builder of Jerusalem, Amen!" The rabbi then recited the *Kaddish* and the *El Maleh Rachamin* for all those killed in the fighting to reach this most sacred of places. "*Leshanah hazot, be-sha'ah hazot, beyerushalayim*," Goren repeated over and over again, "This year, at this hour, in Jerusalem."[60] The rabbi's actions were not just the acknowledgment of the providence of God in delivering the city, the Temple Mount, and the Western Wall to the Jews nor devout ritual actions in the return to the most sacred of places. They were also political acts announcing that for him the Status Quo was no longer the ruling paradigm for the governance of sacred space in Jerusalem.

Six years later, Goren was made the Chief Ashkenazic Rabbi of Israel. Within weeks he ruled that religious Jews were permitted by *Halakha* to go up to the Temple Mount if the exact precincts of the Temple could be determined. Indeed, shortly after the war, Goren had set up a small office on the *haram* where he carried out research on the Temple Mount. In early August of 1967, Goren presented his findings to a group of army rabbis. At the end of the meeting Goren and the other rabbis made an extensive tour of the *haram* dressed in their military uniforms. Shortly afterward, Goren announced his intentions to pray on the Temple Mount later in the month of Tisha be'Av, the solemn fast day commemorating the Roman destruction of the Temple. On Tisha be'Av, which fell on August 15, Goren, other army rabbis, and a group of students entered the Temple Mount carrying a Torah scroll and a *shofar*. After their prayer service, Goren blew the *shofar*. Goren contended that some parts of the *haram* were not part of the Temple Mount and therefore the ban against any Jew setting foot on the Temple Mount until the Temple was rebuilt did not apply. Goren had carefully measured areas of the *haram* using the descriptions of the Temple from the Mishnah, the first-century Jewish historian Josephus, and Sa'adia Gaon and Maimonides' descriptions of the Temple from the middle ages against the archaeological evidence from the *haram* itself. Defense Minister Moshe Dayan ordered him to desist from further efforts to pray on the Temple Mount.

In 1977, Goren's colleague, the Sephardic Chief Rabbi, Ovadia Yosef, ruled that it was improper to go there unless those precincts were indeed established, and no one is authorized by religious law to delineate those areas. Ovadia Yosef's decision was prompted by a radio interview in which Goren told reporters that he was completing a book mapping out precisely those areas on the Temple Mount which are "not holy" and on which Jews may walk. One persistent rumor in Jerusalem is that Menachem Begin prevailed upon the Chief Rabbi not to publish his book for fear that this would trigger renewed Jewish attempts to violate the Law for the Protection of the Holy Places or even repeal it. Chief Rabbi Yosef's opinion has held, and therefore today a sign warning religious Jews is posted at the entrance to the Mughrabian Gate of the *haram*: "NOTICE AND WARNING—ENTRANCE TO THE AREA OF THE TEMPLE MOUNT IS FORBIDDEN TO EVERYONE BY JEWISH LAW OWING TO THE SACREDNESS OF THE PLACE—the Chief Rabbinate of Israel."[61]

Nevertheless, Goren's efforts to pray on the Temple Mount, and the state's decision to clear away many houses in the Mughrabian Quarter of the Abu Madyan *waqf* in order to create a larger plaza in front of the Western Wall, triggered renewed fears among Jerusalem's Muslims that the Israelis were intent upon taking the entire *haram*. Almost immediately after Goren's prayer service on Tish be'Av, the Muslim religious authorities published a *fatwa* or religious pronouncement which stated that the question of the Western Wall had been fixed after the 1929 riots. The Western Wall was Muslim religious property, although Jews have the right to visit it. This they believed "ended the Jewish-Arab debate on the subject of this Holy Place . . . This debate should not be re-opened as it has been resolved through judicial means."[62]

Just as the Revisionists used the wall as a stage to confront the Arabs before the state was founded, so radical Israeli nationalists who want to intensify Jewish sovereignty in Jerusalem and extend it to Judea and Samaria have engaged in efforts both to assert Jewish ritual rights on the *haram* and to profane Islamic sites there. Since 1967, there have been two dozen separate violent assaults on the *haram*. While some of these assaults have been undertaken by individuals, like the Christian fundamentalist Dennis Rohan, who set fire to al-Aqsa mosque in 1969 and who saw the destruction of al-Aqsa and the Dome of the Rock as a singular event which would catapult the world into the messianic age, most have been acted out of the active messianic Jewish tradition. The most dangerous of these assaults was that planned by members of "the Jewish Underground" which was uncovered in 1984. In the wake of the murder in 1980 of six settlers in Hebron by Palestinians, a small number of Gush Emunim settlers organized an underground cell which targeted for physical attack members of the Palestinian National Guidance Committee which had been formed in 1978. The settlers perceived that security in the West Bank and Gaza was slowly deteriorating. The brutal murder of another Hebron yeshiva student in 1983 confirmed their suspicions. They opened fire on students at the Islamic College and planned to attack Bir Zeit University. Their plan to detonate bombs concealed on five Palestinian buses was uncovered shortly before hundreds of Palestinians riding those buses would have been killed and injured. The members of the cell were arrested, tried, and found guilty.

Beyond their violent attacks on Palestinian political elites and educational institutions, they had also attempted to blow up the Dome of the Rock. Their plan, initiated after the Hebron attack in 1980, was not simply revenge. The plotters believed that the destruction of the Dome of the Rock would initiate a national redemption movement within Israel. Human action to purify the Temple Mount of the Muslim "abominations" would lead them and the nation toward Israel's transcendent goal. They were not worried about the consequences of their attack. After all, when Rohan had set fire to al-Aqsa mosque, the Arab states did comparatively little.

The plotters broke into a munitions depot and stole an Israeli device used to clear minefields. This provided them with the high explosives they would need for their carefully planned attack. They spent hours on reconnaissance missions, observing the Temple Mount through telescopes and binoculars from several locations. Every movement was logged and studied. One group observed the Temple Mount from a location between Mount Scopus and the Mount of Olives, while another group watched from the roof of Yeshivat Ha-Kotel in the Jewish Quarter of the Old City. A third group watched the Temple Mount from the belfry of the Church of the Redeemer in the Christian quarter. Some members disguised themselves as tourists and entered the Temple Mount itself. To do this, they found rabbinic rulings which permitted a Jew to enter the Temple Mount in order to maintain it or to cleanse it of impurity. Before their visits, they would immerse themselves twice in a *mikveh* or ritual bath. They also planned to deliver a tape recording explaining their reasons for destroying the Dome of the Rock just minutes before the timers were set to explode, and planned to have a photographer stationed on the Mount of Olives to commemorate the historic event.

The evacuation of Yamit, a Jewish settlement to be dismantled as part of the peace treaty with Egypt, in the winter and early spring of 1982 accelerated the momentum to carry out the plot. The destruction of the Dome of the Rock would put an end to the Camp David Accords and Egypt, under Arab pressure, would quickly back out of its new treaty relationship with Israel. However, the illness of one of the plot's three leaders and the diversion of their attention to Yamit, forced them to postpone the mission. Shortly after the withdrawal from Yamit, another Jew, Alan Goodman, who was totally unrelated to the plotters, attacked the Dome of the Rock. Security was intensified around the Temple Mount, and a new series of lights on the eastern wall meant that the plotters could not scale the wall without being seen. It was decided to shelve the plan until some indefinite time in the future. The explosive charges were sealed in watertight packages and hidden in a bomb shelter, whose door they sealed with cement. When the members of the cell were arrested over a year later, the news that they had carried out the attack on the mayors and upon the students at the Islamic College as well as planned to destroy the buses, shook the settlement movement to its very core. Moments before the beginning of Shabhat, immediately after the initial arrests, a Jerusalem lawyer who had met one of the cell's members in jail telephoned Ophra and spoke to Yisrael Harel, the secretary general of the Settlement Movement. He told him that there was something else that they had planned to do—destroy the Dome of the Rock. Harel was visibly shaken. "God help us," he said. "If the plan had gone through, Israel's sovereignty would have been a dead letter. The Americans and the Russians would have sent U.N. forces here to impose order." Harel told this to Haggai Segal, who only hours later would also be arrested for his participation in the underground.[63]

"THE TIME OF YOUR REDEMPTION HAS ARRIVED"

Rabbi Goren's decision to hold a Tisha be'Av prayer service on the Temple Mount in August of 1967 was just the beginning of what now is over twenty years of struggle to reverse the decision of the Knesset to grant the Muslims exclusive control there. On the twentieth anniversary of the Six-Day War, Rabbi Goren recalled how he had made his way to the Western Wall ahead of the generals who had engineered the stunning victory. When he arrived there he declared: "We have taken the City of God. We are entering the Messianic era for the Jewish people." Immediately after completing his prayers at the Western Wall, Goren rushed to the Mount of Olives to visit the grave of his mother. Like every other Israeli, he had been prohibited from visiting that cemetery since the armistice ending the 1948 war.[64] For many Jews, the experience of exile or *galut* was not ended by the formation of the Jewish state in 1948. Secular Israelis might believe that for some Jews their status in the world was forever changed by the creation of the state. The *haredim*, often called the "ultra-Orthodox" anti-Zionist Jews, continue to view the state as the exact opposite of any messianic kingdom. For them, living in the state is a continuation of the exile. The Gush Emunim understood the war to be still another step in the messianic drama, calling Jews to settle in the very heartland of the ancient Jewish nation.

For Rabbi Goren the unification of the Jerusalem in the Six-Day War was the end of "the trauma of the 2,000 year exile." This trauma had not ended with the creation of the state, but only with the unification of Jerusalem. Quoting the Midrash, Goren would say, "the time of your redemption has arrived." Goren understands that Jewish history is divided into four epochs—each lasting between 400 and 1,000 years—held together by *Halakha* and prophecy. The first period, which he calls the Period of Judges, runs from the first judge of ancient Israel, Joshua the son of Nun, to the last judge, Samuel. The common features of this period were that "there was no national government or national army to defend the people against their enemies, nor a temple for their entire nation. Everything operated on a local family or tribal basis." He calls the second the Period of the Kings, which spans the kingdom of David and Solomon, through the kings of Israel and Judea, or the First Commonwealth, the Babylonian Exile, and ends with the destruction of the Temple by the Romans, bringing to a close the Second Commonwealth. He believes that this period was characterized by Israel's national independence in its land, interrupted briefly by the Babylonian Exile, which lasted forty-nine years.

For Rabbi Goren the third period, which he calls the Period of the Long Exile, extends from the destruction of the Temple to the Six-Day War. Drawing from rabbinic sources, Goren believes that this exilic period was unlike the earlier Babylonian Exile. The reasons for the Babylonian Exile and its duration were revealed in the Torah and in the Prophets. However, the reasons for and the end of the Long Exile, as he calls it, were not disclosed to Israel. Many early rabbis believed that this exile would be brief, and their religious laws were predicated upon their hope that the Temple would speedily be rebuilt. For Goren, there were even false starts which seemed to confirm the rabbis' feelings that the exile would be short-lived like the first. The Emperor Hadrian, according to rabbinic texts, ordered the Temple rebuilt until the Samaritans informed him that if it were completed, then Jerusalem would once again become rebellious.[65] Two hundred years later, the Emperor Julian, who Goren believes was kindly disposed toward the Jews, granted them permission to rebuilt the Temple. Unfortunately for the Jews and Julian, the emperor was killed shortly thereafter in his war with the Persians, and his successor, who was not so positively inclined, ordered the building project ended.

However, the most important factor in this period of the Long Exile was the rabbinic debate over whether or not the rebuilding of the Temple depended upon the Messiah. Goren found one text from the Talmud of the land of Israel which stated that the Temple would be rebuilt before the reestablishment of the Kingdom of the House of David or before the advent of the Messiah. This opinion was contradicted by Maimonides, who argued that the Kingdom of the House of David would be established first and then, and only then, would the Temple be rebuilt. Other medieval interpreters suggested that the third Temple would be brought down ready-made from heaven without any human construction. Even though there are two interpretations of when the Temple would be rebuilt, he believes that there is nothing to prevent the Jews from adopting the first position and indeed, that from the time of the great rabbinic sages in the second through the sixth century, "there have been numerous attempts to renew the sacrificial service on the Temple Mount."

Goren calls the fourth period the Third Commonwealth. The Six-Day War, with its liberation of Jerusalem, "raised the hopes, visions and aspirations that our salvation was drawing near and our righteousness was about to be revealed." For many this was the dawn of the Third Commonwealth. Jews cannot, however, immediately begin to reconstruct the Temple. For one thing, the Dome of the Rock occupies much of the site of the ancient Temple, although Goren's sustained study of the Temple Mount since 1967 has proven to him that the holy of holies, the central part of the Temple, was outside the Muslim structure. He calls areas of the Temple Mount outside the hallowed ground of the Temple *tosefet hordus*, "Herodian additions," referring to the expansion of the Temple's esplanade executed by Herod the Great. Goren has also read articles of Asher Kaufman, a distinguished physicist of Hebrew University, who believes that the real Temple of Solomon was not located on the site now covered by the Dome of the Rock, but approximately 100 meters to the north. Professor Kaufman has studied the Temple Mount for almost twenty years and has collected what many believe is overwhelming evidence to support his conclusion.[66]

Equally important, Goren argues that "we lack the prophetic and halakhic information that is vital for the rebuilding of the Temple. Hence, we must have faith and await the coming of the Great Herald of Redemption, Elijah the Prophet, who will teach us the Temple boundaries, plans, forms, designs, laws, the exact spot of the altar, and the pedigree of the priests of Aharonic descent who are permitted to carry out the sacrificial service in the Temple." Goren's argument is, then, that while rebuilding the Temple cannot be accomplished at the present time, there is nothing forbidding Jews from entering the Temple Mount, as long as they steer clear of those areas which made up the site of the Temple and have immersed themselves in a proper ritual bath before entering the Temple Mount.

Yet the Six-Day War produced a bitter truth—Jews were denied access to the Temple Mount by their own government. Goren recalls that

I personally received a message from the Minister of Defence, the late Moshe Dayan, stating that it had been decided to turn over the administration of the Temple Mount and all of its installations to the Moslem Wakf. This was followed by a decision of the ministerial committee on the holy places not to allow Jews to pray on the Temple Mount. . . . The committee's decision, dated August 13, 1967, was personally addressed to me. Paragraph 1 stated: "The committee charges its chairman with meeting with General Rabbi Goren, and with informing him that he must desist from organizing prayers, measurements and the like on the Temple Mount." Paragraph 3 states that "when Jews who wish to pray appear at the entrance of the Temple Mount, they will be diverted by the security forces to the Western Wall."

These decisions crushed all the hopes that had been ascribed to the Six-Day War. These decisions, which Goren believes were approved by all the components of the Israeli government, including Menachem Begin's Herut, effectively turned over the holy of holies to the Muslims and denied Jews the right to set foot on the Temple Mount. In his memorandum in response to the committee's decision he wrote: "My request is that the gates of the Temple should be opened wide for prayer by Jews and all people and that racial segregation that forbids Jews to come and pray on the Temple Mount as the spirit moves them be abolished.

In the empty area, under the open sky, without requiring the favours of the Wakf administrators or functionaries, we can preserve the fruit of our victory for the foreseeable future." Still the answer was no. Rabbi Goren continued to press every Israeli government since the war to reverse the decision, but without results.

Even more difficult for Goren to understand was Menachem Begin's response to the Temple Mount issue after he became Prime Minister in 1977. "In fact," he said, under the leadership of Begin "the plight of Jews who wished to pray on the Temple Mount actually worsened, and the sovereignty of the Wakf over the area became a factor." Goren feared that the Camp David Accords would create a situation in which the Temple Mount might fall prey to political bartering over Judea and Samaria. Begin tried to still his fears, writing to him that "one cannot imagine that we would agree to have a foreign flag wave over the Temple Mount." On the twenty-second anniversary of the unification of Jerusalem in 1989, Goren would tell his nation that

our position on the Temple Mount has worsened tenfold; even the small remnant of Jewish sovereignty over the Temple Mount has almost completely slipped from our hands. If, on this 22nd celebration of Jerusalem Day, we should attempt to define the historical and Halakhic status of the State of Israel, and the nature of our period in history, it is doubtful that we could give a clear-cut positive response. Is our period the continuation of the Great Exile or is it the "Beginning of the Flowering of Our Final Redemption" and the opening of the Fourth Historical Period—The Third Temple Period?[67]

Rabbi Goren's most recent activity has been more subtle. In 1987 Goren attempted to place a Holocaust memorial on the roof of the Idra Yeshivah overlooking the plaza in front of the Western Wall. The memorial was designed by the Israeli artist Ya'akov Agam and had six Jewish stars situated in flames burning in fountains. Goren told a reporter that while the memorial directly recalls the Holocaust, it also symbolizes the libations and sacrificial offerings of the Temple.[68] The municipality fought Goren through the courts, arguing that Goren had not received the necessary permits and the memorial was in violation of the overall plan for the Jewish Quarter of the Old City.[69] But Goren's plan was not only to symbolize the sacrificial cult of the Temple, but also to make a small inroad in the Status Quo. In late 1988, Goren was able to erect the memorial.

THE VERY BEST BATTLEGROUND

While Israeli courts had granted the abstract right of Jews to pray on the Temple Mount, the Law for the Protection of the Holy Places had turned over complete control of the Temple Mount to the Muslim Council, and they denied access for prayer to the Jews. The Temple Mount did not even appear in the official list of Jewish holy places published by the Ministry of Religion.

Religious Zionists, many of them in the active messianist tradition, continue to find this situation intolerable. For example, Yisrael Medad, a Knesset aide to Geula Cohen in the Tehiya party, who had pushed for Jewish prayer on the Temple Mount, told us: "There was a certain civil rights element to it . . . There's a law on the books that says anybody who interferes with your rights, with your feelings, not only your access, but your feelings for your holy places will be sentenced to between five to seven years of imprisonment. Here, the only group in Israel which cannot get the full measure of protection from this is *davkah* [of all things], Jews."[70]

The assertion of Jewish ritual rights on the Temple Mount became a way for militant Zionists who were willing to gain territory wherever it might be. "If I can prove," Medad told us, "that the Arabs are not willing to do the minimal . . . to make a minimal concession, then why should we do the maximum on the other side? Instead of giving back Sinai and then saying what are we going to do, let's see first if we can solve the problem of Jerusalem. Are the Arabs going to let us live in Jerusalem? Are they going to share the Temple Mount? Are they going to share in the Old City? . . . It would be a proof of what we call the salami process. First they get the Sinai, then they get this and then that, and eventually the march is on to Jerusalem."

Medad believes that the *waqf* administrators on the Temple Mount have paid close attention to Zionists who wish to press their claims to the Temple Mount. Like Rabbi Goren, Medad doesn't want to pray in al-Aqsa or in any other building on the Temple Mount. "There is enough room outside which is in the open air along the west and the south which is outside the confines of the Temple," he told us. "But the Muslim *waqf* began building prayer platforms so as to restrict the open space as much as possible." In spring 1982, Knesset member Geula Cohen announced to the Israeli lawmakers that the *waqf* was carrying out illegal constructions on the Temple Mount with the intention of making use of every foot of open space. Medad told us that "now you cannot walk on the entire southern portion of the Temple Mount. They claim that there is a prayer niche here, a *miqrab*, you know, a prayer direction, and this whole area from 1,300 years ago was made a holy site. So you can't even walk up there even if you don't have a *kippah* on your head and you're wearing a cross. I have seen Dominican monks go up there and be chased away!" Geula Cohen's strategy was to raise the issue as a civil matter. If they were building prayer platforms on the Temple Mount, this would be a clear violation of the Status Quo. She also argued that the *waqf* had intentionally destroyed archaeological evidence on the Temple Mount which might be used to confirm the exact location of the ancient Temple. Photographic evidence of the destruction of archaeological remains was published along with an editorial by Hershel Shanks, the editor of *Biblical Archaeology Review*, which concluded that "Israel has not only the right but the obligation to assure that this [i.e., that no ancient remains, either exposed or unexposed, are destroyed] is the case. The archaeological remains on the Temple Mount belong neither to Israel nor to the Moslem authorities (both are only the custodians); the ancient remains belong to all mankind, and not just to this generation, but to generations past and yet unborn."[71] Cohen also argued that the Temple Mount was being used for political purposes and she pointed to a memorial for the victims of the Sabra and Shatilla massacre of 1982 which was erected on one of the outdoor prayer platforms.[72]

The *waqf*'s chief architect, Issam Awad, denied that there had ever been deliberate destruction of archaeological remains, telling us flatly, "We respect history." Awad has lived his entire life in Jerusalem. He studied architecture in Jerusalem and then studied preservation of art for an additional year in England. He began working on the restoration of al-Aqsa almost immediately after the fire set by Dennis Rohan had been extinguished. For him it is a lifelong project. We asked him about the charge made by Geula Cohen that the *waqf* has built additions to the existing structures of the *haram al-sharif*. "We are only preserving what is here, that's all," he answered. "But for the open spaces here what we are doing here is paving some areas and planting gardens. But these are not additional things. We don't do anything here which adds to anything. . . . I studied to be an architect and conservator. Conservation means to keep and not to add. We don't even correct mistakes made by others. I'm not really an architect here, because architects create things. I don't create anything. I am only preserving what is already here."

Issam knew all about the Jewish nationalists' efforts to reverse the Law for the Protection of Holy Places, and we asked him whether he thought that it is possible for Jews and Muslims to use the *haram* for prayer. "No, no," he answered and continued, "I don't think it is possible. But I hear that in the Jewish faith they say that no one should set foot here and there are signs that say that, because no one knows where the Temple once stood. And the only way when someone is going to rebuild the Temple is with the Messiah. When the Messiah comes, then I will share. Let the Messiah decide. That seems to be the best solution."[73]

Knesset discussion of Cohen's charges was tabled because of the attempted break-in by Rabbi Ariel's students in March 1983. It wasn't until late 1985 that the matter reached the Interior Committee. They voted to look over the Temple Mount themselves. In early January 1986, the ten committee members, headed by their chairman, Dov Shilansky from Herut, visited the Temple Mount, but they had not even gotten through the Mughrabian Gate before a huge crowed of Muslims formed, blocking their entrance. The *waqf* guards refused to let them enter, they said, because the cameras of the television reporters were strictly forbidden on the Temple Mount. The loudspeakers on the Temple Mount began blasting, "Jews have approached al-Aqsa and the mosque is in danger!" A shoving match broke out. Geula Cohen was shoved backwards by a *waqf* guard.

She bellowed at him, "You are not the boss here. In your mosque you can tell us no cameras. But not here!"

Shilansky shouted back, "We shall return! Our flag will yet fly over the Temple Mount, and we shall go there freely and the Temple shall be rebuilt."[74] Later he told reporters that the incident was terribly humiliating.

A few days later, a larger delegation of Knesset members tried to enter the Temple Mount. A full-scale riot exploded when Knesset member Rabbi Eliezer Waldman and another Tehiya party member took out prayer books and began the recitation of the Kaddish. This time, al-Aqsa's loudspeakers blared, "The Jews desecrate this place" and "We are the Sword of Muhammad!" Over six hundred border police were required to end the rioting, and tear gas had to be used to disperse the mob.[75] Meanwhile, outside the Temple Mount, four Knesset members from the Citizens' Rights Movement staged their own counterdemonstration against the visit to the Temple Mount. Yossi Sarid and Shulamit Aloni spoke for the group and called Rabbi Waldman's actions "a provocative and senseless move." Shimon Peres, who was Prime Minister in the Unity Government at the time, told reporters that Geula Cohen's initiative was unwarranted, for "Israeli sovereignty over Jerusalem needs no further proof or test." Yitzak Shamir, the Foreign Minister, concurred that there was no need for demonstrations to prove Israel's sovereignty in Jerusalem and especially on the Temple Mount.[76]

Since the mid-1980s the issue of the Temple Mount has also become a central issue for the Gush Emunim, the religious nationalist movement which has spearheaded the settlement of Judea and Samaria. In the early years of the decade, the movement's journal, *Nekudah*, hardly ever printed articles on the Temple Mount, but between 1982 and 1986 dozens of articles advocating the takeover of the Temple Mount appeared.[77] On Jerusalem Day in June of 1986, over 12,000 Temple Mount activists, many drawn from the ranks of the Gush Emunim, marched from Merkaz Ha-Rav to the Mount of Olives to view a sound-and-sight presentation entitled "The Temple Mount Is the Heart of the People." A large detachment of soldiers and police was required to keep approximately 100 of these activists from forcing their way onto the Temple Mount.[78] The September 1986 *Nekudah* editorial read: "What is proper regarding the whole Land of Israel must also be proper regarding the Temple Mount . . . if for returning to the whole Land of Israel, and for the establishment of the state, we have pushed to the end, by the same token we must now build the Temple."[79] The following year, for the festival of Sukkot, the Gush Emunim and the Faithful of the Temple Mount together attempted to pray at the Mughrabian Gate. This caused a major riot in which an estimated 2,000 Muslims fought a pitched battle with police and border troops for over three hours. Tear gas and live ammunition were used to bring the rioters under control, and more than fifty Palestinians were injured. Gershon Salomon, the founder of the Faithful of the Temple, told the press, "No power can stop us. We have the will of God."[80] In July of 1988, more than 1,500 police were required to separate Muslims who wished to pray on the *haram al-sharif* on 'Id-al-Adha, marking the end of the yearly pilgrimage to Mecca and Medina, and Jews who wished to pray at the Mughrabrian Gate for Tisha be'Av. Approximately 100 Jews prayed at the gate, but police barred the group from entering the Muslim Quarter. Nevertheless, about twenty members of Tehiya and Kach were able to slip through the police barricades and marched through the area waving Israeli flags.[81] Both journalists and high-ranking military officers warned that it was now only a matter of time before very serious damage was done to the Dome of the Rock and al-Aqsa, and a plan to defend the Temple Mount from Jewish extremists must be implemented immediately.[82]

"THIS IS OUR MOSQUE. IT IS NOT A SYNAGOGUE!"

The Muslims of Jerusalem are just as immovable. Sheik Sa'ad al-Din al'Alami is the Mufti of Jerusalem, the highest Muslim religious authority in Jerusalem and in what he understands as occupied Palestine. In addition to this post, he is also the head of the Supreme Muslim Council and the Council for the *waqf* and Islamic holy places. The Shari'a or religious law of Islam dictates that when Muslim lands are occupied by non-Muslims, the Muslims must elect representatives from amongst themselves to administer their affairs. Shortly after the Six-Day War, a number of Jerusalem's most prominent Muslims formed the Supreme Muslim Council in conformity with the dictates of religious law. This was the very same institution created in 1922 during the early years of the British Mandate.[83] The Jordanians had disbanded it in the early 1950s. The Israelis allowed the council to reconstitute itself after the 1967 war. The Muslims refer to it as the Supreme Muslim Council, but the Israelis refer to it only as the Muslim Council, linguistically hoping to separate it from the council which had exercised so much power under Hajj Amin al-Husayni throughout the Mandate. Sheik Alami was born in Jerusalem in 1911 under Ottoman rule. He has survived British occupation and Jordanian occupation. He intends to survive Israeli occupation too. He is proud of his long family lineage in the city. The first al-Alamis came to Jerusalem with Salah al-Din, and his family has always provided religious leadership for Jerusalem's Muslim community.

Israelis like Rabbi Goren want to worship out of doors, outside al-Aqsa and the Dome of the Rock in those places which are empty of Muslim buildings and structures. For them the Muslim claim to the holiness of the *haram al-sharif* is limited to the space within al-Aqsa mosque and the Dome of the Rock. But the Mufti sees things very differently. "The whole area is a mosque," he told us. "Not the buildings only, but all the land, all 144 *dunams*, all of it is our mosque and all of it we believe is a very holy place for all Muslims in the world. We believe that our Prophet Muhammad came and prayed here. These buildings that you see, the Dome of the Rock and al-Aqsa mosque, were not here then. There were no buildings here at that time. But he prayed in the area and we believe that that was all this area. All of this area is a mosque." Sheik Alami recounted to us the Muslim conquest of Palestine and how the second Caliph, Umar ibn Kuttab, came to the Temple Mount. There wasn't any holy place here to any religion in the world. There wasn't a synagogue. There wasn't a church or anything. There wasn't a holy building to anybody. He built a small mosque here. Sixty years later, the Umayyad caliph, Abd al-Malik, built the Dome of the Rock and, according to Sheik Alami, enlarged the original mosque of al-Aqsa. The Mufti again reminded us that when he built these, there was only the small mosque built by Umar. It made no sense to him that even though the Jewish Temple was here two thousand years ago, the Jews should now say that they want to pray in the *haram al-sharif*. He asked us if we had ever been to Spain, to Cordoba or Granada, and had seen the mosques there? "They changed them from a Muslim mosque to a church, yes? Can I go there and say that this is my mosque and I want it back? This is impossible. Surely, I can't. What can I say?"

Sheik Alami complained to us that the Jews had constantly harassed Muslims and Christians since 1967. He sternly told us that "they put bombs near the churches, near the mosques, several times, and here in al-Aqsa mosque. You know that the Jews burned al-Aqsa mosque in 1969." He continued to catalogue the assaults against the sanctity of al-Aqsa. The Jews had taken the keys to the Mughrabian Gate and allowed whoever they wanted to enter whenever they wanted. They stationed their soldiers on the *haram*. But we interrupted him and suggested that the soldiers might be there to protect the *haram* from Jewish extremists. To have Israeli soldiers on the *haram* is to rub the Mufti's nose in the subordination of Islam within Jewish Jerusalem. He understands that it is the duty of the government to protect the holy places, but they would do that with the police, not soldiers. He sent letters and telegrams to the Prime Minister, the Minister of Defense, and the Minister of the Interior who controls the police, demanding the removal of the soldiers. He shrugged his shoulders and told us, "What can I do? I haven't soldiers to oblige their soldiers to go out. I am asking the government to take them out and it's their duty to take them out. . . . They can put police in the mosque." He believed that the police could handle any threat to the security of the al-Aqsa and the Dome of the Rock and he pointed out that when Jews in 1983 attempted to penetrate the *haram*, the police discovered them, not the Israeli military.

But most disturbing to him were the repeated efforts of Jews to enter the *haram* and to pray there. He underscored several times in our discussion that the *haram* was open to all visitors. "Anybody," he said, "can visit any mosque, any of our mosques, here in al-Aqsa mosque or any other place as a visitor, but not as one who enters to pray and to do as a synagogue here." He repeated himself so that there would be no question about his implacable opposition to Jewish prayer on the *haram*. "This is our mosque. It is not a synagogue!" Even if he could compromise, he didn't believe that the Jews would only be content with the open spaces on the *haram*. For him, the litmus test for the sincerity of the Jews was the Ibrahimmiyah Mosque in Hebron, what the Jews call the Cave of Machpelah. Its tall Herodian walls suggest to the visitor that this is a fortress rather than a tomb, but within are buried the patriarchs and matriarchs of ancient Israel. The building is made up of two floors; the ground floor is traditionally understood as the burial chambers of the patriarchs, while the second floor contains their symbolic tombs. For the Muslims this structure is the tomb of Ibrahim, the Friend of God and the first Muslim, and for the Jews this is the tomb of Abraham, the first Jew. Before the 1929 evacuation of the Hebron's Jewish community, Jews had only been allowed to go to the seventh step of the outside staircase.

Alami narrated how he believed the mosque had been transformed into a synagogue, after the Jews requested only a small amount of time for their ritual prayer. "In 1967, their Minister of Defense, Moshe Dayan, went to the Mayor of Hebron, Sheik Jabbari, and he asked him to give him permission for the Jews to enter and visit the mosque. Sheik Jabbari, the mayor of Hebron, said that all our mosques are open to any visitor who wants to visit, Jews, Christians, to any visitor. . . . The mayor gave his permission. What has happened after that? First of all, they began to enter and visit after they took their shoes off. Then after a few days or a few weeks, they began to enter with their shoes on. Then they began to enter and pray. Then they brought their material for praying, benches and tables and so on. Then they began to pray most of the time and they don't let the Muslims enter to pray inside. If you go to see the mosque, you don't know whether it is a synagogue or a mosque. That's what has happened to our mosque in Hebron."

Sheik Alami is absolutely uncompromising. He will not allow what has happened to the Ibrahimmiyah Mosque to take place at the *haram*. "We have now one million Muslims and Christians" in the West Bank and Gaza, he tells us. "When they will kill all this million, the Muslims and the Christians, they may enter, but not before. All the Christians and all the Muslims are ready to die before letting anyone into the mosque. I told you that we have one million Muslims and Christians and we have one billion Muslims outside. No one will enter and change anything to let them pray in our mosque. All the Muslims will come here. If they kill all of them, after that they may do whatever they want, but not before. Not as long as there is one Muslim still alive in this area." Many of Jerusalem's longtime administrators believe that this talk is not just rhetoric.

The Mufti was keenly aware that a significant proportion of the Palestinian population is Christian, but he believed that there was nevertheless an essential unity among all Palestinians. "Here in Palestine," he told us, "we believe that all of us are Arabs. It doesn't matter with me that this one is a Christian and goes to pray in a church and I go to pray in my mosque. After all we are good friends. All the Christian leaders are my good friends. And I love them and we are the same. Christians and Muslims, we all believe that we must be Arabs!"

He told us that beginning in 1982 he began receiving menacing letters from anonymous individuals who he believed were members of Rabbi Meir Kahane's Kach party and others threatening to enter the *haram* and to pray. The letters told him that if he persisted in refusing Jews the right to enter, then the Dome of the Rock, al-Aqsa mosque, the Church of the Holy Sepulchre, and other Christian holy places would be destroyed. The letters also threatened to kill both Christians and Muslims and he told us, "to take their blood to build Israel, for the Jews to drink it." Another letter attempted to offer a bribe of one million Jordanian *dinars* to leave the *haram* and Jerusalem and another an explicit death threat. The threats only strengthened his resolve to resist efforts to change the Status Quo. "I'll not let them kill any Christian or Muslim!" he drummed. "I'll not let them destroy the *haram al-sharif* and al-Aqsa mosque. I will protect them.

I myself will go to the Holy Sepulchre and I'll protect the Holy Sepulchre and all the holy places for the Christians and Muslims. Also, all the Christians will come here and aid me to protect our mosques. All of us here see ourselves as Arabs."[84]

Sheik Alami is a public man who knows that his sermons and interviews with the foreign press are closely watched by the Israelis. But he is also a sophisticated politician who wields considerable influence on the West Bank, and even after King Hussein cut his ties to the area in August 1988, he continues to administer a huge Jordanian-funded bureaucracy of Islamic officials. The center of King Hussein's power base in Jerusalem and on the West Bank has always been the *waqf* and the religious court system. These have functioned as vehicles to extend the king's patronage and to generate loyalty to him rather than to Palestinian nationalist causes. The king has retained the nucleus of his infrastructure and he has not ceded his authority over the management of religious affairs in Jerusalem or in the West Bank. Sheik Alami remains an important player in Hussein's dreams to realize his grandfather's claim to the *haram al-sharif*. Alami's public persona and his ties to an extensive patronage machine are very much unlike other Muslim religious leaders, such as Sheik Ibrahim Yazuri, Sheik Ahmad Yasin, Sheik Abd al-Aziz Odeh, and Sheik Fathi Shqaqi, all of Gaza and all involved in the emergence of resurgent Muslim groups such as the Islamic Jihad or the Islamic Resistance movement.[85] The Islamic Jihad first appeared in 1987, well before the beginning of the Intifada. However, the Islamic Resistance Movement is a product of the uprising and is widely known through its acronym, HAMAS or in Arabic "zeal." Both groups are spinoffs from the Muslim Brotherhood which has had a long history in Gaza, where the British, the Egyptians, and the Israelis used it to undercut Palestinian nationalism. Both groups would replace Israel with an Islamic state. HAMAS' "covenant" defines all of historic Palestine, both Israel and the occupied territories, as "an Islamic *waqf* for all generations of Muslims until the resurrection." The covenant also rejected any two-state solution, stating that "various initiatives, peace proposals and international conferences [here perhaps referring to the diplomatic moves of the PLO in the fall of 1988] run counter to the principles of the Islamic Resistance Movement, since giving up part of Palestine is like giving up part of religion." It also ruled out any international peace conference which might be set up to mediate the Israeli-Palestinian conflict, since it would "give the infidels the role of arbiter over the land of the Muslims. When have infidels ever dealt justly with believers?"[86] Sheik Yassin is widely believed to be the chief organizer of HAMAS and was jailed by the Israelis in June 1989. However, in an interview a few months earlier with the *Jerusalem Post*, he said that "I want to be a citizen of Palestine, with full rights, social and political. My aspiration is to have a Muslim state, but I'll accept the decision of the majority. If the PLO wins, I'll accept, but at the same time, I'll continue with my [religious] preaching."[87]

These resurgent Muslim groups have also tried to control the meaning of the *haram* and assimilate its power to their efforts to define the Palestinian struggle against Israel. In April of 1989, there were massive disturbances on the *haram* which coincided with the beginning of Ramadan. The disturbances were widely believed to have been organized by members of HAMAS who had come to Jerusalem from the Gaza Strip. Huge boulders and stones, which had been stored on the *haram* according to police sources, were hurled down onto the Jews praying at the Western Wall. Police retaliated with tear gas and rubber bullets.[88] The Israelis responded on the following Friday, restricting entrance to the *haram* only to those Muslims who were from Jerusalem. In order to keep the HAMAS people from gaining their symbolic center, roadblocks on the highways leading from the West Bank and Gaza to Jerusalem stopped many who wanted to pray in al-Aqsa. Soldiers and border police, who manned checkpoints in the Old City and at the entrances to the *haram*, scrutinized every person's identity card so that only Muslims from Jerusalem could enter.[89] Approximately 7,000 Muslims were allowed onto the *haram*, but police had earlier estimated that 35,000 or more Muslims would attempt to pray in Jerusalem. The following week Sheik Alami, through his spokesman, called for Muslims to pray in al-Aqsa. The spokesman said that if the Israelis "prevent them from entering the mosque, they are to pray in the Old City of Jerusalem. If they are barred from entering the city, they are to pray on the roads leading to Jerusalem."[90] HAMAS and the Islamic Jihad were unwilling to adopt the position of the Unified Command and the Intifada which in 1988 and early 1989 pushed the PLO toward a two-state solution with the Israelis. Their exclusion from the leadership of the uprising because of their position meant that their only power could be generated from the symbolic center of the Palestinian community, and during Ramadan 1989 they began to use that power with effectiveness.

In comparison to these movements and their leaders, Sheik Alami appears to be a moderate. Throughout our discussion Alami told us that he is a religious man and wants only peace and justice, not only in Jerusalem, but also in the world. He was willing to countenance a two-state solution to the Israeli-Palestinian conflict. "I want Israel," he told us, "to return back to its boundaries in 1967. Let us Palestinians be free in our part and let them be free in their part. And let us be good neighbors. That is the best way, I think." He rejected violence as a way to achieve this two-state solution. "I don't want war. And I don't want a single Jew to be killed or any Muslim or Christian. I want justice and peace." Yet in November of 1988, when firebombs were hurled at buses in Jericho and Jerusalem, killing a Jewish mother and her three children and seriously injuring another woman, Sheik Alami was on the other side. He reportedly made statements about Israeli soldiers' torturing and burning Palestinians alive. This brought back a blistering attack from Mayor Kollek, who told him in a letter that his statements were groundless and intended only to incite violence. "Your first duty," Kollek wrote to the Mufti, "is to condemn the shocking crime by young Arabs whose victims were a Jewish mother and her children, who were burned alive." The mayor went on to say that "it's very strange that we didn't hear or read any denunciation from you and your colleagues about that."[91]

BETWEEN A ROCK AND A HARD PLACE

The Knesset's legislation giving full control over the Temple Mount to the *waqf* was motivated by a profound sense of religious freedom in a liberal democracy and an awareness of how politically sensitive the Temple Mount might be. The solution was but a holding action.

Islamic control over the Temple Mount remains a fundamental contradiction for large numbers of Zionists, and there remains substantial support to remove the contradiction. To many, sovereignty without control over the central site of sacrifice is incomplete. To others, it is an infringement upon Jews' religious freedoms in their own capital. To still others, it represents a failure to pursue the human activity necessary to bring on redemption. Since 1967 various polls have sought to measure the Israeli attitude toward the Temple Mount. In 1983, for example, 18.3 percent of Israeli Jews supported the idea of rebuilding the Temple before the coming of the Messiah.[92]

The debate over the Knesset's Law of Holy Places with regard to the Temple Mount recapitulated the conflicts that had begun in the early years of the British Mandate. Militant Zionists are acting out the very same symbolic claims acted out by the Beta youth in 1929. Sheik Alami is driven by the very same symbolic logic that drove Hajj Amin al-Husayni in the 1920s. And just as Hajj Amin al-Husayni attempted to harness the power of the *haram* to reach for leadership of the Palestinian community, so too are the resurgent Muslim groups attempting to seize control of the meaning of the *haram* to lead the Palestinians toward an Islamic polity. But at the same time that the *haram al-sharif* has become once again a privileged platform for Palestinians, the central irony is that they must rely on the power of the Israeli state to protect them from the incursion of the new Jewish nationalists and to maintain their exclusive control over that space.

The Islamic elite is deeply apprehensive that what happened at the Cave of Machpelah, or the mosque of Ibrahim, in Hebron immediately after the 1967 war, allowing Jews for the first time in centuries to enter and pray in the structure, will also happen on the *haram al-shariff*. The Cave of Machpelah is in fact much more important and less threatening to the symbolic claims of the Jewish state than the Temple Mount. The Cave of Machpelah established the symbolic right of patrimony, while the secular Israeli state has a more ambiguous relationship with the Temple Mount, the symbol of priesthood. The Temple and its priesthood undercuts the symbolic legitimacy of the state in a way that the Cave of Machpelah does not.

As we have shown, this sacred site is a source of enormous social power, control over which has been contested between and within the Israeli and Palestinian communities. It has been used repeatedly to mobilize within each community and against the other community. It is the state which must ultimately adjudicate these inter- and intracommunal conflicts. The use to which this sacred space has been put has enormous implications for the content of the state's legitimacy, that nature of the discourse in which political power is understood and exercised. There is an intimate connection, then, between the organization of sacred space and the material and cultural organization of power. Sacred space is socially constructed. Its meaning is made, and that making has implications for the doctrines which motivate those who claim it as their own.

Political violence cannot be understood as simply the irrational acts of desperate men. Violence, no matter how how distasteful we find it, is a normal part of political conflict and must be understood as such. Typically it is a strategy used by those who are intensely motivated and have few other resources at hand. What we have shown in the case of Jerusalem is that it is the same for symbolic violence. Groups in both communities have chosen to desecrate the others' sacred space. Rabbi Orenstein's text with which we began this discussion noted that the Western Wall had been "brutally desecrated." This desecration continues to the present, whether it be an individual who carries out a murderous assault on the *haram al-sharif* or a grenade attack at the precise moment that Israeli soldiers are being sworn into the army. These are not simply acts of violence. They are a symbolic discourse about the status of a symbolic place.

Bruce Lincoln recently published a brilliant interpretation of one of the most curious events of the Spanish Civil War in which the bodies of hundreds, if not thousands, of Spanish priests and nuns were exhumed. The mummified remains of priests, bishops, and nuns were ritually desecrated in the streets of Barcelona. Churches were burned, ritual images and statues were disfigured and decapitated. Ecclesiastical paraphernalia were appropriated in parody of the church. Francisco Franco's Nationalists immediately seized upon these acts of anticlericalism among the forces of the Communists and Republicans as examples of inhumanity, barbarism, and bestiality. But Lincoln finds something else in these symbolic acts which he calls a "profanophany." He defines this term as "a revelation of the profanity, temporality, and corruption inherent in someone or something."[93] These profanophanies were intended "to demonstrate dramatically and in public," he writes, "the powerlessness of the image and thereby to inflict a double disgrace on its champions, first by exposing the bankruptcy of their vaunted symbols and, second, their impotence in the face of attack."[94] He concludes by stating:

Although the exhumations have consistently been presented as an aberrant and impious act of violence, such a simplistic analysis is untenable. Like all anticlerical violence throughout Spanish history, they were not an assault on religion per se, but rather on one specific religious institution: an institution closely aligned with, and subservient to, the traditionally dominant segment of society. At the same time that the exhumations were a ferocious assault on and mockery of that institution, they were also an assault on the segment of society with which it is symbiotically entangled, and what is more—they were a ritual in which the traditionally subordinate segment of Spanish society sought by means of highly charged discourse of gestures and deeds to deconstruct the old social order and construct a new radically different order in its place.[95]

Violence is a form of communication. Symbolic violence is an adjunct to material violence. Symbolic violence, profanation, is used by members of one community or movement in order to mobilize their own communities, to make their definition of reality the dominant one, to demonstrate the ultimate powerlessness of the other, and to redefine the other as radically alien, as profane. By profaning the other's sacred place you make the other profane, an alien with no claim to possession of that space. Symbolic violence is a way to mobilize intense opposition, to polarize the situation using a very few resources. It is a way to delegitimize those political forces who would treat the disposition of territory as a matter to be negotiated between normal states. If the United States and the Soviet Union on the one hand, and Israel and the PLO on the other, move towards a negotiated solution to the Israeli-Palestinian conflict, we can expect even more violence at the sacred center of Jerusalem.

NOTES

1. Amos Elon reprints a number of entries from Rabbi Orenstein's diary in his *Jerusalem: City of Mirrors* (Boston: Little, Brown and Company, 1989), pp. 84–87.

2. Cited in Taysir Jabara, *Palestinian Leader Hajj Amin al-Husayni: Mufti of Jerusalem* (Princeton, N.J.: The Kingston Press, 1985), p. 81.

3. "Jerusalem: Holy City of Three Religions" (Jerusalem: Israel Universities Study Group for Middle Eastern Affairs, 1977), p. 3.

4. Dov Joseph, *The Faithful City: The Siege of Jerusalem, 1948* (New York: Simon and Schuster, 1960), p. 58.

5. Larry Collins and Dominique Lapierre, *O Jerusalem* (New York: Simon and Schuster, 1972), pp. 385–86.

6. Alan Hart, *Arafat: Terrorist or Peacemaker?* (London: Sidgwick and Jackson, 1984), pp. 72–74.

7. See, for example, Miriam Lichtheim, "The Praise of Cities in the Literature of the Egyptian New Kingdom," in S. M. Burstein and L. A. Okin, eds., *Panhellenica: Essays in Ancient History and Historiography in Honor of Truesdell S. Brown*, (Lawrence, Kan.: Coronado Press, 1980), pp. 15–24.

8. See especially his *La Poétique de l'espace* (Paris: Presses Universitaires de France, 1957) and *La Terre et les rêveries de la volonté* (Paris: J. Corti, 1948).

9. Otto von Simpson, *The Gothic Cathedral* (Princeton, N.J.: Princeton University Press, 1962), and John James, *Chartres: The Masons who Built a Legend* (London: Routledge and Kegan Paul, 1982), esp. pp. 83–112.

10. *L. A. Freeway: An Appreciative Essay* (Berkeley: University of California Press, 1981).

11. See his essays "Sacred Architecture and Symbolism" and "Barabudur, the Symbolic Temple" in Diane Apostolos-Cappadona, ed. and trans., *Symbolism, the Sacred and the Arts* (New York: Crossroad Publishing Company, 1985), pp. 105–42.

12. *Religion in Essence and Manifestation*, trans. by J. E. Turner (Gloucester: Peter Smith, 1967), 2: 393.

13. Ibid., p. 402.

14. Joachim Wach, *Sociology of Religion* (1944; rpt. Chicago: University of Chicago Press, 1971).

15. "Universals in Religion," in *Types of Religious Experience: Christian and Non-Christian* (1951; rpt. Chicago: University of Chicago Press, 1971), p. 34.

16. *Traité d'histoire des religions* (1949; rpt. Paris: Payot, 1970), p. 35.

17. "Mircea Eliade and the 'History' of Religions," *Religion* 19 (1989): 106.

18. *Patterns in Comparative Religion*, trans. by Rosemary Sheed (Cleveland and New York: World Publishing Company, 1963), p. 7.

19. *Banaras: City of Light* (London: Routledge and Kegan Paul, 1983), pp. xiv-xv.

20. Jonathan Z. Smith, *Map is Not Territory: Studies in the History of Religions* (Leiden, Netherlands: E. J. Brill, 1978), p. 291.

21. Jonathan Z. Smith, *Imagining Religion: From Babylon to Jonestown* (Chicago and London: University of Chicago Press, 1982), p. 52.

22. David Harvey, "Monument and Myth: The Building of the Basilica of the Sacred Heart" in *Consciousness and the Urban Experience: Studies in the History and Theory of Capitalist Urbanization* (Baltimore: John Hopkins University Press, 1985), pp. 221–50. A parallel study is Mona Ozouf, "Le Panthéon," *Les lieux de mémoire*, vol. I, *La République*, ed. by Pierre Nora (Paris: Gallimard, 1984), pp. 139–66.

23. Johanna Broda, David Carrasco, and Eduardo Matos Moctezuma, *The Great Temple of Tenochtitlán: Center and Periphery in the Aztec World* (Berkeley and London: University of California Press, 1987), p. 156.

24. David Carrasco, "Toward the Splendid City: The Study of Mesoamerican Religions," *Religious Studies Review*, 14.4 (1988): 298.

25. The most complete discussion of the Nebi Musa Mosque is Samuel Tamari, "Maqam Nebi Musa Near Jericho," *Cathedra* 11 (1979): 153–80.

26. For example, James Fin,, *Stirring Times or Records from Jerusalem Consular Chronicles of 1853 to 1856* (London: C. Kegan and Paul Co., 1878), 1: 204.

27. The most comprehensive description of the pilgrimage is Tewfik Canaan, *Mohammedan Saints and Sanctuaries in Palestine* (1927; rpt. Jerusalem: Ariel Publishing House, n.d.), pp. 206–14. See also G. E. von Grunebaum, *Muhammadan Festivals* (London: Curzon Press, 1976), esp. pp. 81–83.

28. Philip Mattar, *The Mufti of Jerusalem and the Palestinian National Movement* (New York: Columbia University Press, 1988), pp. 16–17.

29. Cited in Y. Porath, *The Emergence of the Palestinian-Arab National Movement 1918–1929* (London: Frank Cass, 1974), p. 98.

30. Ibid., pp. 192–93.

31. The term *waqf* literally means a "pious foundation" of either real estate or buildings set aside by specific families or government officials. *Waqf* property cannot be taxed and its entire income must be devoted to charitable uses. Technically, there are two forms of *waqf*. The *zurri* is *waqf* intended for family usage, while *mahbus* is *waqf* intended for public charitable use.

32. The most comprehensive history of this *waqf* is A. L. Tibawi, *The Islamic Pious Foundations in Jerusalem: Origins, History and Usurpation by Israel* (London: The Islamic Cultural Centre, 1978), esp. pp. 10–15.

33. See the comprehensive study of Schmuel Berkovicz, "The Legal Status of the Holy Places in Israel," Doctoral Dissertation, Hebrew University, 1978.

34. The British knew, for example, that in the winter of 1918, Syrian and Palestinian Cairenes came together, fearing the establishment in Palestine of Jewish administration or state. On their mind was the expected large-scale Zionist purchases of Arab-owned land, and the possibility that the Jews would rebuild the Temple and thus cause sectarian strife in the county. See Muhammad Y. Muslih, *The Origins of Palestinian Nationalism* (New York: Columbia University Press, 1988), p. 185.

35. Taysir Jabara, *Palestinian Leader Hajj Amin al-Husayni: Mufti of Jerusalem* (Princeton, N.J.: The Kingston Press, 1985), p. 78.

36. Ibid., p. 79.

37. Philip Mattar, *The Mufti of Jerusalem*, p. 36.

38. Jabara, *Palestinian Leader Hajj Amin al-Husayni*, p. 81.

39. Ibid., pp. 106–7.

40. Mattar, *The Mufti of Jerusalem*, p. 40. The first modern reference to the wall belonging to the Abu Madyan *waqf* is in 1840. For a history of Jewish interests, see Itzhak Ben-Zvi, "Eretz-Yisrael under Ottoman Rule, 1517–1917," in Louis Finkelstein, ed., *The Jews: Their History* (New York: Schocken Books, 1972), p. 464,.

41. Mattar, *The Mufti of Jerusalem*, p. 40.

42. Ibid., p. 46.

43. Jabara, *Palestinian Leader Hajj Amin al-Husayni*, p. 95.

44. Mohammed K. Shadid, "The Muslim Brotherhood Movement in the West Bank and Gaza," *Third World Quarterly* 10: 2 (1988): 658–82.

45. See Walter Zander, *Israel and the Holy Places of Christendom* (New York: Praeger Publishers, 1971), p. 88 and Gabriel Padon, "The Divided City, 1948–1967," in Alice L Eckardt, ed., *Jerusalem City of Ages* (New York: University Press of America and American Academic Association for Peace in the Middle East, 1987), esp. pp. 134–42.

46. On King Hussein's control of the *haram al-sharif* since his disengagement from the West Bank in the summer of 1988, see Adam Garfinkle, "Getting it Right? US Mideast Policy in the Bush Administration," *The Jerusalem Quarterly* 52 (1989): 55–78.

47. The complete text of the Proclamation is found in Itamar Rabinovich and Jehunda Reinharz, eds., *Israel in the Middle East: Documents on Society, Politics and Foreign Relations, 1948–Present* (New York and Oxford: Oxford University Press, 1984), pp. 13–15. For the text of the "Law for the Protection of the Holy Places" see Zander, *Israel and the Holy Places of Christendom*, pp. 102–3.

48. Meron Benvenisti, *Jerusalem, The Torn City: A Study of a Polarized Community* (Jerusalem: The West Bank Data Base Project, 1983), Research Paper No. 3, p. 41.

49. One recent example of Israel as a theological category for Islam is Mohammad H. Al-Asi, *The Duality of the Palestinian Issue: Islam, al-Intifadah, the Future* (Bethesda, Md.: Islamic Trend of North America, 1988). Here, Israel is the ideology of the nation-state which carves up the unitary *umma* (pp. 4–5, for example). See also Ronald L. Lettler, *Past Trials and Present Tribulations: A Muslim Fundamentalist's View of the Jews* (Oxford and New York: Pergamon Press, 1987), which notes that Muslim religious authorities looked with discomfort at the European emancipation of the Jews (pp. 19–20).

50. See Arie Morgenstern, "Messianic Concepts and Settlement in the Land of Israel," in Richard I. Cohen, ed., *Vision and Conflict in the Holy Land* (Jerusalem and New York: Yad Izhak Ben Zvi and St. Martin's Press, 1985), pp. 141–62, and *Messianism and the Settlement of Eretz-Israel* (Jerusalem: Yad Izhak Ben Zvi Publications, 1985).

51. Jody Myers, "Attitudes toward a Resumption of Sacrificial Worship in the Nineteenth Century," *Modern Judaism* 7 (1987): 35. But see also her "Seeking Zion: The Messianic Ideology of Zevi Hirsch Kalischer, 1795–1874," Doctoral Dissertation, University of California, Los Angeles, 1985.

52. Menachem Friedman, "The State of Israel as a Theological Dilemma," in Baruch Kimmerling, ed., *The Israeli State and Society: Boundaries and Frontiers* (Albany: State University of New York Press, 1989), pp. 203–4.

53. Charles S. Liebman and Eliezer Don-Yehiya, *Civil Religion in Israel: Traditional Judaism and Political Culture in the Jewish State* (Berkeley and Los Angeles: University of California Press, 1983), p. 159.

54. Yeshayahu Leibowitz, *Judaism, the Jewish People and the State of Israel* (Jerusalem: Schocken, 1975), pp. 233–335. Leibowitz's position on the sanctity of the Western Wall is parallel to the position taken by Gershom Scholem after the riots in 1929. See David Biale, *Gershom Scholem: Kabbalah and Counter-History* (Cambridge, Mass., and London: Harvard University Press, 1979), p. 179.

55. Perhaps one of the most comprehensive discussions of this transformation is Ehud Luz, *Parallels Meet: Religion and Nationalism in the Early Zionist Movement 1882–1904* (Philadelphia: Jewish Publication Society of America, 1988), esp. pp. ix–xvi.

56. Charles S. Liebman and Eliezer Don-Yehiya, *Religion and Politics in Israel* (Bloomington: Indiana University Press, 1984), p. 74.

57. Zvi Yehudah ha-Cohen Kuk, *On the Paths of Israel* (Jerusalem: Menorah, 1969), p. 160.

58. Among the most important studies of the Gush Emunim are David Biale, "Mysticism and Politics in Modern Israel: The Messianic Ideology of Abraham Isaac Ha-Cohen Kook," in Peter Merkl and Ninian Smart, eds., *Religion and Politics in the Modern World* (New York and London: New York University Press, 1983), pp. 191–204; Janet Aviad, "The Contemporary Israeli Pursuit of the Millennium," *Religion* 14 (1984): 199–222; David Newman, ed., *The Impact of the Gush Emunim; Politics and Settlement in the West Bank* (London: Croom Helm, 1985); Eliezer Don-Yehiya, "Jewish Messianism, Religious Zionism and Israeli Politics: The Impact and Origins of Gush Emunim," *Middle Eastern Studies* 23 (1987): 215–34; Gideon Aran, "From Religious Zionism to Zionist Religions: The Roots of Gush Emunim," in Peter Y. Medding, ed., *Studies in Contemporary Jewry* (Jerusalem and Bloomington: Institute of Contemporary Jewry of the Hebrew University of Jerusalem and Indian University Press, 1986), 2: 116–43, and "Eretz Israel: Between Politics and Religions," The Jerusalem Institute for Israel Studies, No. 18 (Jerusalem: The Jerusalem Institute for Israel Studies, 1985).

59. Gideon Aran, "A Mystic-Messianic Interpretation of Modern Israeli History: The Six Day War as a Key Event in the Development of the Original Religious Culture of Gush Emunim," in Jonathan Frankel, ed., *Studies in Contemporary Jewry* (Jerusalem and Oxford: Institute of Contemporary Jewry of the Hebrew University of Jerusalem and Oxford University Press, 1988), 4:263–75, described how many intellectuals of Gush Emunim interpreted the Six-Day War as marking the beginning of a new historical era, the era of Redemption. See also Uriel Tal, "Contemporary Hermeneutics and Self-Views on the Relationship between State and Land," in Lawrence A. Hoffman, ed., *The Land of Israel: Jewish Perspectives* (Notre Dame: University of Notre Dame Press, 1986), pp. 316–38.

60. Uzi Narkiss, *The Liberation of Jerusalem: The Battle of 1967* (London: Vallentine, Mitchell, 1983), pp. 252–56. See also Abraham Rabinovich, *The Battle for Jerusalem,*

June 5–7, 1967–20th Anniversary Edition (Philadelphia: The Jewish Publication Society, 1987), esp. p. 370.

61. For a description of Rabbi Goren's activity immediately after the Six-Day War, see Meron Benvenisti, *Jerusalem, The Torn City,* pp. 287–90.

62. Cited in Meron Benvenisti, *Jerusalem, The Torn City,* pp. 290–91.

63. Haggai Segal, *Dear Brothers: The West Bank Underground* (Woodmere: Beit-Shamai Publications, 1988), p. 20.

64. Dan Fisher, "6-Day War: The Legacy of Conflict," *The Los Angeles Times,* May 31, 1987.

65. J. Theodor and C. Albeck, *Midrash Bershit Rabbah* 64:10 (Jerusalem: Wahram Books, 1965), 2: 710–11.

66. See Asher Kaufman, "New Light upon Zion: The Plan and Precise Location of the Second Temple," *Ariel* 43 (1984): 63–99; "Where the Ancient Temple of Jerusalem Stood," *Biblical Archeology Review* 9 (1983): 40–58; and "The Meaning of HAR HA-BAYIT and its Northern Gate," *Niv Ha-Midrashiah,* 18–19 (1984–85): 97–109. See also Abraham Rabonivich's essay on Professor Kaufman, "The Professor in Search of the Temple," in *Jerusalem on Earth: People, Passions and Politics in the Holy City* (New York: The Free Press, 1988), pp. 141–48.

67. Shlomo Goren, "The day of Jerusalem: Our hopes and aspirations," *The Jerusalem Post,* June 2, 1989, p. 10.

68. Cited in Ian Lustick, *For the Land and the Lord: Jewish Fundamentalism in Israel* (New York: Council on Foreign Relations, 1988), p. 324, n. 43.

69. Andy Court, "Rabbi Goren loses first round in court," *Jerusalem Post,* April 18, 1988.

70. Our interviews with Yisrael Medad were conducted on February 26 and March 11, 1984.

71. "Ancient Remains on the Temple Mount Must Not Be Destroyed," *Biblical Archaeology Review* 9 (1983): 61.

72. Yisrael Medad, "Inside the Temple Mount," *Counterpoint: Perspectives on Israel and the Jewish People* 1 (1984): 8.

73. Issam Awad, personal interview, January 15, 1984.

74. Dan Fisher, "10 Israeli Lawmakers, Arabs Clash at Holy Site," *Los Angeles Times,* January 9, 1986.

75. Thomas L Friedman, "Another Incident on Temple Mount," *The New York Times,* January 15, 1986.

76. "Left, Right trade charges over Mount," *The Jerusalem Post: International Edition,* January 25, 1986.

77. See, for example, Motti Nachmani, "What is going on with the Temple Mount," *Nekudah* 47 (September 3, 1989): 7; Yigal Ariel, "The Temple Mount as *waqf* property," *Nekudah* 58 (May 17, 1983): 18–19; Shabbatai Ben-Dov, "Fasts of the Temple Destruction," *Nekudah* 61 (July 18, 1983): 8–9; Yisrael Eldad, "In the Den of Numerologists," *Nekudah* 78 (September 21, 1984): 14; Baruch Lior, "To Prepare the Generations for Prayer and War," *Nekudah* 85 (April 5, 1985): 12–13; Yisrael Medad, "Battle on the Temple Mount," *Counterpoint* 3 (1986): 8–9; Moshe Ben-Josef, "Prelude to the Mount," *Nekudah* 97 (March 25, 1986): 8. See also the editorials "The Temple Mount is Not in Our Hands," *Nekudah,* 87 (May 24, 1985): 4; "The Fuse," *Nekudah* 95 (January 21, 1986): 4; and "Messiah Now," *Nekudah* 105 (September 5, 1986): 5.

78. Lustick, *For the Land and the Lord: Jewish Fundamentalism in Israel,* pp. 170–71.

79. Cited in ibid., p. 172.

80. "Israeli Police, Arabs Clash in Jerusalem: Jewish Group's Plan to Pray at Temple Mount Sparks Violence," *Los Angeles Times*, October 12, 1987.

81. "2 West Bank Arabs Killed; Security tight in Jerusalem," *Los Angeles Times*, July 25, 1988.

82. See Lustick, *For the Land and the Lord*, pp. 172–73. Brigadier General Yoel Ben-Porat stated in *Ma'ariv*, May 10, 1987, a report translated in *Israel Press Briefs*, No. 53 (May-June 1987), that he personally knew of messianic fighters from elite IDF units (pp. 14–15).

83. On the formation of the Supreme Muslim Council see Y. Porath, *The Emergence of the Palestinian-Arab National Movement, 1918–1929* (London: Frank Cass, 1974), esp. pp. 194–207.

84. Sheik Sa'ad al-Din al-Alami, personal interview, May 25, 1984.

85. For a detailed account of the relationship of these two groups to the PLO see, Matti Steinberg, "The PLO and Palestinian Islamic Fundamentalism," *The Jerusalem Quarterly* 52 (1982): 37–54.

86. Dan Fisher and Dan Williams, "Islamic Group Changes PLO Over Palestine," *Los Angeles Times*, September 5, 1988.

87. Michael Sela, "Resistance is a Moslem duty," *Jerusalem Post*, May 26, 1989. But also see Elain Ruth Fletcher, "Islam and the Strife," *Jerusalem Post*, May 26, 1989; and Daniel Williams, "Rivalry to Control Uprising Grows: Islamic Hard-Liners Impose Strike in Challenge to PLO," *Los Angeles Times*, September 10, 1988.

88. Daniel Williams, "Muslims, Israel Police Clash at Islamic Holy Site," *Los Angeles Times*, April 8, 1989.

89. Sabra Chartrand, "For the First Time, Israel Restricts Palestinians' Freedom of Worship," *New York Times*, April 15, 1989.

90. Dan Izenberg, "Moslems urged to flock to al-Aksa," *Jerusalem Post*, November 11, 1988.

91. Andy Court, "Kolleck urges Mufti to score firebombing," *Jerusalem Post*, November 11, 1988.

92. Cited in Lustick, *For the Land and the Lord*, p. 191.

93. Bruce Lincoln, *Discourse and the Construction of Society: Comparative Studies of Myth, Ritual, and Classification* (New York and Oxford: Oxford University Press, 1989), p. 125.

94. Ibid., p. 120.

95. Ibid., p. 127.

3

The Temple and the Garden of Eden in Ezekiel, the Book of the Watchers, and the Wisdom of ben Sira

Martha Himmelfarb

Judaism is a religion deeply informed by geography. Its historical imagination is shaped by the contrast between other lands and the land of Israel; its stories move back and forth between those poles. I hope that this essay will demonstrate how fruitful attention to geography can be for another aspect of early Judaism, the visionary imagination. The visionaries to be considered here make no distinction between mythic geography and real, but this should not mislead us into dismissing the places they name as unimportant to their message. There is no doubt that we miss the full import of their visions unless we study their geography attentively.

In the concluding vision of his book, the prophet Ezekiel, prophesying in exile in Babylonia after the destruction of the Temple in 586 B.C.E., is taken on a tour of a future Temple in a restored Jerusalem. In one passage he describes a stream flowing from the Temple in terms that recall the Garden of Eden. A similar transplantation of the garden with its tree of life and its rivers to the vicinity of the Temple appears also in the Book of the Watchers in the late third century and the Wisdom of ben Sira in the early second century B.C.E. For the author of the Book of the Watchers as for Ezekiel, the reemergence of Eden in the Temple lies in the eschatological future, but ben Sira claims that the presence of Eden in the Temple has already been realized. Here I hope to show some of the implications of the association of the Garden of Eden with the Temple in these three works.

EZEKIEL'S TEMPLE VISION

The Book of Ezekiel concludes with the prophet's vision of the restoration of the Temple, the city of Jerusalem, and indeed of the land and people as a whole.[1] These chapters (40–48) answer the earlier vision of God's abandonment of the defiled Temple and its subsequent destruction (chs. 8–11). In the future, Ezekiel tells his audience, God will return to a new Temple, reestablished in the land to which all the people of Israel have been restored, even the ten tribes of the northern kingdom lost a century and half before Ezekiel's time.

The vision opens as Ezekiel is taken from Babylonia to "a very high mountain" in the land of Israel.[2] An angelic guide leads the prophet about this city, which is revealed as the Temple compound, measures the dimensions of the Temple that will someday replace the one so recently destroyed, and gives instructions for the performance of the cult in the new Temple and for the behavior of the priests who will serve in it (40:3–44:31). The description of the Temple is followed by the allotment of space to the holy district in Jerusalem (45:1–9), and various laws, including a festival calendar and laws governing the conduct of the prince who is to rule the restored commonwealth (45:10–46:24).

Next the angel takes Ezekiel to see the stream that issues from the Temple, bringing wonderful fertility with it as it flows into the Dead Sea (47:1–12). The vision concludes with the boundaries of the land, the allotment of portions of the land to restored tribes (47:13–48:29), and the enumeration of the twelve gates of the new Jerusalem (48:30–35). The portions of the tribes are equal and symmetrical, as is the structure of Jerusalem. Geographical reality is not allowed to intrude into the symmetry, nor does historical reality play much of a role: the land east of the Jordan is eliminated from the Holy Land (47:18).

In the vision the prophet expresses his understanding of the centrality of the Temple and the Holy Land to God's reconciliation with the people of Israel by drawing on a variety of earlier traditions.[3] The "very high mountain" of 40:2 on which Ezekiel sees the restored Temple is clearly Mt. Zion, the Temple Mount. Ezekiel perceives Mt. Zion as "very high," not because of its physical stature, but because of the mythic qualities it has acquired. Biblical authors did not hesitate to adapt to Mt. Zion motifs associated with the Canaanite mountain of the gods. The inviolability of Mt. Zion and the stream rushing from it in so many biblical texts, for example, have their roots in Canaanite myth.[4]

The vision of the restored Temple also draws on the complex of traditions associated with Sinai, the mountain on which the plan of the tabernacle was revealed to Moses (Exodus 25:9). In the course of the vision Ezekiel functions as a second Moses, the recipient of a revelation about the laws for the proper functioning of the new Temple and the policy associated with it.[5]

Finally the prophet calls on traditions about the primal garden of God.[6] The association of Eden with the Temple is not original to Ezekiel, but the prophet develops it in some detail.[7]

47:7. As I went back I saw upon the bank of the river very many trees on the one side and on the other. 8. And he [the angelic guide] said to me, "This water flows toward the eastern region and goes down into the Arabah; and when it enters the stagnant waters of the sea, the water will become fresh." 9. And wherever the river goes every living creature which swarms will live, and there will be very many fish; so everything will live where the river goes . . . 12. And on both sides of the river, there will grow all kinds of trees for food. Their leaves will not wither nor their fruit fall, but they will bear fresh fruit every month, because the water for them flows from the sanctuary. Their fruit will be for food, and their leaves for healing.

The stream is a prominent feature of the Canaanite mountain of the gods, and it would be a mistake to try to differentiate too sharply elements of the traditions of Mt. Zaphon from elements of the traditions of Eden.[8] But the details of the description of Ezekiel's stream point to Eden in significant ways.

The Garden of Eden as Genesis describes it contains four rivers and "every tree that is pleasant to the sight and good for food" (2:9). On either side of the stream that flows from the Temple stand trees of wonderful fruitfulness. Levenson suggests that the *'etz rav meod* on either bank of the stream in v. 7 should be translated not as a collective, "very many trees," but rather as a singular, "a great tree." In that case the passage alludes to the tree of knowledge and the tree of life as well as to the fruit trees of the tradition of Genesis 2.[9]

But the powers of Ezekiel's Temple stream go beyond the fertility associated with Eden in Genesis 2. The effect of the waters that flow from the Temple is nothing short of miraculous: they cause the Dead Sea to teem with fish. And the trees watered by the stream provide not only fruit for food, but even leaves for healing. Ezekiel's eschatological Eden at Zion surpasses the Eden of the past. And it is the Temple that is the source of the wonderful powers of the stream, as the angel tells the prophet quite clearly (v. 12).

While the prophet is clearly alluding to the Garden of Eden in the passage about the stream, he never refers to it explicitly. But elsewhere in his book Ezekiel does mention the garden by name, in his lament for the king of Tyre (28:11–18) and his oracle against Pharaoh (31:1–18). Both passages use the imagery of Eden to describe the blessed state of these enemies of Israel before their fall so as to make clear the full magnitude of the fall.

The lament in chapter 28 describes the king of Tyre's former glory as a jewel-bedecked resident of Eden and his expulsion by a cherub who guards the garden because of his arrogance and sinfulness. The echoes of the story in Genesis 2-3 are clear; in addition to the story of the fall and expulsion, the details of the precious stones, although not as ornaments, and of the guardian cherub, appear also in Genesis 2–3.

In this passage, too, Ezekiel associates the Garden of Eden with the Temple. The king of Tyre's home is identified first as Eden (v. 13), then as the mountain of God (vv. 14, 16). The jewels of the king of Tyre's dress (v. 13) recall the breast plate of the high priest, as the cherub (vv. 14, 16) suggests the cherubim of the holy of holies. And one of the accusations against the king is that he has "profaned [his] sanctuary" (v. 18).[10]

The traditions behind chapter 31's allegory for the doom of Pharaoh and the land of Egypt show that Ezekiel knew a larger set of traditions about the primal garden than those preserved in Genesis 2–3. The traditions about the world-tree may have come to him from Babylonian sources. The world-tree is a tree of life, an *axis mundi* connecting the upper world with the lower.[11] Ezekiel describes Pharaoh as a mighty cedar in Lebanon, a nesting place for birds, a shelter beneath which animals give birth to their young. With its great beauty and stature, the tree is the envy of all the trees in the garden of God. But once again pride causes destruction. The tree pays for its pride in its stature with its destruction at the hand of foreigners.

Thus the Garden of Eden figures prominently in Ezekiel's prophecy. In the vision of the restored Temple motifs drawn from Eden suggest a restoration better than anything history could possibly offer.[12] Their use also sheds light on certain peculiar aspects of Ezekiel's prophecy.

By heredity a priest, Ezekiel is deeply concerned with the details of the cult, the only prophet to offer a set of laws for the daily operation of the Temple. For some scholars these are interests unbecoming a prophet, and Ezekiel is seen as untrue to his title.[13] But whatever complaints the modern reader may have about Ezekiel, the power of his imagination can hardly be denied. And this powerful imagination conceives of the Temple, the arena of the everyday cult, in mythic terms. Its cherubim are God's chariot throne, and its mountain is the cosmic mountain. In the midst of the dry legal material appears the stream that flows from the future Temple, recreating the fertility and plenty of the primal paradise, no, surpassing them. The use of traditions about the Garden of Eden in relation to the restored Temple, so surprising at first glance, appears on closer consideration quite characteristic of Ezekiel.

THE BOOK OF THE WATCHERS AND THE TOUR TO THE ENDS OF THE EARTH

The Book of the Watchers, written in Aramaic by a Palestinian Jew in the third century B.C.E., is one of the earliest apocalypses.[14] It has come down to us as chapters 1–36 of 1 Enoch, a collection of five Enochic apocalypses preserved in Ethiopic. The Book of the Watchers (chs. 6–11) tells a more detailed version of the story of the sons of God and daughters of men alluded to so briefly in Genesis 6:1–4. According to the Book of the Watchers, the sons of God are angels known as watchers who abandon their heavenly duties because of lust for the daughters of men. The encounter between the heavenly beings and the earthly women creates havoc on earth. The offspring of their union are giants who inflict terrible damage on the earth and its inhabitants; in addition the angels reveal to the women secrets best kept from humanity, like metalworking, cosmetics, magic, and astrology. In Genesis the flood follows immediately on the story of the sons of God and daughters of men, but without any explicit indication of a causal relationship; here it is represented as the means of cleansing the earth from the corruption and violence caused, directly and indirectly, by the fallen angels.

Enoch appears in the Bible only in the context of genealogies, most notably in Genesis 5:21–24, where the notice of his career breaks the pattern of the notices for the other antediluvian patriarchs. The others live a certain number of years, beget their first born, live more years, begetting more sons and daughters, and then die. At the age of sixty-five, after begetting his firstborn, Methuselah, Enoch "walked with God" for three hundred years and begat other sons and daughters. The concluding notice tell us that unlike his forebears and his descendants, Enoch did not die. Rather "Enoch walked with God, and he was not, for God took him." As with the compressed notice of the interest of the sons of God in the daughters of men in Genesis 6, this notice about Enoch suggests the existence of a more extensive body of traditions about the patriarch. Here in the Book of the Watchers we find the development of such traditions, but a development undertaken with the biblical text in view.

Enoch enters the narrative of the Book of the Watchers in his professional capacity as scribe, when the watchers who remain in heaven send him with a message of doom to their fallen brethren. Upon hearing this message, the fallen watchers ask Enoch to draw up a petition on their behalf, asking God's forgiveness (chs. 12–13). In order to carry out the mission entrusted to him by the watchers, Enoch ascends to heaven (chs. 14–16). There before God's throne Enoch presents their petition. Although God emphatically rejects the plea for mercy and insists that the watchers deserve eternal doom, Enoch himself is treated with great honor. He is able to pass through terrifying outer courts to stand before God's throne as the angels do. When he falls on his face in awe before the throne, God sends an angel to raise him and speaks to him "with his own mouth" (14:24).[15]

Enoch's ascent to heaven, the first in Jewish literature, is deeply indebted to the chariot vision of Ezekiel 1, where God's glory descends to earth to encounter the prophet by the River Chebar in Babylonia. One sign of the debt is the throne of cherubim with its wheels on which Enoch finds God seated. While in Ezekiel's vision the wheels and winged creatures of the throne[16] serve a function, to make the throne mobile, that function has been lost in the Book of the Watchers.[17] More broadly Enoch's ascent to heaven draws on the imagery of the theophany of Ezekiel 1 to describe God's heavenly abode.[18]

The Book of the Watchers' interest in a heavenly Temple reflects a certain discontent with the early Temple and its personnel. The author uses the story of the fall of the watchers to criticize the corrupt priests of the Jerusalem Temple.

As the angels fail to perform their duties in heaven, these priests fail to fulfill their responsibilities in the earthly Temple, and for some of the same reasons, like inappropriate marriages.[19]

The assumption that temples on earth have counterparts in heaven, or to put it more accurately from an ancient point of view, that temples on earth correspond to heavenly archetypes, is widespread in the ancient Near East and appears in a number of biblical texts.[20] But the heavenly archetype can serve either to lend glory to its earthly counterpart or to make its shortcomings more obvious. In the eighth century B.C.E., Isaiah of Jerusalem meets God enthroned in the Jerusalem Temple (ch. 6); for Isaiah the earthly Temple is a worthy dwelling place for God. The attribution of cosmic qualities to Mt. Zion is part of the same phenomenon. But in the period of the second Temple the earthly Temple appears in a less favorable light. It is at best an inferior version of the first Temple, at worst a place of corruption whose offerings are unacceptable to God.[21] For the author of the Book of the Watchers as for many of his contemporaries, God's presence must be sought in the heavenly Temple.

After his ascent to heaven, Enoch undertakes a journey to the ends of the earth with angels as his guides. This journey concludes the Book of the Watchers, and it takes up almost half the work. The companionship of the angels reinforces the point made by the ascent that Enoch is fit company for angels. The tour includes many wonderful sights, and one major function of the tour, made explicit at the end, is to assert God's greatness as creator.

And then I saw, I blessed, and I will always bless the Lord of Glory who has made great and glorious wonders that he might show the greatness of his work to angels and to the souls of men, that they might praise his work, and that all his creatures might see the work of his power and praise the great work of his hands and bless him for ever (36:4).

If the Book of the Watchers no longer shares the optimism of the Book of Proverbs and some of the psalms that the wonders of nature loudly proclaim God's glory to all mankind, it is not so pessimistic as Job, with its claim that the wonders of creation are beyond human understanding. For the Book of the Watchers, these wonders are accessible to at least one particularly pious human being, and his concluding praise of God claims that all God's creatures can see his great work and draw the appropriate conclusions.[22]

Like the ascent to heaven, Enoch's tour to the ends of the earth is deeply indebted to Ezekiel. On strictly formal grounds, the best precedent to Enoch's tour is Ezekiel's tour of the restored Temple and its environs. Not only is this passage the only full-blown tour in biblical literature; it also includes comments to Ezekiel from his angelic guide in the form of explanations that begin with demonstrative pronouns or adjectives. In the Book of the Watchers the spare explanations of Ezekiel's tour have developed into dialogue; Enoch's questions and exclamations elicit rather elaborate demonstrative explanations from his guide. The tour to the ends of the earth was no doubt influenced by other traditions like the Greek *nekyia*, but the use of demonstrative explanations indicates that the primary model in the author's mind was Ezekiel.[23]

The tour to the ends of the earth is in fact composed of two sources, a rather short tour (chs. 17–19) that was expanded, probably by the author of the Book of the Watchers in its present form, to create a longer tour including many of the same sights but also some significant new ones (chs. 20–36). Only the last of the sights in chapters 17–19, the abyss that will serve as a prison for the fallen watchers (18:12–19:2), is explicitly related to the story of Enoch and the watchers.[24] Many of the sights are described very briefly; they consist of heavenly phenomena like the places of the luminaries and the treasuries of the stars, thunder and lightning (17:3), or features of earthly geography like the living waters, the fires of the west that receive the setting sun, a river of fire, and the great rivers (17:4–5).[25] One further sight should be noted here because of the way it will be developed in chapters 20–36. In the course of his travels Enoch comes to seven mountains, each made of a different jewel; the middle one is "like the throne of the Lord" (18:8).

Enoch's itinerary in chapters 20–36 begins with the sight most intimately related to the narrative of the fall of the watchers, the place of their punishment (ch. 21). It continues with a related sight, the mountain in the west where the souls of the dead await the last judgment (ch. 22). The fate of human souls is a natural outgrowth of the concerns of the narrative of the Book of the Watchers.

Next Enoch sees the burning fire in the west (ch. 23) and seven magnificent mountains, one the throne of God,[26] with the tree of life (chs. 24–25). The seven mountains and the mountain throne of God of the second tour are a more elaborate version of the same phenomena in the first tour. The presence of the tree of life at the mountain throne represents a conflation of Eden and Zion traditions; the gems of the mountains recall the precious stones of Eden in Genesis 2–3.[27]

In relation to this sight, the angel tells Enoch,

This high mountain which you saw, whose summit is like the throne of the Lord, is the throne where the Holy and the Great One, the Lord of Glory, the Eternal King, will sit when he comes down to visit the earth for good. And this beautiful fragrant tree— and no *creature* of flesh has the authority to touch it until the great judgment when he will take vengeance on all and will bring *everything* to a consummation for ever— this will be given to the righteous and humble. From its fruit life will be given to the chosen; towards the north it will be planted, in a holy place, by the house of the Lord, the Eternal King (25:3–5).[28]

In the last days, then, the tree of life will be transplanted to the Temple, and the righteous will eat of its fruit. Like Ezekiel, the author of the Book of the Watchers transplants Eden to the Temple—in the eschatological future. In Enoch's time, and presumably the author's as well, the tree of life remains inaccessible, at the mountain throne of God.

Now Enoch comes to the "middle of the earth" (26:1), that is, Jerusalem, which Ezekiel explicitly designates the "navel of the earth" (38:12). Jerusalem is described as a blessed land with trees; in it stands a holy mountain with a stream flowing out of it to the south (26:1–2). Again our author is indebted to Ezekiel. Next to the holy mountain lies a cursed valley in which the eschatological judgment will take place (26:3–27:5). This is Gehinnom, the valley in Jerusalem that later tradition removes from its earthly location for a long career as a place of punishment for the wicked.

Now Enoch travels east to a wilderness full of trees and plants, watered by a gushing stream (ch. 28), with several stops for spice trees. Enoch finds a group of mountains planted with more spice trees. Beyond these mountains, "far towards the east," Enoch comes to the Garden of Righteousness, full of trees including the tree of knowledge (ch. 32).[29]

What is the relationship of the Garden of Righteousness here in the east to the mountain throne of God and the tree of life in the west? First it should be noted that although the extant texts of both Greek and Ethiopic contain *seven* mountains over which Enoch passes to reach the Garden of Righteousness (32:1), the Aramaic fragment of this passage refers to mountains without specifying their number. Given the ease with which the mountains that stand before the Garden of Righteousness could be associated with the seven mountains in the west, it seems likely that the number seven here is an addition of the Greek translator that then made its way to Ethiopic.[30] Indeed a close examination of the eastern and western sights suggests that the mountain groups have less in common than it first appears. The mountains in the east are not part of the Garden of Righteousness; Enoch crosses them on the way to the garden, but they are separated from it by the Erythrean Sea and another sight (32:2).[31]

Still the presence of the Garden of Righteousness in the east, after the tree of life in the west and other motifs associated with Eden have appeared in the west, requires some explanation. Grelot argues that the author of the Book of the Watchers doubles the Garden of Eden in an attempt to reconcile contradictory biblical traditions about the location of the garden, the eastern site of Genesis 2–3, and the identification of the garden with the holy mountain in Ezekiel 27.[32]

I am inclined to think that Grelot is right in seeing the influence of Ezekiel on the association of the mountain throne and the tree of life, although I suspect that Ezekiel 40–48 is a more important influence than Ezekiel 27. We should not be surprised that the author of the Book of the Watchers has a rather unusual approach to the Garden of Eden. The Book of the Watchers, after all, tells a story about how evil came into the world notable for ignoring or, indeed, contradicting the story Genesis tells about events in the Garden of Eden.

Our author, as we have seen, detaches the tree of life from the Garden itself and associates it with Mt. Zion and the Temple. While the tree's eschatological significance is emphasized, its connection to the Garden of Eden is played down. It is interesting that when our author comes to describe the garden in the east in terms that cannot help but recall the Garden of Eden of Genesis, he names the

Garden not Eden, but the Garden of Righteousness. And it is a rather diminished version of Eden. With the tree of life transplanted to the mountain throne of God and the precious stones relocated to the seven mountains, the great glory of this garden is the tree of knowledge.

This tree our author describes as "the tree of wisdom from which they eat and know great wisdom" (32:3). The reference to those who eat of the tree of knowledge and attain great wisdom is presumably eschatological, a counterpart to the eating of the tree of life in chapter 24. Later traditions depict the Garden of Eden as the place of reward for the righteous after death, much as Gehinnom has become the place of punishment for the wicked. But if this is the author's view, he does not make it explicit. Nor does the angelic guide wax enthusiastic about the qualities of this tree as he did about the qualities of the tree of life. I suspect that this is because the tree of knowledge inevitably and forcefully recalls the story in which it plays its role in Genesis, the story of the disobedience of Adam and Eve. To lavish attention on this tree is to remind the reader of that story.

Having mentioned the tree of knowledge, the author can hardly avoid some acknowledgment of its role in the drama of primal disobedience. When Enoch exclaims about the beauty of the tree, the angel Raphael says to him, "This is the tree of wisdom, of which your old father and your aged mother, who were before you, ate, and learnt wisdom; and their eyes were opened, and they knew that they were naked, and they were driven from the garden" (32:6).

Thus Raphael manages to offer a compressed version of the story of Adam and Eve's fall without any mention of their sin. The only indication in Raphael's account that Adam and Eve did something they shouldn't have done is that they are driven out of the garden. A reader who did not know the story in Genesis 3 might be puzzled about why learning wisdom and realizing your nakedness should lead to expulsion from paradise.

Of course it is difficult to imagine a reader of the Book of the Watchers who did not know that story, and this certainly raises the question of why our author chose to include the Garden of Eden at all, under any name, in Enoch's tour. It appears to be Ezekiel's influence that leads him to depict the mountain throne of God with motifs drawn from Eden, but the presence of the Garden of Righteousness itself cannot be thus explained.

One way to make sense of the presence of the garden, with the conflicts it suggests with the narrative of the fallen angels, is to see it as such a fixture of mythic geography that no author could ignore it. Or perhaps our author chose to include it so that he could exercise a sort of damage control. By depicting it as he did, perhaps he felt that he could subtly diminish its importance, making his readers less likely to sit up from his work and say, "Yes, but what about the fall of Adam and Eve?"

From the Garden of Righteousness Enoch continues on "to the ends of the earth," where he sees beasts and birds, perhaps inspired by the proximity of the garden, and the portals of the heavens (ch. 33). Through these portals he sees the courses of the stars, described to him by the angel Uriel. To the north, west, and south, he sees more portals, through each set of which come winds, dew, and rain (34:1–36:1), and finally to the east a last set of portals with small portals above them through which the stars are visible (36:2–3). The last sights of the tour, then, point to God's greatness as creator and are a suitable means of eliciting from Enoch the praise with which the book concludes.

With Ezekiel, the prophet who most influenced him, the author of the Book of the Watchers condemns the present reality of the Temple in the name of the ideal. Much of the interest in the Temple and priests in the Book of the Watchers is acted out in the heavenly Temple, but the earthly Temple is not forgotten. Despite the difficulties the use of traditions of the Garden of Eden creates for him, our author follows Ezekiel in drawing on them for a striking image of the life-giving qualities of the eschatological Temple, the transplantation of the tree of life to its precincts.

WISDOM IN THE TEMPLE IN BEN SIRA

An association of the Garden of Eden and the Temple, not as eschatological hope but as present reality, appears in Wisdom's praise of herself in chapter 24 of the Wisdom of ben Sira. Ben Sira was an aristocratic wise man and teacher who wrote his book in Jerusalem about 180 B.C.E. He may have been a younger contemporary of the author of the Book of the Watchers; in any case he lived not many decades later.[33]

Ben Sira's book contains a range of different kinds of material, from proverbs reminiscent of the collection in the biblical Book of Proverbs to ben Sira's own reflections on the meaning of history, a subject almost completely ignored in biblical wisdom literature. The work stands in close relationship to the biblical wisdom tradition, but it is clearly the product of a later time. While ben Sira is deeply indebted to the Proverbs, his appreciation of its optimistic attitudes was anything but unselfconscious, as Mack has recently pointed out.[34] The wise men of Proverbs in the royal courts of Judah before the exile saw the world as permeated by God's order and expected the wise, who follow God's ways as revealed in the world he created, to prosper.

But the view of the order of the universe that came naturally to the authors of Proverbs could be maintained by ben Sira only by an act of will. Ben Sira faced the problem, now centuries old, of the gap between Israel's self-understanding as God's chosen's people and their actual status as a subject people in a great empire. Even the rebuilt Temple, as we have seen, was tainted in the eyes of many.

But in the extended meditation on Israel's past in his praise of the fathers (chs. 44–50), ben Sira claims that Israel's present circumstances represent not a fall from a more exalted past but the height of glory. Ben Sira treats the Temple and the high priesthood, the central political institutions of the period after the exile, as a completely inadequate replacement for the kingship of the past. In part he does so by stressing the continuity of the postexilic leadership with the period before the exile. The two heroes allotted the most space in the praise of the fathers are Aaron, the founder of the priesthood (45:6–22), and the recently deceased high priest, Simon the Righteous (50:1–21). Ben Sira goes so far as to claim that the time of Simon was a high point in Israel's history.

But, as Mack insists, ben Sira's picture of continuity, stability, and glory in his own time is best understood as an effort to overcome a far more natural response, that his own time is a time of decline. This is why his claim that Eden is to be found in the Temple even as he writes is so striking; after all, Ezekiel and the author of the Book of the Watchers reserve the appearance of paradise at the Temple for the eschaton.

Ben Sira brings Eden to the Temple through the other great religious institution of his time, the Torah. In chapter 24 ben Sira identifies God's wisdom, present with him at creation, with the Torah God has revealed to Israel. This identification is made here for the first time, and it will have a long and significant history. It is this wisdom that embodies the aspects of Eden to be found in the Temple.

The poem in ben Sira 24 is deeply indebted to the poem in Proverbs 8, Wisdom's praise of herself. The understanding of wisdom as the order of creation is dramatized in the earlier poem in Wisdom's claim to have stood by God's side as he created the world. But like the early wisdom tradition generally, the poem is cosmopolitan in its outlook. Wisdom is present at the creation of the entire world; she is available to all who seek her. There is no suggestion that she is the specific property of Israel.

Ben Sira's Wisdom also claims to have been present as God began the work of creation: "I came forth from the mouth of the Most High / and covered the earth like mist" (24:3).[35] This is apparently an allusion to the second creation story in Genesis: "A mist went up from the earth and watered the whole face of the ground" (2:6).[36] But after her tour of the newly created cosmos, ben Sira's Wisdom, unlike her predecessor in Proverbs, longs for a permanent home, and so at God's direction she takes up residence in the Temple at Jerusalem. "In the holy tabernacle I ministered before him, / and so I was established in Zion. In the beloved city likewise he gave me a resting place, / and in Jerusalem was my dominion" (24:10–11).

Now that she is established in the Temple, Wisdom describes herself as a tree or vine:

> I grew tall like a cedar in Lebanon,
> and like a cypress on the heights of Hermon.
> I grew tall like a palm tree in En-gedi,
> and like rose plants in Jericho;
> like a beautiful olive tree in the field,
> and like a plane tree I grew tall.
> Like cassia and camel's thorn I gave forth the aroma of spices,
> and like choice myrrh I spread a pleasant odor,
> like galbanum, onycha, and stacte,
> and like the fragrance of frankincense in the tabernacle.

Like a terebinth I spread out my branches,
and my branches are glorious and graceful.
Like a vine I caused loveliness to bud,
and my blossoms became glorious and abundant fruit (24:23–17).

In the background to the identification of Wisdom/Torah as a tree stands
Proverbs 3:18: "She [Wisdom] is a tree of life to those who lay hold of her."
Ben Sira has developed this theme in considerable detail. The spice trees so
important to the tour to the ends of the earth appear here in their relationship to
the Temple service. Gilbert points out that the place names associated with the
trees to which Wisdom compares herself outline the borders of the Holy Land.[37]
I would like to suggest that the trees are also meant to make us think of the
Garden of Eden.[38]

To begin with, ben Sira has already invoked Genesis 2. In a passage from
the poem that we will consider shortly he compares Wisdom to five rivers, four
of them the rivers of Eden according to Genesis 2. Thus Eden is obviously on
his mind. Further, the cedar of Lebanon (ben Sira 24:13) is the greatest tree of
the garden according to Ezekiel 31. The image of the terebinth sending forth
its branches (ben Sira 24:16) also echoes the description of the great cedar of
Ezekiel 31. The link to Ezekiel 31 strengthens the case that ben Sira intends
us to associate wisdom as tree with the trees of the Garden of Eden—a tree of
knowledge whose fruit is healthful.

Now ben Sira makes explicit the identification of Wisdom and Torah: "All
this is the book of the covenant of the Most High God, / the law which Moses
commanded us / as an inheritance for the congregation of Jacob" (24:23).[39] At
this point the comparison to the rivers begins.

It fills men with wisdom, like the Pishon,
and like the Tigris at the time of the first fruits.
It makes them full of understanding, like the Euphrates,
and like the Jordan at harvest time.
It makes instruction shine forth like light,
like the Gihon at the time of vintage (24:25–27).

Here the allusion to Eden is clear. Each of the four rivers of Eden according
to Genesis 2 is mentioned, with the addition of the Jordan, the great river of
the land of Israel. Now, since ben Sira has already fixed wisdom in the Temple,
his comparison of wisdom to the rivers of Eden serves to associate Eden and the
Temple. The apparently anomalous mention of the Jordan is quite purposeful in
this reading: it affirms the association of Eden with the Temple in Zion, where
the nearest great river is the Jordan.[40]

Ben Sira goes on to mark out his own relationship to the river of Wisdom.

I went forth like a canal from a river
and like a water channel into a garden.

> I said, "I will water my orchard
> and drench my garden plot";
> and lo, my canal became a river,
> and my river became a sea.
> I will again make instruction shine forth like the dawn,
> and I will make it shine afar;
> I will again pour out teaching like prophecy,
> and leave it to all future generations (24:30–33).

Here ben Sira makes the striking claim that he and presumably other teachers as well have inherited the mantle of prophecy. His image of the canal becoming a river and the river becoming a sea may be intended to recall Ezekiel's stream flowing from the Temple to bring fertility to the Dead Sea.[41]

Ben Sira claims the presence of paradise in the Temple so many others viewed as corrupt by depicting Wisdom as a tree and river of life. Ben Sira parts company with Ezekiel and the author of the Book of the Watchers, who bring these aspects of Eden to the Temple only in the eschatological future. Of course eschatology does not figure prominently in ben Sira's work. In this he stands in continuity with the earlier wisdom tradition.

But ben Sira's insistence that Eden is to be found in the Temple in his own time is not a sign of genuine contentment with the present. Rather it is an attempt to ignore the failings of the present, to insist on its essential continuity with the past. Wisdom, now equated with the Torah, provides him with a vehicle for doing so. Wisdom transcends time, and her presence in the Temple allows Eden to be recreated there even as it turns ben Sira into a prophet at a time when others believed prophecy to be a thing of the past.

NOTES

1. The prophet's authorship of these chapters is the subject of some dispute. Perhaps the most detailed study of their composition is Hartmut Gese, "Der Verfassungsentwurf des Ezechiel (Kap. 40–48) traditiongeschichtlich untersucht," *Beiträge zur historischen Theologie* 25 (Tübingen: J.C.B. Mohr [Paul Siebeck], 1957). Gese sees a complex development, with a considerable portion from hands other than the prophet's. Moshe Greenberg, "The Design and Themes of Ezekiel's Program of Restoration," *Interpretation* 38 (1984): 181–208, is inclined to accept the essential unity of the section and to attribute it to the prophet himself. Any assessment of authorship is necessarily colored by assumptions about Ezekiel's outlook. See, for instance, the remarks of Walther Eichrodt, *Ezekiel: A Commentary*, The Old Testament Library, trans. Cosslett Quin (London: SCM Press, and Philadelphia: Westminster Press, 1970), pp. 548–51. In what follows I am interested primarily in Ezekiel's influence on later writers. The author of the Book of the Watchers and ben Sira surely took Ezekiel to be the author of all of chs. 40–48.

2. All translations from the Hebrew Bible are taken from the Revised Standard Version.

3. For a full treatment of these traditions, see Jon D. Levenson, *Theology of the Program of Restoration of Ezekiel 40–48*, Harvard Semitic Monographs 10 (Missoula, Mont.: Scholars Press, 1976), pp. 5–53.

4. Ibid., pp. 7–24, and Richard J. Clifford, *The Cosmic Mountain in Canaan and the Old Testament*, Harvard Semitic Monographs 4 (Cambridge, Mass.: Harvard University Press, 1972), 131–60.

5. Levenson, *Program*, pp. 37–53.

6. Ibid., pp. 25–36.

7. Ibid., pp. 27–28, for a discussion of Psalm 36:8–10. The J source in the Torah gives one of the rivers of Eden in Genesis 2 the name of the spring that was the source of Jerusalem's water supply, Gihon (Ibid., p. 29).

8. Ibid., pp. 30–31.

9. Ibid.

10. Carol A. Newsom, "A Maker of Metaphors—Ezekiel's Oracles Against Tyre," *Interpretation* 38 (1984):161–64. The Hebrew of Ezekiel 28:18 reads "sanctuaries," plural, and the RSV follows the Hebrew. I follow Newsom and other commentators in amending to the singular, following some of the manuscript and versional evidence (see *Biblica Hebraica Stuttgartensia*).

11. Eichrodt, *Ezekiel*, p. 425.

12. Levenson *Program*, pp. 21–33, offers an interesting discussion of suprahistorical implications of Eden as opposed to Zion.

13. See, for instance, Paul D. Hanson, *The Dawn of Apocalyptic*, rev. ed. (Philadelphia: Fortress Press, 1979), pp. 228–34. See also Eichrodt, *Ezekiel*, pp. 550–51, where Ezekiel is rescued from these charges by the claim that large parts of the vision are not his.

14. For an introduction to the Book of the Watchers, see George W. E. Nickelsburg, *Jewish Literature Between the Bible and the Mishnah* (Philadelphia: Fortress, 1981), pp. 48–55.

15. The translation of the Book of the Watchers used here is that of M. A. Knibb, "1 Enoch," in H.F.D. Sparks, ed., *The Apocryphal Old Testament* (Oxford: Clarendon Press, 1984), pp. 169–319.

16. The living creatures of the chariot throne in Ezekiel's vision are identified as cherubim in Ezekiel 10:20. While many modern scholars regard this identification as editorial, the author of the Book of the Watchers would have assumed it.

17. In Knibb's translation the throne has no wheels, and there is the sound rather than the sight of cherubim. But Knibb translates a single Ethiopic manuscript. The Greek is very difficult here, and the Aramaic is not extant at the crucial point. I follow here the reading of other recent translations: Matthew Black in consultation with James C. Vander Kam, *The Book of Enoch or 1 Enoch: A New English Translation* (Leiden, Netherlands: E. J. Brill, 1985), and George W. E. Nickelsburg, "Enoch, Levi, and Peter: Recipients of Revelation in Upper Galilee," *Journal of Biblical Literature* 100 (1981):579. For a discussion see Black's note to 14:18 and J. T. Milik, *The Book of Enoch: Aramaic Fragments from Qumram Cave 4* (Oxford: Clarendon Press, 1976), pp. 199–200.

18. See, for example, Nickelsburg, "Enoch," pp. 576–82.

19. Nickelsburg, "Enoch," pp. 584–87; David S. Suter, "Fallen Angel, Fallen Priest: The Problem of Family Purity in 1 Enoch 6–16," *Hebrew Union College Annual* 50 (1979):115–35.

20. Clifford, *Cosmic Mountain*, pp. 177–80, and Martha Himmelfarb, "From Prophecy to Apocalypse: *The Book of the Watchers* and Tours of Heaven," in Arthur Green, ed.,

Jewish Spirituality: From the Bible to the Middle Ages (New York: Crossroad, 1986), pp. 150–51.

21. For example, 1 Enoch 89:73.

22. Himmelfarb, "From Prophecy," pp. 158–60.

23. Martha Himmelfarb, *Tours of Hell: An Apocalyptic Form in Jewish and Christian Literature* (Philadelphia: University of Pennsylvania Press, 1983), pp. 41–60.

24. The dialogue between Enoch and his guide takes place primarily in the second tour; the only instance of dialogue in the first tour appears in relation to this sight. The presence of the device there is probably not accidental, but a means of emphasizing the single sight in the tour that is linked to the narrative of Enoch and the watchers.

25. The meaning of the first sight Enoch sees, a place of creatures of flaming fire who can appear like men (17:1), is far from clear. Pierre Grelot, in "La géographie mythique d'Henoch et ses sources orientales," *Revue Biblique* 65 (1958):38, thinks that these fiery beings may be the cherubim of the Garden of Eden according to Genesis 2–3.

26. This mountain, which, like the mountain in the first tour (18:8), is first described as like the throne (24:3), is later identified as the throne (25:3).

27. It is not clear whether the gems of chapter 18 are intended to suggest Eden. In one case at least, an allusion to another set of traditions appears to be intended; the sapphire of the summit of the middle mountain surely recalls Exodus 24:10, where Moses and the elders of Israel see a sapphire pavement beneath God's feet and Ezekiel 1:26, where God's throne is of sapphire.

28. Italics in Knibb's translation indicate words that do not appear in the original, but are added to improve the English.

29. J. T. Milik, "Hénoch au pays des aromates," *Revue Biblique* 65 (1958):70–77, sees this stage of Enoch's journey as reflecting two routes traveled by spice merchants from Palestine, one south to Arabia, the other north and east, through the Caucasus to India.

30. Ibid., p. 74, and Milik, *Books of Enoch*, p. 232, for the Aramaic fragment (4QEn[el] xxvi, lines 17–18).

31. "Darkness" is the reading of the Aramaic for this other sight (4QEn[el] xxvi, line 21, in Milik, *Books of Enoch*, p. 332). The Aramaic may explain the unintelligible readings of the Greek and Ethiopic (see Milik's note to line 21, p. 232).

32. "Géographie mythique," pp. 41–44. Grelot suggests that the author of the Book of the Watchers drew on a tradition of exegesis of Genesis 2–3 that understood God to have removed the tree of life from the Garden of Eden after the fall.

33. For an introduction to the Wisdom of ben Sira, see Nickelsburg, *Jewish Literature*, pp. 55–65.

34. Burton L. Mack, *Wisdom and the Hebrew Epic: Ben Sira's Hymn in Praise of the Fathers* (Chicago and London: University of Chicago Press, 1985), pp. 84–87, 150–56. Mack argues that the personification of wisdom in Proverbs 1–9 can also be viewed as a response to crisis (pp. 142–50). My treatment of the praise of the fathers below is much indebted to Mack.

35. All translations of ben Sira are taken from the Revised Standard Version Apocrypha, where the work is titled, "Ecclesiasticus, or the wisdom of Jesus the Son of Sirach."

36. Maurice Gilbert, "L'éloge de la Sagesse (*Siracide* 24)," *Revue Théologique de Louvain* 5 (1974):341–44.

37. Ibid., p. 332.

38. Alain Fournier-Bidoz, "L'arbre et al demeure: Siracide XXIV 10–17," *Vetus Testamentum* 34 (1984):1–10, discusses the biblical background to ben Sira's use of trees in considerable detail. He too sees the language of this passage as suggesting the tree of life from the Garden of Eden (p. 8).

39. For a discussion of the critical problems with this verse, see Gilbert, "L'éloge," pp. 336–38.

40. Ibid., pp. 338–39.

41. Ibid., pp. 340–41, and Otto Rickenbacher, "Weisheitsperikopen bei Ben Sira," *Orbis Biblicus et Orientalis* 1 (Göttingen: Vanderhoeck & Ruprecht, 1973), pp. 168–69.

PART II

CHRISTIANITY

4

The Iconic Self: Luther, Culture, and Landscape in Finland

Ronald Bordessa

Finland is a Lutheran country. Approximately 90 percent of its inhabitants are members of the Evangelical-Lutheran Church of Finland. The church is responsible for some functions that are often state-managed elsewhere, for example, the maintenance of local population registers and cemeteries. From cradle to grave the Evangelical-Lutheran Church of Finland is a powerful presence, recognized if not always accepted by the Finnish population. Moreover, the church has enjoyed its dominant place in Finnish society for almost five hundred years, as Finland came within the spheres of first Sweden and then imperial Russia before emerging independent in 1917. Centuries of subjugation and the relative isolation to which this led, added to the geographical marginalization that has exacerbated the xenophobic orientation of Finland, producing a nation which is only now emerging as an "international" presence. Naturally there are many instances of Finns venturing out into the world (notably, for example, Pehr Kalm to North America in the eighteenth century), and of international activities on the part of the Finnish government long before the present day. Yet Finland was not part of the "Age of Discovery": controlled by Sweden, through whom Luther's message was imposed upon her, she was engaged in another quest, an inner one which sought the meaning of this new message.

That voyage, and its impact on Finland, is examined in this chapter.

FINLAND: A BRIEF REVIEW OF RELIGION

At the time of Luther's ascendancy Finland was part of the Swedish Kingdom. The Swedes under Gustavus Vasa rejected Roman Catholicism, adopted Lutheranism, and then imposed it upon Finland. The spread of Lutheranism in Finland began with Peter Särkilahti's preaching in 1524. But it was Mikael Agricola who left an indelible mark on Finnish religion and culture. Agricola was, in the mid-sixteenth century, Bishop of Turku (then known as Abo). His translation of the Bible into Finnish, a language which until then had not been written, has earned him the honor of being "the father of Finnish literature." Indeed, the written word became central to Lutheranism, as it did to the development of Finnish culture. Luther's insistence on the direct connection of the Word and the individual required a programmatic approach to literacy under the auspices of the church which reinforced Lutheran doctrine as it built a more homogenous culture than elsewhere.

Finland's marginalized geographical location had ensured a relatively homogenous indigenous population, mostly bypassed by the migration streams that had thoroughly mixed populations elsewhere. Now the stress on basic literacy served to reduce variations within the Finnish population. And knowledge of Luther's catechism as well as the ability to read and write were taken very seriously—permission to marry, for example, was contingent on demonstrable competence in these skills.

From its beginnings, the Lutheran Church in Finland benefited from the protection of the Swedish king and the harnessing of evangelism to the development of a national culture. That culture was distinctive enough to withstand the transference of Finland from one ruler to another, and from one cultural sphere to another. In 1809 Finland became a Grand Duchy of the Russian Empire. The czar allowed the Lutheran Church to remain as a state church, but also granted the Orthodox Church official recognition.

Independence in 1917, and the civil war associated with it, swept the Lutheran Church into the mainstream of civil affairs. Luther's strong support for civic authority and legal order clearly guided the church's actions at that time. During the civil war, "virtually the entire clergy supported bourgeois Finland. Ties between the church leadership and the organized working class remained distant, while the victors began to see the church as the protector of the legal order, the national tradition and Western culture."[1] The fact that the clergy remained silent over the deaths of thousands has not been forgotten to this day and has caused tension between Finnish socialists and the church.

Whatever the merits of the position of the church in the civil war, there is no doubt that it became a rallying point for nationalist fervor in the Winter War against the Soviet Union in 1939–40. National survival was at stake and the Lutheran Church stood as a pillar of Finnish identity, a natural institution to which to turn. After World War II, religion in Finland became subject to the same secularizing tendencies that have characterized the rest of the Western world.

The Lutheran Church has published an assessment of its role in Finnish society. In it, secularization is identified as a principal trend at the present time in Finland. However, Heino et al. conclude, "We seem to be dealing with a change in religiosity, rather than a decrease of religiosity or religious interest."[2] They then argue that religion, for an increasing number of people, "has become a sphere of life separate from their everyday existence, only coming to the fore with certain life situations, such as church ceremonies or feast days. The domain of the sacred has drifted away from the profane, and the connections of many spheres of life with religion and the church have become more tenuous. The dimension of the hereafter in religion has become less significant and has lost ground, superseded by social, psychological, and therapeutic considerations."[3]

The re-centering of religion in the world of everyday affairs reinforces the post-World War II trend towards the integration of Finland into the international economy. Emergence from the inward-looking tendencies of Lutheranism into the mainstream of Western civilization brings the material benefits of modernity at the cost of a loss of traditional direction and comfort. Given Finland's entry into the mainstream of the modern world, "from the Church's point of view, the problem is largely whether it can adapt itself to the new cultural situation and answer the real questions that arise in the lives of modern people without forsaking the foundations of its Lutheran faith in the process. The problem is thus once again one of contextualization of religion."[4] On the surface it would seem that there is a general drift away from the church, and this is certainly supported by a fall in membership and participation rates. Nevertheless, about 90 percent of all Finns remain Lutheran, pay the mandatory church tax, and feel entitled to use the church, whatever their level of conviction. Heino et al. conclude, "Evidently, we are not dealing with a difference between the traditional image of God and a new one, but rather a reluctance to become dependent on the Church's authority and teaching. The privatization of religion is, in fact, related to a more extensive change in culture, with an emphasis on a striving for individuality, independence and freedom from control of any kind of authority. Religion is seen as a personal conviction and spiritual experience, rather than a matter involving the community."[5]

Yet "three out of four Finns have a favourable attitude towards the Lutheran Church."[6] The Lutheran Church is a cultural anchor and a people's church in the sense that it is seen as responsible for making itself accessible. Neither of these perceptions has been undercut by the trend to secularization and internationalization. Perhaps we can conclude that the Finns appear to be nominally Lutheran, but are strongly attached to the church as a national symbol and as a ready sanctuary to fulfill their personal needs. The truer this conclusion is, the hastier will be the integration of Finns into Western consciousness and the speedier the softening of those edges of national character that give Finland its current coherent identity.

We now turn to the attempt to make some connections between Lutherism and the culture, national character, and landscape of Finland.

ICONICITY TURNED INWARD: LUTHER AND SELF

Luther's break with Rome, inevitable as it now seems, came after painful realization that reform from within could not be attained. Indulgences triggered Luther's growing dissatisfaction, as he pinned his "Ninety-Five Theses" to All Saints Church in Wittenberg, but they were only an indicator of a wider gulf that separated his thought from Rome. The established church had cultivated its icons, and Luther's vision could not accommodate to them. Despite his own ambivalence with respect to the French iconoclasts, Luther was, intellectually, an iconoclast who sought to replace what amounted to Roman idolatry with a purified church that abjured mediation between God and the individual soul.

Yet opposition to idolatry and iconoclasm may be an illusion. As Mitchell points out, "one might argue that iconoclasm is simply the obverse of idolatry, that it is nothing more than idolatry turned outward toward the image of a rival, threatening tribe. The iconoclast prefers to think that he worships no images of any sort, but when pressed, he is generally content with the rather different claim that his images are purer or truer than those of mere idolaters."[7] If the icons of Roman ecclesiastical art forms and a mediating priesthood obscured the true path of God, Luther's vision contained an alternative route—a direct one connecting the Word and the individual human mind. All that was required was a Reformation that would give strength and courage to those who trusted that faith, as revealed in the Word, would provide a direct path to their salvation. But as Feuerbach and Marx, both anti-Semites, have noted, iconoclasm and idolatry are not as far removed from one another in the history of monotheism as we might suppose. The Jews substituted the idolatry of God for the idolatry of graven images, but in the process secured for themselves, as custodians of God's domination over nature, a license to practice accumulation and consumption rather than contemplation. This latter consequence, in Marx's view, also captures the Protestant position, which in this respect is closest to the Jews. As Mitchell points out, the conclusion to Marx's argument is that "the modern Christian iconoclast *is* the idolater; commodity fetishism *is* an iconoclastic monotheism that destroys all other gods."[8]

If the church of Rome nurtured early icons in the service of its understanding of God and if Judaism made "an 'idol of the egoistic will' in the form of Jehovah as creator, and in the practical life of the Jew as a mere consumer," what icon did Luther's revolution bring to the fore?[9] Central to Luther's vision was a distrust of structure, especially of hierarchy in spiritual matters, and an unabridged certainty that faithful acceptance of revelation was necessary to secure a place in heaven. God was a given for Luther. Roman icons were a problem, not a solution; they were barriers to, rather than facilitators of, the attainment of genuine faith and salvation. What was left was a new figure in human history, the appearance of which marks the transition from medieval to modern—the self-determining individual soul. Luther saw this reality more clearly than most, and was therefore able to give shape and identity to this emergent concept of human being.

MacIntyre has pointed out that in Luther (as well as in Machiavelli) "there appears a figure who is absent from moral theories in periods when Plato and Aristotle dominate it, the figure of 'the individual.' "[10] Luther enthrones the individual as a new icon. Only the spiritual side of the individual, however, is worthy of any attention with respect to questions of salvation. Actions, however obnoxious and laudable they may be, are of no weight compared to "the faith which moved the agent" to action.[11] For this reason, energy directed towards any form of questioning of authority is energy taken away from spiritual matters, and it is, therefore, to be roundly suppressed.

A new icon—the sacrosanct individual soul—insulated from the secular world, though nuclear to it, is Luther's pathway to God. This icon is free of the corruptions of consumption, to which Feuerbach charges the Hebrew conception of Yahweh leads, as it is also unblemished by various mediating forms cultivated by Rome. The removal of secular corruption legitimized by spiritual belief, and of spiritual corruption legitimated by secularized modes of hierarchical authority, left Luther with a purified spirit, distanced from the secular realm, and single-mindedly capable of reaching God through faith alone. Here indeed was a suitable candidate for the status of icon.

Iconoclasts and iconophiles are locked into their positions by social and political contextualizing conditions that themselves observe the undercurrents of consciousness. Whether those undercurrents are by themselves sufficient to effect changes in the material conditions of social life, or whether rupture and revolution is necessary to achieve a genuine re-balancing of human affairs, continues to separate philsophers and political thinkers (and actors) alike. Luther's thought was certainly responsible for varying consequences along the continuum running between reform and revolution, but these secular issues lay outside his theological program. Far more important was Luther's focus on the interior of the individual—a focus that was to become the essential underpinning for the foundationalist conception of the world that is at the very core of modernity. Buried in the interior of the individual is the means by which to approach God. Exterior icons become redundant, whether they take the form of priests, paintings or statuary, or bountiful nature transformed according to whatever interpretation of God's injunctions is applicable. The iconic self becomes the only authentic representation of the power of God, and the effort of will required to locate it becomes the only recipe for an appropriately led spiritual life.

It must also be noted that faith for Luther was closely bound to his insistence that the newly empowered individual was responsible, as a consequence of empowerment, for his own salvation; the individual had sovereignty over his own spiritual affairs. It was only later that Luther's gift of spiritual sovereignty spilled over into secular realms. One must not confuse the later rise of individualism or liberal democracy with Luther's program, which constituted only a spiritual challenge to the hierarchy of the Roman church. Yet inevitably the lines between the spiritual and the secular autonomy of the individual became less distinct than they had been in Luther's own understanding, and any attempt to interpret the impact of Luther in the actual course of history or on the geography of place cannot fail to take into account the variety of ways in which his thought was appropriated and expanded.

Despite, then, the statistically demonstrable secularization of Finland, which is part of a general Western phenomenon, it cannot be automatically concluded that Luther's flame has been extinguished, and the torch handed over to bearers of some economic stripe. As we have noted, while Heino et al. recognize secularizing tendencies in Finland and the loss of some ground by the Lutheran church, they reiterate the sense of connection the vast majority of Finns continue to feel with the Lutheran Church.[12] More importantly, what appears to be secularization may in fact obscure a rather different process, namely, the retreat into a self that is better achieved in the absence of church structure. Seen from another perspective, Luther's Reformation may be said to have resulted in Finland in a sense of divided identity, in which the individual must relate simultaneously to the domain of the divine and to the domain of the secular. Finland adopted the Lutheran Church, and the Finns have, for close to five centuries, attempted to pay homage to God and tribute to Caesar simultaneously. That is not to say that Finland reflects the values of deep spiritual isolation, of a struggle with the doctrine of predestination, and an inability to look to sacrament for succor, which lead, in Max Weber's view, to "that disillusioned and pessimistically inclined individualism which can even today be identified in the national character and the institutions of the peoples with a Puritan past."[13] Finnish religion is not the Protestantism of this Calvinist severity. The connections between the divine and secular spheres which Lutheranism fosters have saved the Finnish nation from the overly dismal consequences to which Weber alludes. Inwardness is characteristic of the Finnish religious personality, but this inwardness is ultimately optimistic, not pessimistic. In Luther, we have essentially iconoclastic thought which leads to a new view of the relationship between humankind and God. Luther created the icon of the individualized self. Our task is to take this central thesis and reflect on it in the context of the cultural geography of Finland.

THE LUTHERAN LANDSCAPE OF FINLAND

The interdisciplinary study of geography and religion contains a strand which attempts to uncover "concrete expressions of religious ideology on the landscape."[14] Charles Heatwole, for instance, relates church architecture to the variations in religious ideologies exhibited by conservative, liberal, and moderate Mennonite congregations.[15] It is difficult, however, to demonstrate a clear connection between an entire landscape and a religious ideology. Elaine Björklund's examination of a part of southwestern Michigan dominated by the Dutch-Reformed community hypothesizes "that ideology, as one of the major parts of culture, contains the basis for the organization of areas."[16] In this conservative and closely knit community, Björklund is able to make links between ideology and "human establishments and institutions," but is unable to identify the general landscape with Dutch-Reformed Christianity.[17] On the contrary, she concludes: "To the casual observer traveling through Michigan and State Highway 21, which cuts across the heart of Dutch-Reformed territory between Grand Rapids and Holland, Michigan, there are only subtle visible manifestations of the distinctive ideology."[18] In another vein, however, Salter and Lloyd begin a discussion of the "signatures of sacred space" by asserting that "the architectural signatures that denote sacred space offer a tangible expression of underlying religious systems."[19] They further note that "sacred space involves more than a simple, straightforward expression of a cultural system. It is not only the architecture of the shrines that one must understand in the analysis of the cultural landscape, but also the thought systems that invest space with its sacred quality."[20]

We may begin, then, with the assertion that landscape, the humanly created transformation of nature, bears witness to the pattern of consciousness underlying cultural identity, of which religious ideology is a key aspect. In Finland, Luther's centering of the way to salvation in the self-reflective human being, directly informed by the Word of God, does not fit well with the construction of edifices testifying to an acceptance of the Christian message in majestic architectural forms. Naturally, simplicity of architectural expression can be thought of as leading the searching soul away from aesthetic experiences and towards the inner self where grace is to be obtained. Many modern Finnish churches reflect this view; brick or concrete interiors and exteriors with unrelieved façades and minimal light shafts are typical. Even Engel's beautiful neoclassical cathedral in Helsinki's Senate Square is faithful to the motif of simplicity: of design, materials, and decoration. But perhaps the Temppeliaukio Church, "the Church in the Rock," best expresses Luther's vision transformed into architecture. This church was built—excavated is a more appropriate term—in the 1960s, following an architectural design competition which was won by an unusual concept. The winning design called for a circular church blasted into a granite hill, creating a bowl, over which a copper cap was placed, supported by an entire circle of glass, separating concrete trusses running from the rock to the cap. "The unique atmosphere of the Temppeliaukio Church is created by the diffused light filtering down from the windows far overhead, the infinite subtle variations in the color of the granite, the dusky gleam of copper, and the muted lilac furnishing."[21] To sit and reflect in this church is to become a tiny point, alone and encircled in an excavated auditorium, from which deliverance can be found by looking up to the sky, as it radiates light from every direction overhead. This is the only source of natural light, and one reaches toward God as one turns upwards towards it, even if the fact that this church has become one of Finland's premier tourist attractions, subjected to a steady stream of bus tours, often puts such moments under a heavy strain.

In another vein, Finland's Lutheran heritage has sensitized the Finns to the claims of the inner life and cultivated an artistic sense that is reflective of the need to nurture, rather than to consume, God's kingdom on earth. Forest policy and the law in Finland have been especially attentive to this impulse, and even today forest ownership patterns reveal an unusually high proportion of small-scale owners. Until the 1960s, when economic pressures began to take their toll, the family farm dominated agriculture, and only in the last generation has the rural-to-urban migration pattern taken hold. Yet an orientation towards smallness and affinity to nature remains a feature of Finland's urban centers. Helsinki, for example, is remarkable for the extent to which it has retained its skyline at an almost uniform height. Very few architectural monuments to humankind's technological progress pierce the sky, while the streetscapes are muted and relatively uniform.

Finns express creativity by attending to the fine rather than to the grand. Finnish design is thus notable for its lasting qualities, rather than its ephemeral attractions—an orientation to the future, rather than to the present, which is typical of Finnish culture. Finnish building is characterized by a sense of inner expression, rather than outward display. Alvart Aalto's Finlandia House in Helsinki epitomizes this tendency. In assessing the achievements of Aalto, William Mead and Wendy Hall lend weight to the argument that the Lutheran focus on cultivating the inner self has given the Finns a predisposition to thoughtful transactions with their environment rather than to damaging acts which are contextualized by momentary desires. Of Aalto, Mead and Hall have written: "In the early thirties he had already established himself as a master of the modern idiom, in the best sense of the expression. From the late forties onward he showed more and more his brilliant combination of the organic and the inventive; so that his buildings can stimulate and delight without evoking either shock or surprise. He has mastered that most difficult of all tasks—the harmonizing of a modern building with the vast Finnish landscape which surrounded it, and of making modern man feel equally at home in a large concrete structure as in a forest."[22] Similarly, James Maude Richard's assessment of Finnish architecture speaks of Aalto's "heroic stature" in international circles, yet also notes that he is only one among many architects to whom "the architects of other nations look up and to whose buildings they make respectful pilgrimage."[23] Richards links Finnish architecture to "the Finnish people's consciousness of their long drawn out struggle to assert and maintain their independence."[24] Perhaps the national feelings that repression engenders can find a creative outlet in the resources of the land itself. For Aalto, for example, "wood is the material with which his most personal designs are especially associated, and this again is wholly consistent with the way Finland and its landscape were with him and within him, whatever he did."[25] In fact, similar factors characterize Finnish designs in glass and fabric, as well as in building.

Aalto's remarkable career is a reflection of the Finnish context that has nurtured it. Nature, as a continuing expression of God's work on earth, holds sway over

Finns. For example, the chapel at the Technical University in Otaniemi is built *into* nature, with a glass wall behind the altar allowing the worshippers to feel that they are sitting in God's forest. As Hall and Mead remind us, "Despite rapid development and widespread building, Helsinki still manages to keep some contact with nature. . . . The Finns are by temperament conservationists, whose concern for natural features is such that they will build a flight of steps round a tree rather than cut the tree down."[26] Nowhere is this respect for God's creation more evident than in the construction of new towns in Finland. Tapiola is typical. A new town for Helsinki's overflow population, Tapiola was begun in 1952, a period not noted elsewhere for its sensitivity to environment. The town has become a remarkably prophetic example of the capacity to construct urban landscapes which sculpt themselves to nature, rather than ride roughshod over it. Compared, for example, with the sterility of new towns around London, England, built immediately after World War II, Tapiola affords its population housing, employment, and recreation in a designed environment that preserves woodland and rock outcrops and allows nature its voice. In this respect, Tapiola stands as a testament in urban planning to horizons which go beyond the pragmatic needs of an expanding population. It is a typically Finnish solution that seeks to solve a human problem with environmental care as well as with economic expediency. In a retrospective book on the Tapiola story, Heikki von Hertzen, the driving force behind the private nonprofit housing foundation (Asuntoäätiö) which constructed it, recalled that "the starting point for planning was the individuality of man and his proximity to the natural environment."[27] Beyond that, von Hertzen also believed that "in every part of the earth towns should grow from topography, climate, and local character. New towns should be created to respond to the indigenous way of life."[28] Reliance on one's own resources, unaided by a government weighed down with war rebuilding priorities, and the creation of urban design forms that provide opportunities for privacy even within urban densities, variously express the extent to which the Finnish urban landscape embodies and expresses the Lutheran stress on inwardness in the contemporary world. As an achievement of technological progress, Tapiola has succeeded because it humanizes the landscape and establishes connections between humankind and their natural surroundings.

Clearly, the natural environment is of extreme importance to Finns as a physical locus and an inspiration in the quest for inward peace. This is especially true of the forest. Luther and history have reinforced an attraction to the forest as a site for inwardness which has long been characteristic of Finnish culture. As Mead has pointed out, during the medieval period there was "a sense of oneness with [the forest], not alienation from it; a sense of satisfaction deriving from the mere process of accommodating in it or of resistance to it."[29] A folktale in Finland relates the story of a Finnish man, alone but not lonely in his forest abode, secure in his isolation. One day he sees smoke rising from the chimney of a new settler. It is time to move on. Civilization has drawn too close, and withdrawal to a place where the inward quest can be continued without distraction is necessary. The importance of privacy and retreat, increasingly difficult to secure in an urbanizing Finland, is increased by Luther's doctrine of personal salvation and by the anguish of subjugation which is still keen in the Finnish national memory. The forest is a locus of survival, a place of quiet and seclusion in which the soul can be regenerated. It is a therapeutic environment as well as a shelter in which national culture has been kept alive—a comfortable home ground which no warring adversary has ever been able to conquer. The forest is a symbol of disengagement as much as it has historically been the source of lifegiving food and shelter and protection from enemies. By turning inward to themselves and their environmental home, the Finns have cultivated a strong sense of national affinity. The mixing of the world's peoples during the last fifty years has had very little influence on Finland, which has only about 15,000 foreign residents and extremely conservative immigration, refugee, and guest worker policies. Only now, as Finland emerges as a strong economic presence, are questions of interaction coming to the fore. There is little yet to suggest that Finland is ready to let its own economy be penetrated by counter-flows of international capital. The psychology of the forest still prevails, as Lutheran inwardness strives to retain its grip on Finnish culture.

CONCLUSION

It is one thing for the Finns to respond to the reality of our commercial world and to go out and participate in it. This participation can be achieved without losing sight of their central motivating devices; Finns can meet the world more or less successfully on their own terms. But it is quite another thing to invite the world, with its own set of motivating forces, into their own house. That possibility sparks a note of caution in a nation that has grown accustomed to disengagement and has lost its sense of strong connection, entailing as it does reciprocal interpenetration of ideas and practices. Yet this interpenetration is the very problem with which Finland must grapple, as it attempts to find a new niche for itself in a secularized and pluralized world which threatens to overrun those isolated pockets that have best survived the homogenizing trends of the modern age. The tension within Finland is thus one of preserving inwardness while also reaching outward, that is, of acquiring the skills of interaction which disengagement has left them deficient in, while retaining the consciousness of inner spirit that was the gift of disengagement. Finland's response to a secularizing world thus contains two moments: on the one hand, there is the general element, in which moral and spiritual identity must be determined and balanced; and on the other hand, there is the second, more particular moment, in which the call to inwardness of the spirit must be balanced against outward disturbances to its stability. In this respect, Finland has been able to achieve a unique, and recently much admired, stance with respect to international strategic relations, because its resources of mind have been attuned to inner reflection, which has oriented Finns toward patient and pacific survival in a world bent on impatient acquisitiveness and self-destruction. Centuries of inwardness have yielded a resource that Finns have always been able to draw on—a national propensity to march to their own drummer. But there is a recognition in Finland that, while it must enter the race toward secularization and internationalism, it must also strive to retain a balance between the Finnish vision of inner self and salvation and the human urge for material comfort. With respect to both the urban and the natural landscapes, tradition and national culture are tenaciously upheld in Finland, and the Lutheran Church is supported as perhaps the chief guardian of these values. Luther's insistence on faith and God's grace is a firm reminder that truth and certainty are never fully within the control of the human subject. Just here is the humility that underlies Luther's imprint on Finland.

NOTES

1. Harri Heino, "Churches and Religion in Finland," in *Finnish Features* (Helsinki: Ministry for Foreign Affairs, 1989), p. 6.

2. Harri Heino, Juha Kauppinen, and Risto Ahonen, *The Evangelical-Lutheran Church in Finland 1984–1987* (Tampere, Finland: The Research Institute of the Lutheran Church in Finland, Pub. No. 38, 1989), p. 10.

3. Ibid., p. 9.

4. Ibid., p. 10.

5. Ibid., p. 10–11.

6. Ibid., p. 11.

7. W. J. Thomas Mitchell, *Iconology: Image, Text, Ideology* (Chicago: University of Chicago Press, 1986), p. 198.

8. Ibid., p. 200.

9. Ibid., p. 199.

10. Alasdair MacIntyre, *A Short History of Ethics* (London: Routledge and Kegan Paul, 1967), p. 121.

11. Ibid., p. 11.

12. Heino et al., *Evangelical-Lutheran Church in Finland*.

13. Steven Lukes, "Conclusion," in Michael Carrithers, Steven Collins, and Steven Lukes, eds., *The Category of the Person: Anthropology, Philosophy and History* (Cambridge: Cambridge University Press, 1985), p. 96.

14. Janel M. Curry-Roper, "Contemporary Christian Eschatologies and Their Relation to Environmental Stewardship," *Professional Geographer* 42 (1990):157.

15. Charles A. Heatwole, "Sectarian Ideology and Church Architecture," *The Geographical Review* 79 (1989):63–78.

16. Elaine M. Björklund, "Ideology and Culture Exemplified in Southwestern Michigan," *Annals of the Association of American Geographers* 54 (1973):228.

17. Ibid.

18. Ibid., p. 229.

19. Christopher Salter and William J. Lloyd, *Landscape in Literature* (Washington, D.C.: American Association of Geographers, Commission on College Geography, Resource Papers, No. 76–3, 1977), pp. 16–18.

20. Ibid.

21. Matti A. Pitkänen, *Helsinki* (Helsinki: City of Helsinki, 1979), pages not numbered.

22. William R. Mead and Wendy Hall, *Scandinavia* (London: Thames and Hudson, 1972), p. 22.

23. James Maude Richards, *800 Years of Finnish Architecture* (Newton Abbot, England: David and Charles, 1978), p. 153.

24. Ibid.

25. Ibid.

26. Mead and Hall, *Scandinavia*, p. 90.

27. Heikki von Hertzen and Paul D. Spreireger, *Building a New Town: Finland's New Garden City, Tapiola* (Cambridge, Mass.: M.I.T. Press, 1971), p. 217.

28. Ibid., p. 216.

29. William R. Mead, *An Historical Geography of Scandinavia* (London: Academic Press, 1981), p. 47.

5

Diversities of Divine Presence: Women's Geography in the Christian Tradition

Ellen Ross

INTRODUCTION

The physical world functions as a medium for the absence and presence of God in the lives of spiritual women throughout Christian history. This chapter explores the variety of ways space and place function in women's religious expression; it considers six distinct but related models or ideal types that explain how geography and religion interact in the spiritual understanding of women.[1] This exploration is not intended as a complete summary of all possible patterns, but rather as a typological survey to draw attention to the question of the place of geography within Western religious thought and experience. It must be said at the outset that it is as yet too early in this nascent field of study to make any conclusive comparative assessments about the similarities and differences between women's and men's use of geographical categories and imagery in their writings and self-understandings. The more productive enterprise at this time is to undertake a thorough and selective study of texts by women and men separately, in order to isolate the patterns which shape religious uses of geographical imagery, and to leave comparative statements until a time when they can be more adequately substantiated in the light of the data now being collected and analyzed.

Two provisos must, therefore, be kept constantly in mind: First, the kinds of spiritual understanding discussed are not exhaustive of all possible ways women experience the divine, but are rather suggestive of some of the dominant patterns one finds in a survey of the Christian tradition; and second, I am not arguing that these are patterns found only in the lives and writing of women. Only further comparative studies will determine whether some of these patterns are found more often in the experience of women, or with unique configurations in texts by women with texts by men. Having admitted these caveats, however, let me briefly set out the models or ideal types I will use as heuristic devices for the interpretation of the role of spatiality in women's spiritual experience in the Christian tradition, and point to some initial points of intersection among them. I consider six ways in which women spatially experience manifestations of the divine. In a chronological manner that includes the Hebrew Scriptures' Ruth, Paula, and Egeria (4th c.), Margery Kempe (d. 1438), five nineteenth- century women who were slaves, and the contemporary journalist Sara Maitland, these paradigmatic expressions embody different ways in which women use geographical categories and vocabulary to express their concrete, physical, landed encounters with the sacred.

The first type I refer to as the "Land as Sacred Presence." Using the Hebrew Scriptures' Book of Ruth (dated prior to 700 B.C.E.) as an example, I argue that in this type of literature the community's relationship with God happens through its interaction with geographical space as such, not with a specific plot of land characterized by any physical, literal features; but rather the concept of "land" in general has the function of symbolizing God's presence.[2] Spectacular appearances of the Divine do not characterize this model because the land itself symbolizes the enduring presence of the sacred, and one's interactions with the land are symbolic of one's interactions with the Divine. This model bears out Walter Brueggemann's thesis that "the land is the means of Yahweh's word becoming full and powerful for Israel."[3]

The second type, "Historical Place as Sacred Presence," describes the situation in which specific geographical locations that have gained recognition on account of their association with particular historical events within the Christian tradition's concept of salvation history function to connect believers to the Divine. While the kind of experiences one has in relation to the historical places in this model are not absolutely unique, they tend to be spiritually invigorating and emotionally powerful encounters with the Divine which emerge in part from imaginative identification with the historical events commemorated in the sacred space. Early Christian pilgrimages of Paula (d. 404) and Egeria (late 4th c.) to the Holy Land including Jerusalem, Antioch, and Constantinople, and also the late medieval travels of Margery Kempe (d. ca. 1438) to Spain, Rome, and Jerusalem exemplify this model of geography as a means of interaction with the Divine.

The third type, "Created Space as Sacred Place," names the phenomenon in which ecclesial structures created by women and men are invested with sacrality through ritual tradition. Here, unlike the first model where all land has potential for manifesting divine presence, and unlike the second, where only those places historically touched by the salvation tradition do so, specific humanly created spaces (e.g., churches) which commemorate "ordinary events" are invested with spiritual significance and become "power" centers where the Divine manifests itself with regularity and authority.[4] The sacred manifestation can be like that of the first model where there is a steady and symbolic but relatively silent presence, or the manifestation can be experienced in dramatic ways by believers (model 4 below). The medieval English prophet and mystic Margery Kempe exemplifies both aspects of this third model.

Fourth, I will also briefly consider a subcategory of the first type, "Landed Eruptions of the Sacred," where the Divine manifests itself to communities or individuals through the land, now not in a steady, continuing, pervasive way, but in a spontaneous, occasional, and frequently dramatic fashion. In common with the parent model described above, the Divine's presence is perceived through the physical, natural world and is not bound by any salvation-related, historically determined delineation of sacred space. This model of interaction is present in the autobiography of the medieval Margery Kempe and in the nineteenth-century American slave narratives of Harriet Jacobs (d. 1897) and Lucy Delaney (cd. 1891) considered below.[5]

In the fifth type, "Space as Apocalyptic Presence," the focus is not so much on the manner of divine presence through a tangible, physical medium (models 1–4), as it is upon dimensions of the divine influence in a dualistic, third-worldly, and otherworldly dichotomy. The features of this geography are not determined by physical, territorial boundaries, but by spiritual categories of bondage and freedom. A literal, physical situation obviously parallels the spiritual geography (e.g., the historical condition of slavery parallels the realm of spiritual bondage), but while the Divine is present in this earthly realm, the dimension of human experience which partakes in God's way of being is derived from participation in a heavenly realm, or as a situation in which the heavenly impinges on this world. We see this pattern in American slave narratives of the nineteenth century.

In the sixth and final model, "Figural Nature and the Sacred," the natural world provides images for expressing human persons' relationship to the Divine. This model can take the form found in women's slave narratives in which categories from nature provide images to describe how human persons experience the Divine; that is, the natural world is a sacred simile, so to speak, where God is understood as being like a river, a mighty wind, a safe harbor. The identification is not literal, as in the first model, but figural. The emphasis is not on God's presence in the river, but rather on the ways in which God's being with us resembles the characteristics of a river. One sees this in Margery Kempe and in the slave narratives of the nineteenth century. This sixth model can also take the form in which spatial categories derived from nature (and often rooted in Scripture) describe not how God acts in relationship to us, but how we chart our own continuing relationship to the Divine. The contemporary Scottish journalist and novelist Sara Maitland's use of categories from map making to convey the character of women's journeys towards spiritual growth and religious influence provides a clear example of this figural use of nature to express our experiences in relationship to the Divine.

LAND AS PRESENCE

The Book of Ruth in the Hebrew Scriptures narrates the stories of Naomi and Ruth and culminates in the birth of Obed, grandfather of King David. The cycle from "land to landlessness, from landlessness to land, from life to death, from death to life," which Walter Brueggemann observes throughout Scripture, structures the Book of Ruth so that the main themes of this narrative, "the gracious rescue of Elimelech's family from extinction by provision of an heir," loyalty, generosity, kinship, and fertility, all emerge in a drama that centers on land and the presence of God through the land.[6]

In the story Naomi and her husband Elimelech leave Bethlehem in Judah during a famine and settle in Moab. Two sons are born to them and the two sons marry two Moabite women. Elimelech dies, and not long thereafter Naomi's two sons die, leaving her to support herself, and seeming to assure the end of her and Elimelech's family line. Now that the land of Moab will no longer sustain her, she decides to return to Judah, urging her daughters-in-law to return to their "mothers'" homes (1:8) in hopes that "you may find a home, each of you in the house of her husband" (1:9).[7] Even after further encouragement to remain in Moab her daughter-in-law Ruth refuses to leave Naomi's side: "[W]here you go I will go, and where you lodge I will lodge; your people shall be my people, and your God my God; where you die, I will die, and there will I be buried" (1:16–17).

They then return together to Bethlehem "at the beginning of barley harvest" (1:22), and Ruth announces to Naomi that she is going forth to the fields to "glean among the ears of grain after him in whose sight I shall find favor" (2:2). (Hebrew law permitted the poor, presumably widows, to glean, or follow after the reapers and collect the missed or dropped grain during harvest time.) Ruth ended up in the field of Boaz, "a man of wealth" (2:1) and, even more, unbeknownst to Ruth, a kinsperson of Elimelech, Naomi's husband. When Ruth asks Boaz's permission to glean in his fields, he not only gives her permission but promises her protection from the rowdy young workers, tells her to drink from the water that the workers have drawn, provides her with food at the mealtime, tells the workers to pull out some ears of grain from the bundles and leave them for her as they go along, and, further, gives her permission to glean until the end of the barley and wheat harvest (2:23). After a successful day in which she gleaned an ephah of barley (two-thirds of a bushel), she returns home to Naomi, relates the story of her day, and Naomi informs her that Boaz "is a relative of ours, one of our nearest kin" (2:20).

Eventually Naomi, who expressed a concern to find a home for Ruth, concocts a plan, telling Ruth to array herself in her best clothes and with perfume, and to go to where Boaz will be, sleeping one night on the threshing floor. "[W]hen he lies down, observe the place where he lies; then, go and uncover his feet and lie down; and he will tell you what to do" (3:4). Ruth follows Naomi's directions except that when the startled Boaz awakens and demands, "Who are you?", she replies that she is Ruth, and she asks him to marry her: "spread your skirt over your maidservant, for you are next of kin" (3:9). Boaz agrees, but with the caveat that there is one relative who is even closer to Ruth who may, if he chooses, play the role of the redeemer-kinsperson, that is, the role of the one in Hebrew law who had rights to the property and spouse of a deceased relative.

In the morning he gives Ruth six measures of barley to take back to her mother-in-law and proceeds to the town gate, where he informs the relative of his (the relative's) rights to the property, which, according to R. L. Hubbard, probably included not only the buying of the land but also the responsibility of providing for Naomi. Boaz adds one more stipulation: "Now on the day you purchase the property from Naomi's hand, also Ruth the Moabitess, wife of the deceased, you thereby purchase in order to raise up the name of the deceased over his inheritance" (4:5). This indicates that while the work of the "kinsman-redeemer" was to buy the land to provide support for Naomi and Ruth, it was further intended to bring about an heir to Elimelech, an heir who would later inherit the property.[8] The relative replies that he cannot be a part of this, "lest I impair my own inheritance." After this turn in events Boaz and Ruth marry, and a child is born which Ruth gives to Naomi. The women of Bethlehem proclaim, "A son has been born to Naomi" (4:17), and they say to Naomi: "He shall be to you a restorer of life and a nourisher of your old age; for your daughter-in-law who loves you, who is more to you than seven sons, has borne him" (4:15–16). The narrator concludes with a genealogy, explaining that Ruth and Naomi's son Obed is father of Jesse, who is father of David (4:22).

The God of the First and Second Testaments is known in this God's transformation of situations from "emptiness to satiation, from death to life, from hunger to bread and meat," and as is clear in the Book of Ruth, this transformation is acted out in relationship to the land.[9] First, one sees the overarching cyclical theme of land in the story as a whole. Naomi and Elimelech leave their home and land in Judah because of a famine; the land is not producing enough to sustain them. When Moab becomes barren—that is, Elimelech and Naomi's two sons die—Naomi leaves Moab to return to Bethlehem and arrives back in Judah at the time of the barley harvest, a stark contrast to the time of famine which initiated her leaving Bethlehem in the first place.

Ruth seeks sustenance for Naomi and herself from the land; God's providence is assured by the landowner Boaz, who promises Ruth access to the land and to support from it. The land that is owned by Elimelech provides the link between Boaz and Naomi. Boaz's processing of the fruits of the land provides the context whereby Ruth can make contact with him, and his giving of grain to Naomi signals his commitment to her cause. Through his rights of access to Elimelech's property, Boaz gains rights to Ruth. Through her presence on the land Ruth had made herself known to Boaz and provided for and supported Naomi. The symbolic return of Naomi to Bethlehem during the "barley harvest" prefigures the fertility of land and people which gives rise to the birth of Obed, grandfather of David. The land is the symbolic center of this story about the survival and perpetuation of the lineage necessary for the emergence of David. And, perhaps most importantly, if Brueggemann's claim is true that "[the land] is presented as a life-giving embodiment of [God's] word," then the story of Ruth and Naomi may be a story about all of Israel, and even the relationship between all people and the God of both Testaments.[10] The presence and behavior of the characters of this narrative in relation to the land provide evidence of, and the stage upon which, the resolution of the story and celebration of the virtues exhibited therein are played out. Naomi left her homeland; Ruth leaves hers, but it is through land in Judah now that Ruth becomes a part of the Davidic heritage, so that Naomi's family can continue.

The Book of Ruth points to one paradigm of women's expression of their experience in relationship to the Divine: God is present in and through the land. Land, in its depths, by its very nature, is a purveyor of the sacred, and it can never be divested of this quality; thus, while God is neither limited nor completely encompassed by literal, physical land, in some sense it is true to say that God and land are synonymous. Land is a symbol, pointing beyond itself to the Divine, and participating in the sacred, so that the earth can never be "mere land." Divine manifestation of this type is not restricted to one or another specifically designated plot of ground; rather sacrality is a quality of all land, regardless of its geographical location. Sacred presence pervades land—it is an enduring aspect of the divine covenant, and one's dealings with the land reflect one's dealings with the Divine.

HISTORICAL PLACE AS PRESENCE

Christianity celebrates history. In the person of Jesus Christ, God was present in the historical, the concrete, and the immediate. As W. D. Davies has pointed out, sacred place became important within Christianity, first, because remembrance of the Jesus of history "entailed the need to remember the Jesus of a particular land" and, second, because the theological outlook of the New Testament, and especially the Gospel of John with its focus on the word become flesh, determined that "physical phenomena . . . are the means whereby the infinite God and spiritual realities are made imaginable and a present challenge."[11] And even more, it is through the historical that Christians obtain the right to salvation.

This salvation-enabling event of God's presence in the historical specificity of Christ radically transforms Christians' experience of the world and of space, which become bearers of the sacred not just in a general sense, as all creation bears the mark of its Creator, but now in all of its particularity as it shows forth the history of the Divine's continuing and active relationship with the world. This sacralizing of historically determined place characterizes Christianity so that tangible, physical, and individualized geographical places associated with salvation history are perceived as potent mediators of divine presence.

Although those traditions associated with the life and death of Christ were central within the Christian tradition, both the Old and New Testaments provided historical detail which elicited religious response, since Christians understood the world and the events of the Hebrew Scriptures as prefiguring the world of the New Testament; so, with the events of Christ's life providing the hermeneutical key to all of Scripture, both the Jewish and Christian Testaments' scriptural traditions were celebrated in their full historical detail as records of God's presence in the world in concrete historical events.

The goal for Christian women who traveled to visit sites mentioned in Scriptures or revered by tradition was not merely to pay homage in a detached yet respectful manner to an event which happened in the distant past, but rather to celebrate, rejuvenate, and nourish their own faiths by immersing themselves in the original places that situated the founding events of the Christian narrative. Visiting the sacred sites of the actual events lying behind their religious beliefs reminded them of the historical rootedness of their faith. And even more important, it invited them to participate in the meaning of those events by reexperiencing such events—through imagination and visualization—at the very places where the events actually occurred. The experience of sharing space with the figures of salvation history evoked an intensity of experience in Christian women visiting sites even centuries after Christ's death.

For many women the outcome of pilgrimage had a reassuring certainty about it. Pilgrimages are to specific historical sites which have a tradition of acceptance as being charged with the divine presence. They are recognized places, tested and found to be successful at evoking the circumstances of their founding. Since their history of recognition ensures that the celebration of historical places as sacred space is largely a communal activity, sacred places have value in this model because communities and not just individuals recognize their power. Visiting historical sites situates women in a community of tradition that traces back to the historical context of commonly recognized founding events. Pilgrimage functions, then, not only to make the past present, but also to link one to a community of believers that stands in a mediatorial relationship to the healing and sustaining power of God in the world.

A fascination with physical places associated with scriptural traditions characterizes the writings of many early Christian women religious leaders. Melania the Elder (d. ca. 410), who had left home in Rome and traveled widely throughout Egypt and Palestine observing monastic life as it was practised by the desert mothers and fathers, eventually founded her own monastery on the Mount of Olives.[12] Paula (d. 404), the close companion of Jerome, established a monastery in Bethlehem, near the basilica built on the reputed site of the birthplace of Christ.[13]

In a letter of consolation to Paula's daughter, Eustochium, after Paula's death in 404 A.D., Jerome recounts in detail the places Paula visited on her travels in

Egypt and the Holy Land. As mentioned above, for Christians both Hebrew Scriptures and the New Testament refer to Christ.[14] Thus, Paula visited both Old and New Testament sites, including the caves where Obadiah had fed one hundred prophets (1 Kings 18:4); Rachel's tomb, where Benjamin was born (Genesis 35:18–19); the home of Sarah and birthplace of Isaac (Genesis 38:1); the place where Christ was born; and the chambers of Philip's daughters, "the four virgins 'who did prophesy' " (Acts 21:8–9).[15]

According to Jerome, Paula's witnessing of the sites of Christian history evoked a response akin to that of a person at the originary events.

> . . . in visiting the holy places so great was the passion and the enthusiasm she exhibited for each, that she could never have torn herself away from one had she not been eager to visit the rest. Before the Cross she threw herself down in adoration as though she beheld the Lord hanging upon it: and when she entered the tomb which was the scene of the Resurrection she kissed the stone which the angel had rolled away from the sepulchre. . . . What tears she shed there, what groans she uttered, and what grief she poured forth, all Jerusalem knows.[16]

Paula seems to relive the events. They are not located in the distant past, but happening in the present, before her eyes. Historical places as bearers of the sacred have the power to transport the spiritual significance of the past to the present, and to enable someone centuries removed to remember and reunderstand what happened.

Another fourth-century religious woman, Egeria, a nun from a western province of the Roman Empire, traveled extensively in the Holy Land visiting sites which included Jerusalem, Alexandria, Galilee, Mt. Sinai, Antioch, and Constantinople. John Wilkinson notes that on her journey of 381 to 384 A.D. Egeria visited three types of holy places: living places associated with holy people of the First and Second Testaments; burial places of martyrs and prophets; and sites associated with Christ's life and ministry.[17]

In a work addressed to her "venerable sisters," presumably those who could not accompany her on her travels, she describes her journey, visiting, among other places, the birthplace of Moses (Numbers 13:23), the site of the burning bush, the city of the King Melchizedek, a site of the ministering of John the Baptist, the burial place of Job, the burial place of St. Thomas the Apostle, the site of Abraham's house, the site of the well from which Rebecca gave water to the camels of Eleazar, Abraham's servant (Genesis 24:15–20), and the site where Jacob watered the sheep herded by Rachel. The scriptural associations of the pilgrimage spots are evidenced by Egeria's remark that "whenever we arrived anywhere, I always wanted the Bible passage to be read to us."[18] She visited the holy women and men who had established communities near the religious sites, and recorded the practices engaged in by those living the monastic life.

Again, as Jerome indicated in his descriptions of pilgrimage, the commemoration of events at their original sites provided spiritual invigoration and evoked emotional identification with the participants of the originary scenes. In detailing the celebrations for Easter, Egeria records that while the passage in which Christ was arrested is being read at the site of Christ's arrest, "there is much moaning and groaning with weeping among the people that they can be heard by all the people of the city."[19] At the Good Friday liturgy at the site of the Crucifixion, when from noon to three readings and hymns recall the events of Christ's death, both Hebrew Scriptures and New Testament passages are read since, as Egeria writes, "the people are taught that nothing happened which was not first foretold, and nothing was foretold which was not completed."[20] The communal remembrance at the site of Christ's death elicits responses from the participants: "At each reading and prayer there is such emotion and weeping by all the people that it is a wonder; for there is no one, old or young, who does not on this day weep for these three hours."[21]

As the examples of Paula and Egeria indicate, in this second paradigm of geographical understanding of specific historical locations, legitimated by their association with the historical events of God's interactions with human persons, historical places are no longer mere historical places; they are now sacred spaces, bearers of a divine presence which has the power to recall the past to the present and to awaken in believers the religious response of the scriptural figures who prefigured and accompanied Christ. For many women, pilgrimage provided an almost guaranteed link to the Divine; women traveled to places recognized by a tradition as being charged with divine presence and experienced there a reliving of of a scriptural world. They experienced the meaning of Scripture by locating themselves in the historical, physical, concrete world where its narratives happened.

CREATED SPACE AS SACRED PLACE

The third author I will discuss exemplifies paradigm two and also draws attention to two further types of the role of geography in women's religion: first, the importance of humanly created, literal, physical places like churches as providing access to the presence of the Divine, and second, the significance of "landed eruptions of the Sacred," remarkable environmental events as manifestations of the Divine.

The fifteenth-century pilgrim and mystic Margery Kempe is one of the more colorful characters of late medieval religious history. In her autobiography, *The Book of Margery Kempe*, Kempe, the mother of fourteen children, records her process of spiritual development from self-centered and sinful brewer of ale to vocal prophet and pilgrim committed to making God's presence known to the world. Hers is a visible witness, marked by shoutings and weepings, and vociferous attempts to awaken Christians to the meaning of their faith.

In keeping with what I have described in the "Historical Place as Sacred Presence" paradigm, Kempe's visits to historical Christian sites, including the site of Christ's birth, the Flood of Jordan, the mountain where Christ fasted for forty days, and the birthplace of John the Baptist, strengthen her love for God.[22] In describing her traversing the path of Christ's passion and death, Kempe (who calls herself "this creature") describes how, as for Paula and Egeria, the site of Christ's passion gave rise to a response "as if" she had been there:

And when they came up on the Mount of Calvary, she fell down because she could not stand or kneel, and rolled and wrested with her body, spreading her arms abroad, and cried with a loud voice as though her heart would have burst asunder; for, in the city of her soul, she saw verily how Our Lord was crucified. . . . And she had such great compassion and such great pain, at seeing Our Lord's pain that she could not keep herself from weeping and roaring though she should have died for it.[23]

When this creature with her fellowship came to the grave where Our Lord was buried, anon, as she entered that holy place, she fell down with her candle in her hand, as if she would have died for sorrow. And later she rose up again with great weeping and sobbing, as though she had seen Our Lord buried even before her.[24]

Her seeing the physical places of Christ's life and death remind her, and even cause her to experience, what Christ's life and death had meant, evoking a response to intense religious identification with Christ and the followers who loved him.

The earthly world of the physical, literal events of Christian history not only recalls historical events to the viewers' minds, but also pushes Christians' spiritual imaginations beyond this world to the sacred and heavenly world lying beyond this earth. "And when the creature saw Jerusalem . . . she thanked God with all her heart, praying for his mercy that, as He had brought her to see his earthly city of Jerusalem, He would grant her grace to see the blissful city of Jerusalem above, the city of heaven."[25]

Her experiences of the literal events of Christ's life, an intense experience prompted by visiting and reflecting on the physical space that Christ inhabited, do not remain at a literal level, but open her mind to the spiritual realities underlying the physical events.

The third paradigm, "Created Space as Sacred Place," points to a further significant feature of women's spirituality: the importance of particular, humanly created, locatable places, and in the case of Margery Kempe, specifically church buildings, which are places of religious gathering and enduring celebration of the presence of God. Churches are humanly created spaces which are built to celebrate and commemorate the Christian story and are regarded as participating in the divine realm with a consistency and to a degree not found in most other created structures. They are "claimed" as sacred space, and consecrated as places of sanctuary and safety, places of communal gathering, of consistent liturgical celebration, and of personal spiritual reflection and development. While churches are places where Kempe participates in everyday religious events, they are also the site of many of her most marvelous and extreme experiences of communication with God.

Churches, like visits to sites of Christ's life and death, function to intensify Kempe's relationship to God. Throughout her narrative she records her experiences of religious fervor, and the vast majority of them happen in churches, as in the following examples:

She was in [the nuns'] church at midnight to hear their Matins, and our Lord sent her such high devotion and such high meditations and such ghostly comforts, that she was all inflamed with the fire of love.[26]

Then as she went one time in the White Friars' Church at Lynne, up and down, she felt a wondrous sweet savor and a heavenly, so that she thought she might have lived thereby without meat or drink, if it would have continued.[27]

When she heard that Master Aleyn, a friend of hers, was sick, "she ran into the choir at Saint Margaret's Church, kneeling down before the Sacrament," and she prayed that Master Aleyn should recover, and he did.[28] It is in churches that Kempe confides her spiritual experiences and finds supporters for her cause. She goes to see a vicar at Norwich to tell him about her experiences. He says he wants to hear what she has to say. "Then he sat himself down in the church. She, sitting a little aside, showed him all the words God had revealed to her in her soul."[29] This vicar listened, and from that point forward became one of her staunchest supporters.

Some of her experiences in church are much more dramatic than those described above. In one mass, at the moment of consecration the host moved "as a dove flickereth with her wings."[30] Christ tells her "in her thought" that this event foretells an earthquake. In another situation a span from a church roof falls, striking her back. Miraculously, though, Kempe feels no pain.[31]

Churches, built by human persons and invested with spiritual power, are intimate spaces which provide clearly demarcated places of the enduring presence of God. For Kempe, and in the narratives of many women of the Christian tradition, humanly created spaces promise access to the sacred and are places of continual reassurance and spiritual contact with God, where the sacraments, liturgies, and prayers are part of the ongoing conversation between human persons and the Divine.

LANDED ERUPTIONS OF THE DIVINE

A third feature of Kempe's spirituality also relies on the tangible and historical, but now without the surety of pilgrimage sites or church buildings. For Kempe, God is omnipresent, but more dramatically present at some times than at others. One of the Divine's most visible forms of manifestation is through the weather, a medium which expresses the power and magnificence of the sacred, while also exhibiting God's concerns for individuals.

One of the most notable ways Kempe exhibits her prophetic capacities is by predicting the weather, a socially significant ability in a culture as closely bound to the earth as late medieval England, and a similarity to the prophets of Hebrew Scriptures (see, e.g., Elijah, in 1 Kings 17–19). At one time while returning from a pilgrimage she was out "sporting" in the fields, and instructing her followers "in the laws of God," Christ told her to go back to the hostel because bad weather was coming. Just as she and her companions arrived back, "the weather fell, as she had felt by revelation."[32]

Even more dramatically, Margery calls upon the Divine to perform a miracle in response to her pleas for help; she calls upon God because God has promised that all will be well in Lynne, but a fire has burned the Guild Hall and threatens to burn the parish church and the whole town. Kempe cries out to God to make it well by sending rain or some weather to quench the fire. It begins to snow, and the fire ceases, a turn in events regarded as a miracle by many (although, as usual, her detractors refuse to credit her with the victory).[33] Manipulation of weather serves as a way of providing sureties for the validity of God's claims on Margery. At one point she asks Christ for a sign in the form of lightning, thunder, or rain, to testify to the fulfillment of Christ's desire that she will succeed in wearing white (a privilege not generally accorded to women who were not virgins). As in Exodus 19:16, when God speaks to Moses, Christ says the sign will be manifest on the third day, and, as promised, the lightning, thunder, and rain appeared and quickly passed away.[34]

Like the First Testament prophets (the paradigms here are Moses and Elijah), God uses the power of weather to support Margery Kempe. Weather manifests God's wrath towards those who threaten Kempe and her followers, as when on pilgrimage in Leicester she is put under house arrest and two of her companions are thrown into prison. God sends such torrents of lightning, thunder, and rain to the town that the people are terrified, convinced that the imprisonment of the pilgrims has elicited God's anger, so they release the prisoners, and "anon, the tempest ceases and it was fair weather."[35]

As in the first type, "Land as Sacred Presence," God is present in and through the natural world, but now although the natural world may by its very nature be a bearer of the sacred, the focus is on nature as manifesting the immense power of the Divine. Tremendous and terrifying power erupts from the earth in the form of lightning, thunder, and rain, reminding human persons of the Creator God's magnificence, and evoking a response of awe, respect, and renewed faith.

SPACE AS APOCALYPTIC PRESENCE

We turn now to a fifth ideal type of use of geographical categories and vocabulary by women, a use which can be described as perceiving "Space as Apocalyptic Presence." Throughout this discussion I will draw on narratives of five women who were at one time slaves: Harriet A. Jacobs (d. 1897); Kate Drumgoold (ca. 1898); Lucy Delaney (ca. 1891); Mattie Jackson (ca. 1866); and Bethany Veney (ca. 1899).[36] While there are marked differences among these writings, they are united in their perception of space as apocalyptic presence, much as the writings of medieval Christian travelers like Egeria and Margery Kempe exemplify the paradigm of "Historical Place as Sacred Presence."

John J. Collins explains dimensions of the apocalyptic worldview, emphasizing that the significance of the apocalyptic outlook lies in its "affirmation of a transcendent world," a world of eventual judgment which endures and demands response from us even as this world "collapses."[37] The world we live in is not celebrated, as in the "Land as Sacred Presence" paradigm, as the enduring medium for sacred activity. Quite the contrary, the Really Real is not here in the world we inhabit, but rather in the transcendent realm of the Divine. The value and even reality that inheres in this present, visible world is there only because it participates in this other and most Real realm, the heavenly realm of God. Central and at the forefront in women's experience in this view of space is the idea that this world is finally only a temporary place of passage on a journey to the eternal realm of the Divine.

In *Incidents in the Life of a Slave Girl*, pseudonymously written by Harriet A. Jacobs (d. 1897), but telling the story of herself under the name of Linda Brent, one sees frequently the dichotomous structure of reality, the contrast between this life—described variously as a desert, "Satan's church here below," "the land of my birth," where "the shadows are too dense for light to penetrate"—and the realm of heaven—a realm depicted as spatially and morally above this earth, where those who had suffered might find "rest in the grave."[38] The heavenly land is the land of the blest, the blessed mansion, the bright mansion above.[39] The confusion and anguish of this world is contrasted with the comfort and rest of the world to come. As "Linda Brent" struggles in a three foot by seven foot roof garret at her grandmother's house, she is consoled by her grandmother: "Let us be thankful that some time or other we shall go 'where the wicked cease from troubling, and the weary are at rest.' "[40] Bethany Veney cites a hymn which describes this world as a "mournful vale" and contrasts with "worlds on high where one can find long-sought rest."[41]

Heaven is described as a place of reunion and reconciliation.[42] "[O]n Monday she [Drumgoold's 'white mother'] heard the call to her to come up to that blessed land where she should be forever with the Lord her dear husband."[43] A woman who holds the last of her eight babies who has just died says, "I wish it could have lived . . . it is not the will of God that any of my children should live. But I will try to be fit to meet their little spirits in heaven."[44] The realm of heaven is the realm of safety, haven, and refuge. After her husband is killed in an explosion, Lucy Delaney's mother consoles her by saying that while her (the mother's) husband is in the South, and she does not know where he is, or what his condition is, "*Your* husband, honey, is in heaven; and mine, God only knows where he is."[45] Hope is much more assured in relation to heaven than it is in relation to the situation of slaves in the South.[46] In response to the deaths of all four of her children by the time they were twenty-four, Delaney rejoices that they were born and died free, and while she laments their deaths, she perceives them as "treasures laid up in heaven."[47]

The demon of this world, slavery, is contrasted with the freedom of the divine realm whose boundaries are established not by literal, physical markers, but by the values of freedom and liberty. After Congress passed the Fugitive Slave Law (1850), which declared that anyone who aided or harbored runaway slaves would be severely punished, Linda Brent, who had escaped to the North but could no longer freely move about because she might be captured and returned to the South, says: "I was doing harm to no one; on the contrary, I was doing all the good I could in my small way; yet I could never go out to breathe God's free air without trepidation at my heart."[48]

Access to this other world is gained through freedom, and freedom is gained through trust in the word of God.[49] Trust and hope provide the connection between the world of shadows, slavery, and imprisonment and the heavenly realm of light and liberty. Events in which trust in God is rejuvenated are central in many slave narratives. When Brent decides that she will risk her life to attain freedom for herself and her children, she goes to the slave burial ground, the site of her parents' graves, and she repeats Job 3:17–19: "There the wicked cease from troubling, and there the weary be at rest. There the prisoners rest together; they hear not the voice of the oppressor, The servant is free from his master."[50] She describes her experience (which also illustrates the "Landed Eruption of the Sacred" paradigm):

The graveyard was in the woods, and twilight was coming on. Nothing broke the death-like stillness except the occasional twitter of a bird. My spirit was overawed by the solemnity of the scene. For more than ten years I had frequented this spot, but never had it seemed to be so sacred as now. A black stump, at the head of my mother's grave, was all that remained of a tree my father had planted. His grave was marked by a small wooden board, bearing his name, the letters of which were nearly obliterated. I knelt down and kissed them, and poured forth a prayer to God for guidance and support in the perilous step I was about to take. As I passed the old meeting house, where, before Nat Turner's time, the slaves had been allowed to meet for worship, I seemed to hear my father's voice come from it, bidding me not to tarry till I reached freedom or the grave. I rushed on with renovated hopes. My trust in God had been strengthened by that prayer among the graves.[51]

In praying with her young son, Benny, and her grandmother, again her trust is renewed: "We knelt down together, with my child pressed to my heart, and my other arm round the faithful, loving old friend I was about to leave forever. On no other occasion has it ever been my lot to listen to so fervent a supplication for mercy and protection. It thrilled through my heart, and inspired me with trust in God."[52]

Early on in her autobiography, Mattie Jackson describes her mother's trust in God who is largely defined by acts of preservation: "But through all her trials and deprivations her trust and confidence was in Him who rescued his faithful followers from the fiery furnace and the lion's den, and led Moses through the Red Sea."[53] Similar themes are apparent in the narrative of Kate Drumgoold.

Echoing the Mosaic language of Exodus, she writes, "When we were in the land of bondage [the Lord] heard the prayers of the faithful ones, and came to deliver them out of the Land of Egypt."[54] Life is described by Jackson as a "weary pilgrimage."[55] The darkness and dreariness of the environment reflect the loathsome events that take place in its shadow.[56] When freedom is obtained, the language is of a new world in contrast to the constant anxiety and pain of slavery and bondage: "The genial rays of the glorious sun burst forth with a new lustre upon us, and all creation resounded in responses of praise to the author and creator of him who proclaimed life and freedom to the slave."[57] The joy of earthly freedom is described as being a share in heavenly, eternal freedom. In describing her reunion with her father, Jackson writes, "We never expected to meet him again this side of eternity. It was Freedom [sic] that brought us together."[58]

The contrast, again, is not that of strict, literal geographically determined territories as much as it is land where one is free versus land where one lives in bondage.[59] The land of bondage is a land characterized by carrying on "battle through life," "a world of sin and distress," and the land of freedom is depicted as the "land of love" and "land of song."[60] As this language suggests, these narratives presuppose a dualism between the fractured and broken world of this earth where experiences of light are fragmentary and limited, and the transcendent realm of the sacred where freedom is uninterrupted. Within this apocalyptic outlook the dichotomy is not absolute, however, as one can experience this world from the perspective of the divine realm, determining one's values in response to it, and understanding the good things of this world as consequences of the transcendent world's impinging on this one. Human persons, then, cultivate living in relationship and response to this "other" world beyond, investing events in this world with importance primarily as they touch or relate to the divine realm. One endures and seeks even to instantiate the transcendent realm, yet to look always to the world to come: the blessed battle is fought on this side, and the victory shall be on the Lord's side.[61]

FIGURAL NATURE AND THE SACRED

As I mentioned at the outset, there are two primary ways in women's writings that natural images are used in a figural way to describe dimensions of the God/human relationship. In nineteenth-century American slave women's narratives images derived from the natural world play a central role in expressing how God protects and nourishes human persons. For Kate Drumgoold, God is the God of the psalmist; a rock, a hiding place, and a shelter in times of storms.[62] In describing her commitment to God, the "Great Emancipator," Drumgoold remarks that while many have forgotten God's work, "his name has a green spot in my heart."[63] She describes how a preacher who has saved many people will appear before God by saying his arms will be full of "blessed sheaves."[64]

Among the natural images used, the theme of water, and more specifically the theme of navigating water, looms large in the stories of these women to express how they experience the Divine. "While in oppression, the eternal life-preserver had continually wafted her [Mattie Jackson] toward the land of freedom, which she was confident of gaining, whatever might betide."[65] Life is a pilgrimage, but even more specifically, a pilgrimage over water: "[The Word of God] . . . guides us through life, points out the shoals, the quicksands and hidden rocks which endanger our path, and at dusk leaves us with the eternal God for our refuge, and his everlasting arms for our protection."[66]

In listening to the accusing testimony at the trial which was to determine her freedom, Lucy Delaney wrote, "As I listened I closed my eyes with sickening dread, for I could just see myself floating down the river, and my heart-throbs seemed to be the throbs of a mighty engine which propelled me from my mother and freedom forever!"[67] In contrast, as she listens to the supporters of her case, she writes: "I felt the black storm clouds of doubt and despair were fading away, and that I was drifting into the safe harbor of the realms of truth."[68] God promises Bethany Veney protection in rivers of woe.[69] Similarly, Kate Drumgoold describes the "streams of God's providence" and God's helping to pilot her through "life's tempestuous sea."[70]

This same paradigm in which nature functions as a simile for the sacred appears in the autobiography of Margery Kempe. God compares the working of the might of the Godhead to God's power in the environment: as the planets obey God and as thunder and earthquakes and mighty winds which blow down houses and steeples instill fear in people, and as lightning sent by God burns down churches and houses, just so God's power works in human souls. And even as the wind which pulls trees out of the earth cannot be seen, so people only feel, but do not see, God's work. "And suddenly as the lightning cometh from heaven, so suddenly come I into thy soul, and illuminate it with the light of grace and of understanding and set it all on fire with love and make the fire of love to burn therein."[71] At another point Christ compares his presence to Kempe with the sun which may at times be obscured by the moon, but is, nevertheless, always present. Here, as in the Book of Ruth, God is present through the land, but now figuratively; the natural world provides a primary simile for describing the Divine's interaction with human persons.

In the nineteenth-century American slave narratives and in the autobiography of Margery Kempe one can see the significance of nature, where God is present not only through nature, but where the spatial world of nature provides categories for naming experiences of the Divine. In the second form the "Figural Nature and the Sacred" model takes, the focus is not directly on how the Divine appears to us, but rather on how we name our experiences in relationship to the Divine. Now the concern is not with how God is manifest to us (e.g., as a river or as a safe harbor), but rather on ourselves and our own locatedness, our own situation in a desert, or wilderness, or on a mountain, and in considering where we are in our relationship to the sacred.

In illustrating this theme the final source I consider here points to the importance of geography in the contemporary situation, a situation of looking forward and seeking to find new ways of being in the world—a situation that characterizes an important movement within the contemporary Christian context for women. The author Sara Maitland, a contemporary novelist and journalist, has a particular interest in relating women's experience to spiritual journeying and map-making. In *A Map of the New Country: Women and Christianity*, Maitland uses cartographical imagery to describe the process she believes Christian women of the twentieth century are called to.

In a fascinating book which explores the variety of forms of women's participation in Christian denominations from a historical vantage point, Maitland illustrates how a sensitive and attuned perspective of history may reveal that women have long participated in a variety of critical ways in church organization and leadership. Like the theologian Rosemary Radford Ruether, she maintains that women's current challenge to Christian churches is the prophetic task of reminding churches of their commitments. Her assessment of women's challenge and situation is steeped in Old Testament language and imagery: The task "is— or can be—the prophetic voice crying in the wilderness for a return to God, to adventure and hope."[72] She argues further that the church needs the "creative and innovative power of women's worship," and she has a strong sense that the journey which map-making language suggests is itself a critical part of realizing women's goals.[73]

Maitland's image of map-making makes a strong plea for women to learn women's history: "[W]e do not have enough competent maps. We are cut off from the experiences of each other and ourselves. We do not know where other women have been or where they are."[74] She draws out her cartographic analogy by explaining how explorers continually outdate the work of map-makers, yet do not render them useless. Stories of the journey, as in the case of Egeria, or Harriet Jacobs, are an encouragement to others to travel these roads, settling along the way, "not only cultivat[ing] the wilderness . . . [but] also creat[ing] a base from which new exploration can take place."[75]

Maitland pictures a promised land, but its description is shrouded in mystery, just as Ruth and Naomi decided to return to Bethlehem, with no clear idea of how their situation would be resolved. But Maitland knows the "journey will lead again into the desert, through the valley of misery, towards crucifixion."[76] The journey "towards the difficult experience of free life" seems to be one of creating one's spiritual identity where one set out without an absolutely clear picture of one's destiny, but knowing that only on and through the journey can one have the possibility of nourishing the situation of "Christian service, equality, justice, and the renunciation of power through love."[77] The journeying and the manner of journeying itself is a part of the destiny, even as the relationship of Naomi, Ruth, and Boaz with the land throughout the narrative was all of a piece with the conclusion.

In this view the promised land is not a transcendent realm with the certainty of that described in the "Space as Apocalyptic Presence" paradigm. In fact, the promised land as future in a transcendent realm has non-reality about it here;

rather, the future is in this world and in the successive generations of women who benefit from the map-making of those who live now. The world understood as a place where spiritual travelers' journeys over mountains, through the desert, and into the wilderness become the means of expressing human persons' capacities to "reveal yet one more aspect of God" in this life.[78] The natural world provides imagery to describe what women's journeys are like, and to name the variety of experiences in which women may not only encounter but also embody the sacred. The goal is not the realm of God in a world other than this one; the goal, rather, is to create a spiritual map that enables women to journey successfully toward a condition—though perhaps not yet an ideal promised land—which affirms wholeness and justice for all people.

CONCLUSION

As I said at the outset, this selection of six categories is intended to be suggestive of the variety of ways in which women in the Christian tradition use geographical imagery and vocabulary to express aspects of their relationships with the Divine. Further studies may add other ideal types, and comparisons with thematic issues in men's writings will help us draw conclusions about male and female similarities and differences with regard to geography's function within their religious imaginations.

I have considered a variety of sources for reflection on the theme of how women use geographical vocabulary in religious expression: texts by women (the fourth-century Egeria; slave narratives by nineteenth-century American women); texts by women, but probably written down by men (the autobiography of Margery Kempe); and texts about women written by men (the fourth-century Paula). One issue here is the problem of possible gender bias in the production of texts about women but written by men. Further study and comparison will help determine whether there are similarities and differences in the way women use geographical categories in their writings and the way men may explain women's experiences using geographical vocabulary. Other resources—poetry, religious art, interviews, life-style commitments of women who choose communal modes of living, liturgical organization—will provide more information and possibilities for expanding our understanding of how women in the Christian tradition use geographical vocabulary to express their experiences of and with the sacred.

These six ideal types draw attention to at least five different kinds of space in women's writing: land, historical place, humanly created space, figurative space and the reality of transcendent, and otherworldly space as a prime determinant of women's experiences. The variety here alerts us to the diversities of divine presence in Christian women's writing and experience: the sacred manifests itself throughout women's lives in a plentitude of place, in the site of the Crucifixion, in the presence of land, in the tremor of a thunderstorm, in the safe harbor towards which all people journey, and in the promised land of women-space which reveals the sacred to the world.

NOTES

1. Throughout this chapter my use of the language of models, types, paradigms, and patterns is indebted to, among others, the following: Max Weber, *The Protestant Ethic and the Spirit of Capitalism* (New York: Charles Scribner's Sons, 1958); Thomas S. Kuhn, *The Structure of Scientific Revolutions*, 2d ed. (Chicago: University of Chicago Press, 1970); Ian Barbour, *Myths, Models, and Paradigms: A Comparative Study in Science and Religion* (New York: Harper & Row, 1974); and Sallie McFague, *Models of God: Theology for an Ecological Nuclear Age* (Philadelphia: Fortress Press, 1987).

2. Great debate surrounds the dating of the Book of Ruth, with some scholars arguing for a preexilic date and others for a postexilic date. For a comprehensive discussion of the arguments, see R. L. Hubbard, *The Book of Ruth* (Grand Rapids, Mich.: William Eerdmans, 1988), pp. 23–35.

3. Walter Brueggemann, *The Land: Place as Gift, Promise, and Challenge in Biblical Faith* (Philadelphia: Fortress Press, 1977), p. 48.

4. The presence of relics in created spaces such as churches did often provide an explicit link to those places literally touched by the events of salvation history.

5. The date given for Lucy Delaney is taken from William L. Andrews, "Introduction," in *Six Women's Slave Narratives*, a volume of *The Schomburg Library of Nineteenth-Century Black Women Writers*, ed. Henry Louis Gates, Jr. (Oxford: Oxford University Press, 1988), p. xxix, which cites a publication date from Russell C. Brignano, *Black Americans in Autobiography* (Durham, N.C.: Duke University Press, 1984), p. 21.

6. Brueggeman, *The Land*, p. 14; and Hubbard, *Book of Ruth*, p. 39; Hubbard discusses these themes on pp. 35–42. Note that as in the story of Abraham and Sarah (Genesis 17), land, fertility, and descendants are interrelated themes. Athalya Brenner provides a marvelous analysis of the Book of Ruth in "Female Social Behavior: Two Descriptive Patterns Within the 'Birth of the Hero' Paradigm," *Vetus Testamentum* 36 (1986):257–73. See also Phyllis Trible, *God and the Rhetoric of Sexuality* (Philadelphia: Fortress Press, 1978), especially pp. 166–99.

7. All biblical quotations are taken from *The New Oxford Annotated Bible with the Apocrypha* (New York: Oxford University Press, 1971).

8. Hubbard, *The Book of Ruth*, p. 244, n. 46.

9. Brueggemann, *The Land*, p. 33.

10. Ibid., p. 498.

11. W. D. Davies, *The Gospel and the Land: Early Christianity and Jewish Territorial Doctrine* (Berkeley: University of California Press, 1974), p. 366.

12. Rosemary Ruether, "Mothers of the Church: Ascetic Women in the Late Patristic Age," in Rosemary Reuther and Eleanor McLaughlin, eds., *Women in Spirit: Female Leadership in the Jewish and Christian Traditions* (New York: Simon and Schuster, 1979), p. 84.

13. Ibid., p. 81. See also the article of Francine Cardman, "Fourth-Century Jerusalem: Religious Geography and Christian Tradition," in Patrick Henry, ed., *Schools of Thought in the Christian Tradition* (Philadelphia: Fortress Press, 1984), pp. 49–64; and Victor Turner and Edith Turner, *Image and Pilgrimage in Christian Cultural: Anthropological Perspectives* (New York: Columbia University Press, 1978).

14. John Wilkinson, *Egeria's Travels to the Holy Land* (Jerusalem: Ariel Publishing House, 1981), p. 15.

15. Jerome, *Epistolae*, in *Corpus Scriptorum Ecclesiasticorum Latinorum*, ed. I. A. Hilberg (Vienna, 1912), Letter 108:8–14; English translation in *Nicene and Post-Nicene Fathers*, ed. Philip Schaff and H. Wace (Grand Rapids, Mich.: William B. Eerdmans, 1892), 6:198–202.

16. Ibid., Letter 108:9, pp. 198–99.

17. Wilkinson, *Egeria's Travels*, p. 15. For a discussion of the dating of the text, see pp. 3, 237–39.

18. Egeria, "The Pilgrimage of Egeria," in *A Lost Tradition: Women Writers of the Early Church*, ed. Patricia Wilson-Kastner, G. Ronald Kastner, Ann Millin, et al. (New York: University Press of America, 1981), 10:96 [chapter 10: page 96 in Wilson-Kastner translation]. See also 15:100.

19. Ibid., 35:121.

20. Ibid., 37:122.

21. Ibid., 37:123.

22. A shift from the fourth to the fifteenth century is visible in that while Kempe does visit some sites of Old Testament importance (the site of the Flood of Jordan, e.g.), she is much more concerned with scenes from the New Testament. It is notable that the socially legitimizing function in the early church of appropriating and adapting Jewish sites to Christian purposes is no longer necessary by the time of Margery Kempe. As we shall see, she does, however, retain Old Testament influences in her relationship to God through the land and in her use of prophetic motifs in her self-understanding.

23. Translations taken from W. Butler-Bowden, ed., *The Book of Margery Kempe* (New York: Devin-Adair Company, 1944). References to the Middle English text are to Sanford B. Meech and Hope Emily Allen, eds., *The Book of Margery Kempe*, in *Early English Text Society*, vol. 212 (New York: Oxford University Press, 1940). References are to the book (1), chapter (28), page number in Butler-Bowden's translation (57), and page number in Meech and Allen's edition (68) [henceforth 1.28:57;68].

24. Ibid., 1.29:60;71. Note the interesting comparisons between Paula and Margery Kempe.

25. Ibid., 1.28:57;67.

26. Ibid., 1.83:184;200.

27. Ibid., 1.71:156;171. See also 1.57:127;139; 1.60:134;147; 1.74:161;176.

28. Ibid., 1.70:155;169.

29. Ibid., 1.17:30;38. See also 1.13:20;27.

30. Ibid., 1.20:38;47.

31. Ibid., 1.9:14;21–22.

32. Ibid., 1.42:88;101.

33. Ibid., 1.67:149;163–64.

34. Ibid., 1.44:91;103.

35. Ibid., 1.47:101;114.

36. For an important discussion of slave narratives, see Marion Wilson Starling, *The Slave Narrative: Its Place in American History* (Boston: G. K. Hall and Co., 1981). See also Melvin Dixon, *Ride Out the Wilderness: Geography and Identity in Afro-American Literature* (Chicago: University of Illinois Press, 1987).

37. John J. Collins, *The Apocalyptic Imagination: An Introduction to the Jewish Matrix of Christianity* (New York: Crossroad, 1984), pp. 214–15.

38. Harriet A. Jacobs, *Incidents in the Life of a Slave Girl: Written by Herself* (Cambridge: Cambridge University Press, 1987; first publ. 1861), pp. 53, 75, 37, 93.

39. Kate Drumgoold, "A Slave Girl's Story," in *Six Women's Slave Narratives*, a volume of *The Schomburg Library of Nineteenth-Century Black Women Writers*, ed. Henry Louis Gates, Jr. (Oxford: Oxford University Press, 1988; first publ. 1898), pp. 14, 16–17.

40. Jacobs, *Incidents*, p. 131.

41. Bethany Veney, "The Narrative of Bethany Veney: A Slave Woman," in *Collected Black Women's Narratives*, a volume of *The Schomburg Library of Nineteenth-Century Black Women Writers* (first publ. 1889), p. 16.

42. Drumgoold, "A Slave Girl's Story," p. 17.

43. Ibid., p. 13.

44. Jacobs, *Incidents*, p. 144.

45. Lucy Delaney, "From the Darkness Cometh the Light or Struggles for Freedom," in *Six Women's Slave Narratives*, a volume of *The Schomburg Library of Nineteenth-Century Black Women Writers* (first publ. ca. 1891), p. 56.

46. Ibid., p. 57.

47. Ibid., p. 59.

48. Jacobs, *Incidents*, p. 195.

49. Mattie J. Jackson, "The Story of Mattie J. Jackson," written and arranged by L. S. Thompson as given by Mattie Jackson, in *Six Women's Slave Narratives*, a volume of *The Schomburg Library of Nineteenth-Century Black Women Writers* (first publ. 1866), p. 42.

50. Jacobs, *Incidents*, p. 90. See also p. 201.

51. Ibid., p. 90.

52. Ibid., p. 155.

53. Jackson, "The Story of Mattie J. Jackson," p. 7.

54. Drumgoold, "A Slave Girl's Story," p. 3. Again, the theme of trust recurs throughout her autobiography, e.g., pp. 3, 5, 21, 50, and 57.

55. Jackson, "The Story of Mattie J. Jackson," p. 11.

56. Ibid., p. 23.

57. Ibid., p. 32.

58. Ibid., p. 35.

59. Drumgoold, "A Slave Girl's Story," p. 6.

60. Ibid., pp. 9, 18, 20.

61. Ibid., pp. 32, 18.

62. Ibid., p. 30. See also pp. 48, 57.

63. Ibid., p. 35.

64. Ibid., p. 40.

65. Jackson, "The Story of Mattie J. Jackson," p. 32.

66. Ibid., p. 42.

67. Delaney, "From the Darkness Cometh the Light," p. 40.

68. Ibid., p. 41.

69. Veney, "The Narrative of Bethany Veney," p. 29.

70. Drumgoold, "A Slave Girl's Story," p. 18.

71. Kempe, *Book*, 1.77:166–67; 182–83.

72. Sara Maitland, *A Map of the New Country: Women and Christianity* (Boston: Routledge and Kegan Paul, 1983), p. 24.

73. Ibid., p. 111.

74. Ibid., p. 193.

75. Ibid., p. 192.
76. Ibid., p. 194.
77. Ibid., pp. xiii, 194.
78. Ibid., p. 188.

6

Mapping an Apocalyptic World

Leonard L. Thompson

In the study of apocalypses, time has passed and space is taking its place; at least space is taking a place alongside time. Millenarians have always emphasized the prominence of the end-times, signs and descriptions of the end, and other temporally oriented elements in apocalyptic literature. More recently Michael Stone, Christopher Rowland, and others have called attention to its interests in cosmology, astronomy, meteorology, geography, climatology, and spatially oriented elements.[1] For example, some of the earliest materials in 1 Enoch (chs. 72–82) give in detail cosmological secrets regarding the movements of the sun and the moon, the twelve winds, the seven mountains, and astronomical laws that establish a solar year.[2] A recent definition that has become standard in the field takes account of both temporal and spatial elements in apocalypses in the following way: an apocalypse is "a genre of revelatory literature with a narrative framework, in which a revelation is mediated by an otherworldly being to a human recipient, disclosing a transcendent reality which is both temporal, insofar as it envisages eschatological salvation, and spatial insofar as it involves another, supernatural world."[3] Spatial transcendence dominates those apocalypses emphasizing heavenly tours and ascents, whereas temporal transcendence dominates those emphasizing historical speculation; but all apocalypses contain, in different degrees, both elements, and it is the presence and interplay of the two which characterize apocalyptic views of the world and its destiny.

In what follows, I shall suggest some of the dimensions to be reckoned with in the mapping of the apocalyptic world, with special reference to the Book of Revelation, the last book in the Christian canon. The Book of Revelation or the Apocalypse of John, as it is also called, is in many ways the apocalypse par excellence. The generic term "apocalypse" derives from that book, so that characteristics of the Book of Revelation set many of the terms for discussing apocalypses. Moreover, Northrop Frye designates the Book of Revelation as "our grammar of apocalyptic imagery." Thus the book not only has shaping power for describing the genre, but it also serves as a template for imagery in Christian mysticism and a broad strand of Western myth. Mapping the world of the Book of Revelation implicates a much larger body of thought and writings.[4]

ELEMENTS IN MAPPING THE WORLD OF REVELATION

Mapping the world of the Book of Revelation creates some particularly complex problems involving various dimensions of space, time, and extended categories. Here, I only suggest some of the basic issues with which any mapping must reckon. In that sense, this is a preliminary study which does not provide a neat map of the final paragraph. It does, however, provide issues which must be considered in the mapping of any visionary literature.

Boundaries

Boundaries are essential in the mapping of a world. As with "mapping," so "boundary" is a term associated with space and spatial demarcations. In common usage "boundary" refers to the outside perimeter of a space: my property is bounded by a curb on the front and a fence behind. This common understanding of boundary develops from the perspective of one who is "inside." If, however, I fly over my land in an airplane, the boundaries will be seen quite differently. From that lofty perspective, a boundary is simply a mark between two things rather than a limit or an outside perimeter. In fact, without the curb and the fence, there would not be two properties, only one. Thus one can say that boundary not only marks differences, it creates them. A boundary separates and delineates, thereby making a difference where otherwise there would be no difference. Further, just as we can learn how land is controlled by noting where boundaries are placed, so we can learn about the seer's world—fundamental distinctions, values, commitments—by noting where he or she places boundaries and creates differences. Through the term "boundary," relationships of various kinds can be described as "topographical arrangement in space."[5] So, for example, a social boundary divides life inside the Christian community from life outside. A literary boundary can be located at Revelation 4:1, where two different types of literature come together. Divisions between good and evil map values and morality in the seer's world. Mapping the boundaries in the seer's world discloses some of the fundamental structures and networks of relations central to the seer's construction of reality.

Boundaries are also places of crossing. That is, boundaries not only mark differences, they also mark the crossing point, the juncture where there are two sides and where something can move from one side to the other. In the Book of Revelation these junctures are always transformational; that is, the movement across the boundary is a transforming movement. For example, a boundary separates heaven from earth, but those boundaries are open to traffic—and in the crossing, transformation occurs. When the seer, John, crosses from earth to heaven, he is transformed "in the spirit." Or, boundaries separate faithfulness from unfaithfulness, but one may pass through those transformational bounds— by the alchemy of repentance or the opposite transformation of "falling" from the faith. When Satan crosses the boundary from heaven to earth, his "falling" is a moral transformation. In brief, passage through a boundary simultaneously transforms the object from what is on one side to what is on the other, earth to heaven, faithfulness to unfaithfulness, good to evil. The phrase "transformational boundary" describes this particular aspect of a boundary situation.

The notion of "transformational boundary" also calls attention to the "permeability" of boundaries. In the world of the seer, boundaries are not impassable, outer limits; they are not hard and impervious. Boundaries are "soft" and permeable, open to passage. Therefore, distinctions between objects in the seer's world are not absolute and categorical; they are relative, with one object blending into the next; they are soft and fuzzy.

Temporal and Spatial Dimensions

As indicated above, both time and space must be folded in as dimensions of an apocalyptic map. This point can be made more specific by considering the Book of Revelation. In the Book of Revelation, the central spatial object is the heavenly throne. The Divine is portrayed as seated upon that heavenly throne, and all else is positioned in relation to it. The initial throne scene—a scene common to apocalypses—is described in detail. The One on the throne is like precious stones, jasper, carnelian, and emeralds (Rev. 4:3). Surrounding the throne are twenty-four additional thrones on which sit twenty-four elders. Seven lamps of fire burn before the throne, and extending out beyond the lamps of fire is a transparent sea-like crystal. Before and around the throne are four living creatures with six wings, full of eyes: one is similar to a lion, the second to an ox, the third to the face of a man, and the fourth to a flying eagle.[6]

The city, Jerusalem, centers John's eschatological, temporal zone. The city of Jerusalem or the "new Jerusalem," though centering time, is laden with spatial language. When the seer sees "a new heaven and a new earth," after the "first heaven and the first earth had passed away," he describes "the holy city, new

Jerusalem, coming down out of heaven from God" (Rev. 21:1-2, cf. 21:10). That eschatological, temporal reality is then described in detail. It has a high wall, twelve gates, three each facing the cardinal directions. Its length, breadth, and height are equal—twelve thousand stadia in each direction. The wall is one hundred forty-four cubits. The river of life flows through the city, and the tree of life grows within it.

At first glance, the eschatological Jerusalem relates to the heavenly throne as a second center in a parabola. We have two centers—one located in the present, the other in the future. Together, they anchor the world of Revelation in a four-dimensional grid. Those spatial and temporal centers are not, however, separable. In the dramatic narration of the end, the eschatological or new Jerusalem not only comes down from heaven (Rev. 21:2), but it also contains within it the throne of God and the Lamb (Rev. 22:1). That connection makes explicit an understanding throughout the book: heavenly (spatial) and eschatological (temporal) are one and the same. Deliberate descriptions identify heavenly throne with eschatological Jerusalem. The same precious stones describe both. Jasper, carnelian, and emeralds as metaphors are found only in the descriptions of those two center symbols (Rev. 4:3; 21:19-20). Aside from the Book of Revelation, precious stones do not typically describe throne scenes in apocalyptic literature; they do, however, describe the new Jerusalem and the Garden of Eden.[7] By using them to describe the throne and then once again the Jerusalem to come, John makes an explicit link between the two. Only the heavenly throne and the new Jerusalem are said to be "fixed" or "situated," the one in heaven (Rev. 4:2), the other as "foursquare" or "cubed" (Rev. 21:16).[8] In both places God is said to dwell with his people (Rev. 7:15; 21:3), and only in those two places will people not thirst, for God will give them water from running springs (Rev. 7:16; 21:6), and God will wipe away every tear only in those two idyllic locations (Rev. 7:17; 21:4). Upward and forward movements are destined to the same location. Heaven and eschaton become one, and the parabola becomes a circle. Space and time curve into one another.

Home Base, Ordinary Life, and Mythic Expansion

Initial reading of an apocalypse may create a false impression that its visions are strictly otherworldly and unrelated in any fundamental way to ordinary human life. For example, the sea and land beasts in Revelation 13 or Babylon the harlot in Revelation 17 appear at first glance to be stories of mythic creatures without obvious connection to everyday reality. In that case, mapping would track the boundaries of an imaginary world that could be separated from a map of ordinary space and time. I argue that a map of an apocalypse—at least of the Book of Revelation—cannot be so understood, for mythic, apocalyptic visions are integrally related to the ordinary.

Here, the spatial and the temporal come to play again. If apocalyptic visions were strictly descriptions of heavenly travels, then one could argue for a spatial separation of heaven and earth; and if the visions were strictly descriptions of the age to come, then there would be a temporal separation between the present age and the future age. The interplay in apocalypses between space and time prevents either type of separation; for the world to come collapses earth and heaven, and the heavenly presence of eschatological life collapses present and future. In short, the presence and interplay of spatial and temporal dimensions in apocalypses prevent a thoroughgoing dualism in which the visions revealed would become a separate set of forces without connection to everyday human activity in ordinary earthy existence. Apocalyptic visions are not (from the viewpoint contained within them) separate literary worlds or symbolic universes; they do not constitute independent alternatives to everyday, earthly existence. Those visions *expand* the boundaries of the known world through esoteric knowledge.[9]

Ordinary social life takes the preeminent position in the Book of Revelation. The structure of the book makes that point clear. The Book of Revelation progresses concentrically, with the end returning to the beginning. A simple example occurs in the Greek order of Revelation 4:1. "*After this* I looked, and lo, in heaven an open door! And the first voice . . . said, . . . I will show you what must take place *after this*." The seer tends to develop his material concentrically into ever-widening rings. So, for example, several of the eschatological promises to "those who conquer—an element in the seven letters of chapters 2 and 3— reappear in the vision of the new Jerusalem in chapters 21–22: at the beginning of the vision of renewal God makes the link to the letters by saying, "He who conquers shall have . . . " (Rev. 21:7, cf. 2:11); the tree of life promised to those victorious at Ephesus (2:7) appears in the city (22:2). The victorious at Smyrna will not be harmed by the second death (2:11), a phrase recurring in 21:8; and to those conquering at Laodicea Jesus promises a seat with him on his throne (3:21), while at Revelation 22:5 his servants reign forever in the city with the enthroned God and the royal Lamb. Elements of the epilogue (22:6–21) circle back to the prologue (1:1–8) to create one grand circularity. At the end, Jesus calls himself the "first and last" (22:13, cf. 1:17), and "alpha and omega" (cf. 1:8), and the "beginning and the end" (cf. 3:14, 1:5). The final trilogy of couplets thus gathers up in a cumulative manner phrases occurring earlier in the book, and it establishes a ring of circularity around the whole work.

In that process of circularity and accumulation, placement in the narrative sequence is a significant factor; for earlier occurrences of a term, image, or motif become a given in the narrative line, to be drawn on in the development of a later scene. That is, a secondary occurrence in the work loops back around the first occurrence of the term, image, or motif, a tertiary occurrence loops back around the first two, and so forth. There is, thus, a kind of recursive process in which an earlier usage becomes a given and provides input into the meaning of a later one.

The first vision given in the Book of Revelation (1:9–3:22) recounts an encounter in which John is ordered to write to seven angels of seven churches: Ephesus, Smyrna, Pergamum, Thyatira, Sardis, Philadelphia, and Laodicea.

Though the seven messages follow a pattern—command to write, identification of speaker, description of church, accusation, call to repentance, warning and admonition, and a promise—each one alludes to the social, religious situation of the particular church being addressed. The seven cities referred to were all cities in the province of Asia within the Roman Empire. When traced on a map of the province, they form a circuit of roadways probably traveled by itinerant Christian prophets such as John, the writer of the Book of Revelation.[10] All of the cities are identifiable from both Christian and non-Christian sources, and most of them were important cities in the province of Asia. Ephesus, for example, was probably the seat of government for Asia; other cities were judicial or religious centers, with their temples having the right to asylum or treasuries with the right to issue coinage. Laodicea had close links with Colossae and Hierapolis, all towns in the Lycus Valley. The conflicts alluded to at Pergamum and Thyatira regarding the eating of meat offered to idols is a conflict which Christians faced elsewhere in the Roman Empire.[11] Sardis was a prosperous city, a wealth that the seer does not approve of. In Christian circles, we know of Smyrna and Philadelphia through the letters of Ignatius, written a few years after the Book of Revelation. Thus the first vision grounds the book squarely in identifiable cities in the Roman Empire where Christian groups flourished.

Given the organizing principles of circularity, accumulation, and recursion in the Book of Revelation, the placement of messages to urban churches in the first vision grounds the subsequent visions firmly in ordinary life; for a term, an image, or a motif first occurs in the messages, and later occurrences loop back to that context of communication with urban churches as an input for later usage. For example, Babylon the harlot (Rev. 17), a cosmic, mythic figure, alludes recursively to Jezebel the harlot (Rev. 2:20–22), a prophetess who lived at Thyatira. Or Satan, who is described as falling from heaven (12:9) and bound in the abyss (20:2), is first mentioned in connection with the churches of Smyrna, Pergamum, Thyatira, and Philadelphia (Rev. 2:8–3:13). In a word, the cities of Asia are "home base" in the visions of Revelation. The seer communicates his visions to Christians in those cities so that they may see their situation correctly. He presents a symbolic structure through which those Christians may comprehend the proper meaning of objects and relationships in their workaday world. John exhorts, warns, and comforts, but more importantly he transmits a structure of meaning that grounds urban, Christian life in a larger, cosmic world. That larger, cosmic concern expands or extends the everyday; it is not an alternative or independent vision of the world.

METAPHOR AND HOMOLOGY: PASSPORTS BETWEEN MYTH AND HISTORY

In review, there is a spatial/temporal center imaged in the throne/city. That center resides in the cosmic, mythic dimension of John's world. Then there is an urban, Asian center which is established early on in the book and to which the later, cosmic dimension returns recursively. In different language, the throne/city centers the mythic dimension of John's world, while Asian cities center the historical dimension of his world. Once again the metaphor or a parabola comes to mind, with the two centers being the ordinary, historical and the mythic, cosmic. The mythic, cosmic throne/city is an extension or expansion of the historical. A boundary exists between the mythic and the historical, and as with all boundaries in the Revelation, it is a transformational boundary, a point of crossing or passing through.

A more complete examination of "passing" must take a linguistic turn, for the world of Revelation is given to us as a book that communicates through language. Two linguistic phenomena are important for understanding how "passing" occurs through the transformational boundary between history and myth: metaphor and homology.

For present purposes, the most salient features of metaphor can be gotten by comparing metaphor and narrative. Narrative involves time, for it takes time to move sequentially from one scene to another or one action to another. Narrative may be described as a horizontal thread that runs through a work. In contrast, a metaphor occurs "all at once." A metaphor consists of simultaneous, vertical layers of language analogous to overlaying transparencies. As a metaphor, "crown of life" must be grasped instantaneously; the metaphor cannot be traced through the letters or the words. A woman appears to John "clothed with the sun" (Rev. 12:1). As metaphor, the clothing is not like the sun, it is the sun; an identity, not a comparison, occurs. In sum, the metaphoric act creates simultaneous identity, not comparative or narrative sequence.

The term "homology" derives from biology, where it refers to similar structures with a common origin, for example, the wing of a bat and the foreleg of a mouse. In connection with the Book of Revelation, I use the term to refer to any correspondence of structure, position, or character in different dimensions of John's world. Those correspondences probably also derive from common origins, but in this case their origins lie in a common order implicated in the different dimensions of John's world. Metaphoric identity and homologous structures (with origins in a common order) form the threads that make John's world whole cloth and provide the devices for transformational movement into John's cosmic expansions.

Consider sky or the heavens. The seer's celestial realm contains the familiar objects of sun, moon, stars, and sometimes the atmospherics of thunder, lightning, and hail. Birds inhabit the sky, a familiar sight to all.[12] When metaphor enters, however, the celestial is extended and opened up. "After this I looked, and lo, in heaven an open door!" (Rev. 4:1). By means of two metaphors, "open door" and "ascent," the seer describes a passage through a transformational boundary. He ascends through the open door, and that ascent forms an homology—a correspondence in different dimensions of John's world; it is simultaneously a movement upwards, a transformation from a normal to a "spiritual" psychological state, and a time warp from the present to the future (Rev. 4:2). "Going up" (spatial plane), "in the spirit" (psychological plane), and "future sight" (temporal plane) form homologies.[13] Once translated into heaven, John is able to see such heavenly visions as the throne of God; the unsealing of the seven seals; the fall of Satan; and finally the new Jerusalem. Elsewhere, a cloud serves as a translating device (10:1), but throughout the book, ascent metamorphoses towards the Divine.

Ordinary life in Asia is extended not only upwards but downwards through similar metaphoric and homologous devices. By "opening" a shaft to the abyss below (cf. the "open door" to heaven), locusts from that demonic plane pass onto the earth (9:1), or Satan and his surrogates move back and forth from earth to the realm below.[14] Since the realm below represents not only the demonic but also death, movement to and from that realm may also occur in the form of transformation from death to life, or resurrection.[15]

There is also traffic between heaven above and the abyss below. In fact, the demonic plane can claim no independent reality, for it derives from the heavenly, divine plane above. Demonic power becomes operative when a "star" falls from heaven and is given a key to open the shaft below (9:1). This "star"— in origin from heaven—is apparently later identified as the angel Abaddon or Apollyon, who rules over the bottomless pit or abyss (9:11), and still later as the scarlet beast (17:8). In chapter 12 a similar transformation occurs when Satan "falls" from heaven. Satan or the ancient serpent or great dragon called the Devil (12:7–12) serves in the divine court in heaven, but is cast out. Through transformational symbols of descent and conflict, Satan—whose authority and power lie behind all other evil forces in Revelation—is seen to metamorphose from the Divine.

A spatial map of John's world, thus, has three divisions—earth, above the earth, and below the earth—and spatial movement up or down carries familiar values: "up" on the map moves toward the Divine, while "down" moves away from the Divine towards evil forces. Or in the jargon of the history of religions, John holds to a sky, not a chthonic, deity. At the same time, the evil forces below do not establish another center equal to "throne/Jerusalem" or "cities of Asia." They are derivative powers from the "throne/Jerusalem," however great an impact they may have upon the cities of Asia. There is ultimately no good/evil dualism in the Book of Revelation, for evil does not have the ontological status of good.

EXTENDING THE MAP

Transformational movement through space has its homologies in other dimensions of the seer's world, for example, in social and religious categories within the churches of Asia. Movement from faith to un-faith is a fall and a movement towards death (23:5; 3:1). Repentance, however, is a reverse movement, implicitly a move upwards towards the Divine (2:5). Even the most blasphemous have the possibility of transformation through repentance and can cross the boundary from un-faith to faith (16:9, 11). All can "open the door" (3:20). Religious and social status may also be couched in terms of clothing and colors. Godliness in the religious dimension is homologous to bright, clean, linen clothing (Rev. 19:7–8; 15:6). Jesus urges the Laodiceans to buy from him white clothing (3:18). Whiteness is homologous to proper garments, righteous deeds, and holiness. When John went "up," he encountered one with "white hair, white as snow" (1:14); those not stained at Sardis will walk with Jesus in white (3:4–5); the twenty-four elders, seated around the throne, wear white garments (4:4), as do the ones under the altar (6:11) and the army of God (19:14). The color "white" thus substitutes on the color plane for righteousness and holiness—attributes of the God above, the new to come, and present faithful Christians. John's opposition within the seven churches of Asia forms homologies with the mythic figures from "below." Satan's throne at Pergamum forms a homologue with the throne of the beast (2:13; 9:11); the synagogue of Satan—at Smyrna and Philadelphia (2:9; 3:9)—also links the church's opposition to forces of evil; the prophetess Jezebel at Thyatira connects with Babylon the whore; the seven heads of the scarlet beast are the seven hills of Rome (17:9). Through these homologies Christians in the seven cities comprehend properly the meaning of Christian groups, other religions, and political-social elements in the Roman Empire.

As we saw above, time must also be mapped as an integral part of the seer's world.[16] John's God is the God of past, present, and future: "the one who is and was and is to come" (1:4; 2:8). The seer views time as a conductor views a musical score; he ranges freely through time, catching patterns and motifs in his mapping of the eons. Just as there is no ultimate dualism in the spatial dimensions of John's world, so there is no sharp dualism in time. There may be two ages (this age and the age to come), portrayed as "the first heaven and the first earth" over against the "new heavens and the new earth" (Rev. 21:1), but the "new" is a transformation of the old. The Greek world for "new" (*kainos*) could be better translated "renewal" or even "restoration," for the portrayal of the "new" borrows heavily from descriptions of paradise from of old.[17] In both space and time there is a U-shaped curve which, when traced, returns to the vicinity of its origins—heaven or paradise. Finally, since the "new" derives from heaven, time moves upward as it moves forward.[18] Or, as stated earlier, the spatial heaven and the eschatological restoration collapse into one center.

The activity of worship serves as another significant homologue to space. Those heavenly figures that surround the throne of God, one of the centers of the Book of Revelation, engage in praise and worship (Rev. 4:8–5:14).[19] The four living creatures sing incessantly a form of the Sanctus or *Kadosh*, the Latin and Hebrew words, respectively, for "holy":

> Holy, holy, holy
> Is the Lord God Almighty,
> the One who was and is to come (Rev. 4:8).

In various versions, this *Kadosh* or Sanctus is the song par excellence of apocalyptic visionaries.[20] The twenty-four elders acclaim God and his worthiness to be praised (Rev. 4:11). Heavenly angels also join in the liturgy (Rev. 5:12). Worship is not, however, limited to the heavenly, mythic dimension. In the throne scene (Rev. 4–5), worship extends to ever wider dimensions until all creation joins in the worship of the one, true God: "And I heard every creature in heaven and on earth and under the earth and in the sea, and all therein, saying, 'To him who sits upon the throne and to the Lamb be blessing and honor and glory and might for ever and ever!' "21 And the four living creatures said, "Amen!" and the elders fell down and worshipped (Rev. 4:13–14). By the end of the liturgy, the whole cosmos joins in singing and praising God. Worship is not bounded by heaven, but flows out through the whole cosmos. From another point of view, heavenly worship is an extension of earthly worship in the churches of Asia. In the mythic, heavenly scenes, the worship is Christian in that it involves worship of the Lamb (the Christian Christ) and God. But whether one looks at the heaven/earth continuum from the heavenly or the earthly end, it forms one community of worship, an egalitarian *communitas* which joins heaven and earth in joint obeisance.22 Put differently, worship also softens the boundaries between heaven and earth (mythic and historical) and keeps them from becoming hard and impenetrable.

Worship around the throne also brings the heavenly and the eschatological together. From a temporal, eschatological point of view, God's rule, just judgment, and act of resurrecting the dead are imminent; but those very themes are celebrated in heavenly worship as immanent in present, cosmic structures.23 Furthermore, in the organization of the Book of Revelation, liturgical celebrations around the throne can act as a surrogate for eschatological drama. So, in the sequence of the blowing of the seven trumpets, the reader is assured that at the sound of the seventh trumpet the *eschaton* will come. Instead, the seventh trumpet discloses *heavenly worship*.24 Through worship Asian Christian congregations participate in the heavenly throne and the eschatological city—which as we saw above are one and the same.

CONTOURS OF A WORLD MAP

Through metaphor and homology, one can map out a whole world in the Book of Revelation as boundaries become soft points of transformation. Any boundary in the seer's world can unwind through quantum leaps into religious, social, political, and psychological realities. Quantums are transformed as they move through a variety of fields, such as time, space, social groups, literary forms, moral commitments, liturgical celebrations, and psychological states. Moreover, the contour or shape of those field-boundaries is replicated in one another, so that one may describe their relationships as *rational* or forming *ratios*. To grasp essential ratios is to comprehend aspects of an inner structure that unfolds to create a comprehensive vision of the world.25 So in the Book of Revelation, God is to Satan as the Lamb is to the beast, as the faithful are to those who deceive, as the Christian minority is to the larger Roman world; heaven is to earth as the eschatological future is to the present, as the temple is to the space around it, as cultic activity of worship is to everyday activity, as being in the Spirit is to normal consciousness. Ratios and proportions can be formed among social, political, religious, theological, and psychological aspects of the seer's vision because all of these aspects unfold an order implicated and replicated throughout the seer's world.

A world map is by definition totally comprehensive; everything must have a place in its "space." Any and every object that John encounters gains meaning by taking its place on a boundary in the seer's world and entering into his network of metaphors, homologies, proportions, and ratios. All "contexts" are transformed as they flow into the seer's multidimensional world, and all then unfold the essential structures of that world: temporally in eschatological expectations, spatially in heaven-earth connections, liturgically in sacral action and sacred speech, and behaviorally in social practices and social relations. In the process, no one boundary can claim a privileged position. Every boundary reiterates every other as proportions are formed among heavenly worship and Christian celebration, appreciation of Roman culture and demonic excess, political power and insubordination before God, Jewish claims and apostasy to Satan, or church boundaries and the boundaries of paradise. Because the contours of the whole are replicated in every boundary situation, any boundary can illumine another, for a boundary situation is nothing more or less than an unfolding in one dimension of an order implicated in all others. Like Einstein's notion of time and space, boundaries in the seer's world are coordinates of a multidimensional reality.

To map an apocalyptic world is to map a cognitive world, a totality of knowledge and experience. An apocalyptic world is an extended world, one that involves more than the here-and-now. Through metaphor and homology, the world is expanded in both space and time, and through that expansion the here-and-now is situated—given a place on which to stand. That is to say, the expansion of the everyday or historical into a mythic dimension offers one means of orienting and grounding human activity within a larger frame of reference. Mythic grounding in the Book of Revelation—whether in a heavenly throne or an eschatological city—is integrally connected to the everyday activities of urban Christians living in the province of Asia. Various homologous structures built out of different materials at different levels—organic processes, social interactions, liturgical acclamations, mythic visions—contribute to that laborious process of adaptation in which the writer of Revelation (and most every other human) engages.

We often map a cognitive world so that certain dimensions are peripheral to others: for example, mythic, religious, and linguistic symbolisms are drawn on the edge, and social, political, and economic aspects of a world at the center. Or the social boundary dividing, for example, Christian and non-Christian is traced in darker hues than liturgical and mythic provinces. Those modes of mapping then invite causal relations: changes in the center cause changes on the periphery. We need to find a different mode of mapping a world. Different dimensions cannot be traced as separate provinces on flat paper. Laminations and overlays offer a more adequate model for mapping: each overlay then fills in more fully aspects of the seer's world, but no one lamination can claim priority over or determination of the others. There is no essential context (e.g., social-historical or psychological) prior to and occasion for other dimensions. Like the surface of a sphere, the dimensions have neither center nor peripheral edge, and like a hologram, the whole is replicated in every part.

NOTES

1. See Michael Stone, *Scriptures, Sects, and Visions* (Philadelphia: Fortress Press, 1980), pp. 42, 113–14; Christopher Rowland, *The Open Heaven* (New York: Crossroad, 1982).

2. For a text and commentary on 1 Enoch, see E. Isaac, "Ethiopic Apocalypse of Enoch," in James Charlesworth, ed., *The Old Testament Pseudepigrapha* (Garden City, N.Y.: Doubleday, 1983), 1:5–89.

3. John Collins, ed., *Semeia 14: Apocalypse: The Morphology of a Genre* (Missoula, Mont.: Scholars Press, 1979), p. 9.

4. On the Book of Revelation and issues of genre, see Klaus Koch, *The Rediscovery of Apocalyptic* (New York: Charles Scribner's Sons, 1969), p. 18. Northrop Frye's quotation is taken from *Anatomy of Criticism* (Princeton, N.J.: Princeton University Press, 1957), p. 141.

5. Karl Jaspers, *Philosophy* (Chicago: University of Chicago Press, 1970), 2:177.

6. Rev. 4:4–8. Cf. Apocalypse of Abraham 18, 2 Enoch 22.

7. For Jerusalem, see Tobias 13:16; the garden of Eden, Ezekiel 28:13. Precious stones also describe the priest's breastplate in Exodus 28:9, 17; 35:9, 27; 39:6, 10.

8. The Greek verb for "fixed" (*keimai*) is used only in those two places. That fixedness contrasts with the seer's more common notion of space (*topos*) as bound up with destiny and contingency (Rev. 12:6; 2:5; 6:14; 20:11). On the importance of the new Jerusalem in the religious imagination, see James Dougherty, *The Fivesquare City* (Notre Dame, Ind.: University of Notre Dame Press, 1980).

9. See, for example, Rowland, *Open*, pp. 92, 175, 475.

10. See, for example, the reference to prophets in the *Didache*, a second-century handbook for Christians (*Didache* 11–13). See, also Adela Yarbro Collins, *Crisis and Catharsis* (Philadelphia: Westminster, 1984), pp. 34–50. On roads, see Leonard L. Thompson, *The Book of Revelation* (New York: Oxford University Press, 1990), pp. 148–49.

11. See Gerd Theissen, *The Social Setting of Pauline Christianity* (Philadelphia: Fortress Press, 1982), pp. 121–43.

12. See Rev. 6:12–13, 8:13, 12:1, 19:17.

13. The Greek word *pneuma* is regularly associated with transformations, sometimes in connection with cultic time (1:10), resurrection (11:11), and prophecy (19:10). At 11:8 nominal transformation is designated by the adverb *pneumatikos*.

14. See Rev. 13:1, 11; 20:1–3, 7.

15. The "firstborn from the dead," for example, has the keys to Death and Hades (1:18) and can thereby control death and life.

16. More generally, on spatial aspects of time, see Yi-Fu Tuan, *Space and Place* (Minneapolis: University of Minnesota Press, 1977), pp. 118–35, 179–98.

17. For example, references to the tree of life (Rev. 22:2) allude to the Paradise of old in Eden.

18. See also Tuan, *Space and Place*, pp. 34–38.

19. Liturgy and ascent are connected in Jewish Hekhalot mystical texts, see Naomi Janowitz, *The Poetics of Ascent* (Albany: State University of New York Press, 1989).

20. See, for example, Isaiah 6:3, which is the origin of the thrice-holy; 1 Enoch 39; 2 Enoch 21; 1 Enoch 35–40; Apocalypse of Abraham 16.

21. Sometimes the universe is divided into three divisions—heaven, earth, and under the earth—and sometimes four—heaven, earth, under the earth, and on the sea.

22. On connections between the earthly and heavenly in worship, see Leonard L. Thompson, "Cult and Eschatology in the Apocalypse of John," *Journal of Religion* 49 (1969):330–50.

23. For kingship, compare Rev. 19:11–22:5 (eschatological occurrence) with Rev. 19:6; 15:3; 4:11 (heavenly worship); for judgment, cf. Rev. 18:8; 19:2 with Rev. 11:18; 14:6–7; 16:7; for resurrection, Rev. 20–21 with 6:9–11.

24. Rev. 11:15. See Thompson, "Cult and Eschatology," pp. 330–50.

25. See David Bohm, *Wholeness and the Implicate Order* (London: Ark, 1983), p. 20. Newton's insight into gravitation can be expressed as a universal proportion or ratio: as the apple falls, so the moon, and so everything (p. 21).

PART III

ISLAM

7

Sacred Circles: Iranian (Zoroastrian and Shi'ite Muslim) Feasting and Pilgrimage Circuits

Michael J. Fischer

Culture—any culture, be it popular or high culture—is like Yazdi *termeh*, a rich silk brocade of threads of many colors. If you look at the front or positive side, you are entranced by a brilliance of color and pattern. If you look at the back or negative side, you see all the strains, compromises, mistakes, conflicts, and broken ends. Today I want to speak of the front or positive side; because the *termeh* which I will describe is in danger of disappearing, and if it does we will all lose something. The loss is inevitable, but what we can do is at least capture its beauty in a verbal photograph, so that we can reflect on it and weave new pieces of *termeh* with new patterns but conserving the aesthetic.

The tapestry I wish to describe is a communal form of life on the Iranian Central Plateau, a form that is knotted in part by pilgrimages and feasting. It happens to be Zoroastrian. I will also make some comparisons with the Muslim patterns, for they are not only similar but interconnected. The conclusions I want to draw are three. They are in the nature of research goals as well as conclusions. First of all I want to establish a way of making a typology of rural communities which takes account of cultural forms: the form I will discuss is one that is probably more egalitarian than most, and thus can serve as a way of modifying the old social theories of village communism by identifying sources of cohesion.

Second, I want to propose a sociology of Zoroastrianism to complement the Orientalist view. And third, I want to explore ways of opening up the folk culture of the Iranian Plateau to analysis.

RURAL COMMUNITIES AND CULTURAL FORMS

First I need a contrast to throw this particular form of community culture on the Central Plateau into descriptive relief. I perhaps can do no better than to call on Gholem Husain Sa'idi's superb description of the ambience along the Persian Gulf, where relations between the spirit world and human beings are mediated by the drumming and singing "plays" (bazi) of the zar, jinn, pari, div, ghul, noban, and mashayekh (the various species of spirit). Sa'idi writes:

The [Gulf] coasts of Iran are favorable striking grounds for psychic disorders and madness. Living on them means a constant exposure and vulnerability to all sorts of fears, anxieties and deprivations. It means a perpetual confrontation with the terrors of thirst, hunger, drowning, ever present sickness, death, exhaustion, and monotony. Sunk into a pervasive state of despondency, the coastal dwellers are forced into a constant preoccupation with themselves. No other shelter or source for security seems accessible to them, facing the hardships of their lives, but with warmth, closeness and affection they can provide for each other individually, or as groups. These have been the grounds through which the beliefs and rituals of the "People of the Air" have so quickly penetrated the population living on the Southern coasts of Iran. . . . [The spirits] are everywhere, searching for human hosts who are suffering from fatigue and despair, whether on land or sea. Whenever the inhabitants of a region are more ridden with anxieties and fears, the Winds [ahl-e hava] assemble in their greatest numbers.[1]

The idiom of interaction between the anxieties or despondencies of the human beings and the spirits is one of possession. The spirits "mount" their human hosts. The hosts must then be cured by participating in a play (bazi) orchestrated by a Mama or Baba. First the patient is isolated, rubbed with ointments, and an attempt is made to frighten the jinn from his body. Cult members then gather for the bazi. The patient is made to drink some blood of a sacrificial animal, there is drumming and tambourines and chanting. The spirit will respond to a particular tune. The patient is entranced, and through him the Mama or Baba can talk to the spirit and negotiate a modus vivendi. This modus vivendi consists of asking the patient to do certain things, make certain gifts, and observe certain taboos. From an outsider's point of view there are two important transformations which occur in the life of the patient by means of the bazi. One is what psychiatrists call abreaction; that is, an image of conflict is suggested to a patient, which he is encouraged to merge with his own emotional conflicts in such a way that, as the image is manipulated by the psychiatrist or Mama, his emotional conflicts are brought to a temporary or more permanent resolution. The second thing that happens to the patient, which is an important support for abreaction, is that he enters into a cult. He is not cured in the sense that he is returned to his previous state before he fell ill. Rather he is given a new social membership, he is given new daily activities such as observing the taboos, and the community is also alerted to treat him in a slightly different way.[2]

Just one final point: not all people are equally vulnerable to the spirits. Those with greater economic security, merchants, captains of large boats, and so on, are rarely afflicted. Sa'idi puts it this way, "They possess the economic resources to guard themselves against all evils and misfortunes; they do this through making pledges, giving charities, and alms of bread."[3] In other words, there is a differentiated social structure. The richer and more secure people are part of the design: they are financial supporters at least in indirect ways (pledges, charities, alms), and thus they do not challenge or undermine the cult. (The fact that many—both rich and poor—may be skeptics and nonparticipants is not in itself a sociologically destructive force upon the cults. Only today, as the entire economic basis of life and the associated social organization undergoes change, are the zar cults likely to decline or change in form. Previous government attempts to outlaw them merely drove them underground.)

A SOCIOLOGY OF ZOROASTRIANISM

The Zoroastrian villages of Yazd on the Central Plateau have a different communal form.[4] There too life was hard, out on the scorching desert where every drop of water and every patch of green were calculated as a jewel of value and beauty. There too the best shelter or source for security lay in the warmth and care people provided one another. But agriculture rather than fishing and pearling was the daily sphere of activity. And agriculture has its own communal organization, intensified among a besieged minority like the Zoroastrians.

There were at least three major sets of communal ties in the villages of the Central Plateau. One was the organization of agricultural production itself: the *boneh* systems, or agricultural work teams, usually of about five men, most fully described by Javad Safinejad, and the *shaban-e ruz*, literally "day and night," but here referring to units of water distribution.[5] In the northern parts of the plateau, work teams consisted of about five men. Each village had a fixed number of such teams, that is, a fixed number of shares or of adult men who had direct access to the land. It was the job of the *kadkhoda* or village headman to arbitrate among the several work teams regarding the rotation of land and distribution of water, and to negotiate with the landlord about the division of the crop. In the Yazd Zoroastrian villages, work teams were not in evidence. These were not landlord-dominated villages. But much land was held as religious endowment (*waqf*), and these endowments supported periodic communal feasts, so that the community had an indirect interest in the product of the land. More important to the communal structure of agricultural production than land itself was the distribution of water. For irrigation and other purposes, water was brought by underground channels (*ganat*), each laboriously dug from an aquifer in the side of a mountain, and sometimes extending for many kilometers. One either rented or bought shares in the operation of the underground channel, its maintenance, and the regular and fair distribution of water.[6]

The other sets of communal ties reinforced the impact of these features of agricultural organization. One was the endogamous marriage pattern, especially where no division of inheritance was formally made for one or two generations. If a man's several children married one another, there would be less need for division (but rather readjustment) than if they married outsiders.[7] Holding of land as either family endowments or community endowments (*waqf*) would reinforce the justification for centrifugal adjustments according to the needs of each generation, rather than "centripetal" separation of each individual's rights. (The standard Zoroastrian explanation as to why so much land was nominally held as endowments is that, in the Qajar period in particular, Muslims exerted great pressure to appropriate Zoroastrian land. The local *ulema* who served as notaries would write out phony deeds of ownership in support of Muslim claims. However, if land were made of endowments, for some peculiar reason, Muslims would respect the claim. I say "peculiar" because litigation over what is and is not an endowment is hardly foreign to Muslim law.)

The third set of communal ties—feasting—which will be a major subject of our consideration here, has to do with the endowment lands, for when they were made religious endowments, such lands were made *ipso facto* to support a kind of communal feast called *gahambar*. *Gahambars* are periodic feasts held every two months for five days.[8] They have a ritual recited by a priest, and originally, as their six individual names indicate, they had to do with the agricultural-seasonal cycle.[9] For a given village, any five-day feast consists of a number of charitable food distributions (*khairat*) in the fire temple and in a number of different houses. Endowment property supports such acts of charity in accordance with the value of the property. Often, of course, today such property will have little value, but the users or holders of the property will distribute food anyway. There are, then, thirty days regularly distributed through the year when the indigent as well as others are treated to free food.

The charity system, however, is more than this. Other food distributions are also held on death memorials and on occasions of the fulfillment of vows. These irregular feasts are interspersed between the periodic *gahambars*. Food is also shared, but less widely, at pilgrimages and "tablecloth" feasts (*sofrehs*). At tablecloth feasts, food is displayed, and women retell moralizing stories about helping others in order to receive divine aid oneself. At these rituals, women also clean chick peas (*nakhod*), which in turn are redistributed from the original ritual setting to bring blessings to those who could not be present. In fact, these rituals may be fruitfully compared with the less systematic, but similar, charity-feasting systems of Muslim villages associated with certain forms of sermon or preachments (*rauzeh*), as well as with occasions used for communal stews, such as Ash-e Iman Husain on Ashura. According to Dr. Robert Dillon, in the villages of Kirman which he studied, there was an obligation on each family to sponsor at least one preachment a year, at which food would be served. He notes that in the village of Pusht-e Shiran, there were well over a hundred preachments, an average of one every three or four days. Unfortunately, however, he does not tell us how they were distributed over the year. One suspects that despite a possible attempt by the local Moslem clerics (*akhunds*) to ensure some distribution, perhaps through an idiom of auspicious and less auspicious days, many of these preachments were clustered in the months of Ramadan and Moharram-Safar.[10]

THE FOLK CULTURE OF THE IRANIAN PLATEAU: AN ANALYSIS

What I hope I have established so far is a *prima facie* set of communal ties rooted in the agricultural activity. I want to turn now to the ideological or cultural structure of these communal ties.

One of the major moral norms behind the periodic feast (*gahambar*) is that everyone should participate. All disputes should be resolved so that people may sit and eat together. Everyone should have a chance to give a *gahambar* as well as to receive hospitality. The last day of a *gahambar*, especially the last *gahambar* of the year (the Hamspathem Gahambar), often has a communal food distribution (*khairat*) given not by an individual, but supported by subscription of, among others, those too poor to give their own. There is a popular story about the Sassanian Shah, Noshiravan Adel, which stresses that charity by each person according to his means is dearer to God than the lavishness of giving by a rich man merely to demonstrate his power. It is said that Noshiravan prided himself on giving the most lavish *gahambar* in the world, but during one of them he dreamt that there was someone else giving a more meritorious one. Noshiravan searched the world for such a man, who had the effrontery not to come to the royal *gahambar*, but had given a separate one. Eventually he found the man: a very poor, crippled Zoroastrian priest (*dastur*), who had been unable to attend the royal feast because of his infirmity and had sold the door to his house to hold one himself, in order to participate in a *gahambar*.

This theme of merit by giving is also a primary theme in the legends and rituals of the several ritual feasts (*sofrehs*) which are common to both Zoroastrians and Muslims, and are primarily women's activities.[11] Central to these traditions are the stories, "Moshkel Goshā," "Bibi Seshambe," "Pir-e Vameru," and "Bibi Shah Pari." Their common theme is that while human beings are limited in knowledge and ability to control events, difficulties and the drudgery of work can at times be facilitated miraculously, and that the giving of help to others is a prerequisite for good fortune. Of these stories, "Moshkel Goshā," literally "Difficulty Solvers," is the clearest in stressing that supernatural help is possible but only if one gives help to others first. Pir-e Kharkan, the hero of the story, begins as a destitute wood gatherer. He is miraculously helped, but told his luck will hold only if he always remembers to give out "difficulty solvers" (*moshkel goshā*), that is, roasted and cleaned chick peas (*nakhod*). He decides to go on the Hajj and delegates this duty to his daughter, who forgets and consequently ends up in jail on false charges. When Pir-e Kharkan returns, he takes his daughter's place in jail. He convinces some passers-by to bring him chick peas, so he can give *moshkel goshā*. At first they refuse and their affairs go awry. They then bring the chick peas, and all problems are solved. The story of Pir-e Kharkan also has to do with chick peas, but it is a work story. It is told as women sit together to do the laborious task of cleaning the chaff off chick peas. One takes chick peas as well as fruit to shrines to be blessed, and then upon one's return from a shrine one hands out the chick peas so that others may partake of the blessing.

The story "Bibi Shah Pari," which has to do with the daughters of a fairy (*pari*), and the story "Pir-e Vameru," which is also about a daughter of Shah Pari, stress more the miraculous quality of luck that appears in the world. Still, at least in "Pir-e Vameru," the protagonist of the story aids the daughter of Shah Pari, even if unwittingly, before the latter aids her. The story tells of a woman hurrying to do much work before her husband returns, work that she has been lax about doing over the long period he was away. The daughter of Shah Pari has a bone caught in her throat, but as she laughs at the sounds made by the wife, the bone comes out. In return, the work is miraculously finished. The other Shah Pari story is a version of a folk story also told in other contexts with other characters. It tells of a prince marrying this daughter of Shah Pari and having offspring whom she gives to a dog. The prince says nothing until his mother dies, and the wife laughs. He asks why she laughs at his loss, when he had never complained about her giving the children to the dog. She says the dog is her mother, and that she was laughing at the misfortune of the queen, so rich and yet not knowing what would happen. She would return the three children, but they would all die premature deaths. Both of these stories are told in ritual fashion around a ritually spread tablecloth with various offerings (*sofreh*), and food is shared among the women. That is, the ritual action which goes with the stories is one of exchange or sharing, even if this is less explicit in the stories themselves.

Similarly, the story of Bibi Seshambe again has the theme of exchange more clearly expressed. A widower is forced by his new wife to abandon his three daughters in the desert. The eldest daughter goes for food and comes upon three daughters of Bibi Seshambe. She offers to help them with their work. She is given food and saves some for her sisters. Then she gives some water to a thirsty horseman who has found them, and places a straw on the water so that he will not drink too fast and catch cold. He turns out to be a prince and proposes marriage. At court, the three girls get into trouble and the daughters of Bibi Seshambe come to their aid.

The story "Bibi Seshambe" is the ritual story told at a *sofreh* which only women are allowed to attend, and it is held for various vows, but especially for illnesses. Although the other rituals I have described admit males and females, all these *sofreh*, if not exclusively women's affairs, are largely female-oriented. All the active supernatural agents, except in the story "Moshkel Goshā," are female.

This is also true of the legends associated with the six major Zoroastrian shrines. Elsewhere, I have argued—against the popular cliché that males are the exclusive culture carriers in the Middle East—that women and female legendary figures are crucial and central both to the actual management and to the conceptualization of health and culture.[12] Ritual tablecloth feasts (*sofrehs*) and pilgrimages give women opportunities to vary their daily routine, to negotiate social affairs with women of other villages, and to rejuvenate an idiom of health, adjustment to the cosmic order, and general well-being, not only for themselves, but for their family community and menfolk as well. In a very simple way, this is the symbolism of bringing back chick peas (*nakhod*) or difficulty solvers (*moshkel goshā*) from shrines. Culturally, perhaps the nature of legend organization can be pushed further, by saying that there is a stress on the centrality and need to protect the feminine. Or rather, let us put it the other way around: what is central is conceptualized as feminine, interior, emotional, and an internal route of security.[13] In any case, shrine legends have a tripartite structure, which provides both historical and sociological entries into village culture.

There are two kinds of Zoroastrian shrines: the six major shrines, which in a sense mark the socio-religious perimeter of Zoroastrian settlement in the Yazd basin; and little shrines around each village, again usually around their perimeters, defining their socio-religious space.[14] In this latter respect, it is worth noting that the center of a Zoroastrian village is marked by a large cypress (*sarv*) tree, either next to or in the courtyard of the fire temple. At any rate, the legends of the six major shrines are all variations on the legend of Bibi Shahbanu associated with the Muslim women's shrine outside Rey. But this is only one of the three parts of the legend.

The first part has to do with the mythical origin of the legend. For the six major shrines, as well as for several others, this mythical origin is a variant of the Bibi Shahbanu legend, namely, that at the time of the Arab invasion a daughter or son or member of the court of Yazdegird III fled before an Arab army towards Khorassan, came to a point of exhaustion near Yazd, called upon God, and was taken into the mountain, rock, well, or cave before the bewildered Arab eyes.[15] The second part of the legend concerns a process of rediscovery. That is to say, the location of these sites of ascension to the next world was lost. Then, in relatively recent times, they were rediscovered by a shepherd, child, or other person in need, to whom the spirit or saint (*pir*) appeared in a vision or dream. This spirit aids the human protagonist by solving the mystery of lost sheep, lost path, and so on, requesting in return that a shrine be built. Finally, the third part of the legend involves a process of confirmation. That is, to validate that the shrine is not just a craziness dreamt by someone, but is indeed a place of supernatural potency, stories of cures and further premonitory or helpful visions are collected.

Two of the six major shrines appear to be quite old, that is, at least 200 years old; these are the two furthest towards Isfahan, the direction from which Zoroastrians migrated when the Safavids destroyed their quarter in Isfahan.

Boyce believes they are much older indeed, going back to pre-Islamic times and the worship of Anahid, the pre-Islamic goddess of the waters, as a representation of water and fertility. Other of these shrines have rediscovery legends which make them only a few generations old. Among the minor shrines, some of the discovery legends contain information about social conditions and ancestors of the present residents. For instance, the legends associated with the Sheikh-e Panhan shrine in Nasrabad-e Yazd has to do with migration of families from the Meybod area, the viciousness of tax collectors, and several illnesses and problems solved by the saint for the present families and their immediate ancestors.

The fact that the legends of the six major shrines are a variant on the Muslim Shahbanu legend is not an isolated example of such borrowing back and forth. There are shrines in the Yazd area, which drew upon legends of Zoroastrian aristocrats fleeing Arab armies; now it is devout Muslims fleeing the armies of Yazdegird III.[16] The legends in both cases serve to state the hostility between the two religious groups; but they need not be taken that way. In a few cases, there is a dispute about whether a shrine is where a Zoroastrian or a Muslim was miraculously saved. In fact, conciliatory Muslims will say it makes no difference, since Zoroastrians are "our *damad*" or sons-in-law, referring to the Bibi Shahbanu legend in which a daughter of Yazdegird is married to Husain, and in some versions is the mother of the fourth Iman. In all cases, the theme of the legends is that God saved his true followers. The sacrifice which Zoroastrians perform at the shrines (and elsewhere) has ancient pre-Islamic roots, but the legend with which modern Zoroastrians associate the ritual is the Abraham-Ishmail story of dedication to God, a Judaeo-Islamic borrowing. And third, while many of the minor shrines are dedicated to Zoroastrian angels (*yazata*) such as Sorush and Bahram, others are dedicated to Islamic figures such as Elias and Haji Khezr, Islamic mythical figures who move back and forth between this world and the next.

The historical and cultural dynamics of legend and shrine formation is not something of which the Zoroastrian villagers themselves are unaware. They undoubtedly know whereof they speak when they say that many of their shrines (*pirangah*) are formed out of watch-rooms and rest-houses for farmers who have to work at night. They carefully insist that the shrines not be mistaken for idolatry, or for worship of men in place of God; the shrines, they say, are a means of making their surroundings pregnant with meaning and memory. The term *pirangah* is even applied loosely to the candle niches in the walls of the village lanes, which gave light before there was electricity, and still do where there is none. Lighting them each evening becomes something like a ritual, particularly since light is the symbol par excellence of divinity. Where there are human souls—in the house, in the alleys, even in the Towers of Silence— there should be perpetual light, natural light during the day and artificial light at night. As one man put it, the spirits (*pirs*) of Zoroastrian shrines (*pirangah*) are not saints or prophets, but merely persons close to God, knowers of God (*khoda-shenasan*). A few of these shrines are indeed dedicated to the memory of the recently deceased, from the assassinated great reformer of the community, Ostad Master Khodabakhsh, to an ordinary young man who died on his way to Pir-e Sabz.

The shrines have a place in the daily, monthly, and annual ritual cycle of the Zoroastrians. Shrines are taken care of daily. The major shrines have pilgrimage times when as many of the Zoroastrian community as are able gather, and indeed make a circuit of the shrines. Women in Yazd (and a few men on occasion) also have a monthly circuit: on the second of the month they go to Pir-e Vameru; on the 16th to a fire temple; on the 20th to Shah Bahram Ize; and on the 26th to Seti Pir.[17] There they may recite the story "Moshkel Goshā" and clean chick peas (*nakhod*). At Pir-e Vameru there is the legend referred to above, which is an integral part of the visitation (*ziarat*). The story of Bibi Pari is similarly part of a ritual at a shrine in the village of Kuche Biuk once a year. The story of Bibi Seshambe is part of a ritual held on three successive Tuesdays, except in winter, in the kitchen of the organizer of the tablecloth feast (*sofreh*).

We have spoken now of three ritual forms: five-day periodic feasts held every two months (*gahambars*), tablecloth feasts (*sofrehs*), and pilgrimages (*ziarats*). In a traditional Orientalist account, they might well be treated as three separate types of activity; *gahambars* would be treated with the liturgical rites of Zoroastrianism; *sofrehs* would be relegated to the less elevated category of women's folk practices borrowed from Muslim folk religion; and the pilgrimages would be linked to ancient pilgrimages. But in the life of villagers these are not separable things: they are all activities which shade into one another. *Sofrehs* are done at shrines, as well as elsewhere; food distributions (*khairat*) are performed at *gahambars* as well as at other times. All are part of a series of ritual cycles, and all relate to an ethic of sharing. All are expressions of a particular form of village solidarity. When the village solidarity breaks up, it is not only that people are changing from sharing access to land and water to more individualistic salaries, but also that forms of exchange, ritual, and folklore change. One of the changes is that food no longer becomes so important and other things can be substituted as charity: clothing for the poor, contributions to scholarships, and so forth. Another change is that the charity system becomes bureaucratized: a voluntary society (*anjoman*) does it with perhaps greater efficiency, but the form, the style, has changed. Let me now pull these brief comments into three conclusions and suggestions for further research.

CONCLUSIONS AND DIRECTIONS FOR FUTURE RESEARCH

Three conclusions may be drawn. First, in the nineteenth century, social theorists speculated about the communal nature of Oriental villages. Often their speculations exaggerated the lack of internal conflict, individualistic initiative, and cultural elaboration of such villages. Today, planners seem often to have the opposite image, equally exaggerated: of anarchic individuals, who cannot cooperate, and for whom, when new agricultural projects are developed, all social organizations must be provided from Teheran. It is as if such planners had no idea how traditional village mediators, work teams, charity systems, and pilgrimages operated. I have tried to contribute a picture of community life which identifies some of the sources of cohesion. Many of these are things might be expected to evolve in their own way if modern agricultural projects encouraged an independent peasantry, rather than industrialized agricultural.

At the same time, not all villages are structured the same way. And I have tried to draw a picture of the Central Plateau villages which would contrast with the fishing and pearling villages of the Persian Gulf. The plateau villages appear more sober, and are built around an egalitarian ideology of exchange intended not to level all to the same income, but at least to ensure that everyone survives. Pilgrimages on the Iranian Plateau serve in part to draw sacred circles around communities. This pattern perhaps contrasts with the more linear pattern of pilgrimages in the Persian Gulf, with certain pilgrimages made to natural shrines established where an Imam or saint has walked, (gadamgahs, literally "footprints"), and with the more egocentric cults of the spirit-figures (ahl-e hava). Although a description limited to Muslim villages would have to differ by paying attention to the Muslim preachments (rauzeh) and to the symbolic world of the Battle of Karbala, which Muslims use as a vocabulary to talk about life, Muslim villages on the Iranian Plateau, I have suggested, are similar to Zoroastrian ones, because ecologically and historically they are intertwined. Also villages which are more sharply stratified may have rituals which regulate and reinforce that stratification.[18] With the Yazdi villages, for instance, one can contrast the mixed agricultural and transhumant villages of Nuristan in eastern Afghanistan, where there is also great stress on feasting, but the feasting there is competitive, a way of gaining prestige and establishing a hierarchy within the village.[19] The point here is that so far we have few cultural descriptions of different village types. At best we have a few sociological parameters in which the way of life experienced is almost entirely missing. Or we have contextless catalogues of strange customs and folktales.

Second, I have tried to demonstrate that Zoroastrian village life is not just a decayed form of some glorious and intellectually coherent ancient past, as Boyce's descriptions would have us believe. Rather, they are forms of social and cultural organization with a vitality of their own. While I support and admire Boyce's efforts to trace the continuities of tradition in Iran, there is no point in pushing them to an extreme. I hope my efforts will be seen not as a contradiction to hers, but as very occasional gentle correctives. Thus, in an admirable article on the Bibi Shahbanu legend, Boyce builds on the work of Nava'i and Parizi and shows us how the legend grew.[20] The earliest historians tell us that the mother of the fourth Imam was a Sindhi or Khorassani slave; it is only in the ninth-century Yaqubi that Harar, a daughter of Yazdegird III, is mentioned as married to Husain, and later other details slowly are added. From this observation, Boyce speculates that tenth-century Zoroastrians encouraged a confusion of Anahid with this wife of Husain to protect the former's shrine, first in Rey, then in the hills behind Meybod-e Yazd, and later again in the hills where now there is the shrine of Pir-e Sabz. There are two tenuous connections: first, that there is water at Pir-e, and when it rains, a torrent at Pir-e Banu; and second, that the Muslim belief in immortals who pass back and forth between this world and the next (*rajal al-ghaib*) would easily be assimilated to Sorush and Bahram, angelic helpers of the Zoroastrian sevenfold aspects of divinity (*yazatas*), whereas Zoroastrian sensibilities would not allow tombs in shrines, as was the normal Muslim pattern.

Boyce thus concludes that Zoroastrian shrines dedicated to Haji Khezr or Elias were similarly Muslim covers to protect shrines to the *yazatas*, and the Zoroastrians later forgot that they were only covers: "Because these are living *pirs*, the Zoroastrians could adopt their names without offending principle. Conversely, so rooted is the cult of the grave among Muslims, that even in their shrines to Khwāja Khedr there is to be found a tomb-shaped object."[21] This is all very nice speculation, but surely, in the Kermanshah example Boyce cites to support her point, the grave was prior, and the attribution to Haji Khezr later. Further, it is unclear why she had to go all across the country for an example of a Muslim Haji Khezr. Closer to Yazd there is a Muslim Haji Khezr hillside shrine in Kuhbanan which has no tomb or tomblike structure. Indeed, it looks like an abandoned village fire temple.[22] Third, it is implausible that all the village shrines are ancient, since the villages are not. And if Zoroastrians can forget that Haji Khezr was really supposed to be Sorush, why can they not just adopt him from the outset, as today they adopt the Abraham-Ishmail explanation for their sacrifices?

The point here, of course—my hidden agenda—is to try to produce an account of how Zoroastrianism has changed over time which is valid both historically and sociologically. Where once Zoroastrianism was an imperial state religion with public royal rituals and occasional heresy hunts and active proselytization, in medieval and modern times it has largely been a village religion and then the religion also of a merchant class, in which priests performed rituals which the community often knew about and often did not even witness, rites once requiring eight priests now are done by two, and proselytization was eschewed. It is unreasonable under these circumstances to say about Zoroastrianism that "essentially and in details . . . the later religion is unchanged from that of ancient Iran."[23] On the contrary, it is an interesting and valid objective to write an historical anthropology of how a great religion had the resources to adapt to a variety of different situations. Ritual may change slowly, but what ought to be a major object of our study is the consciousness, the common sense, the beliefs of those who practice the rituals. It is almost a sin to treat those we can observe and live with, including ourselves, as mere carriers of a half-forgotten tradition, and not as persons, as culturally active persons in our own right.

Third, and least satisfactorily, I tried to pose some suggestions about how one might open up the cultural organization of the Iranian plateau for further analysis. One of these suggestions had to do with the fairly obvious intimate intertwinings of Zoroastrian and Muslim symbols and rituals, a historical result of mutual debate, adaptation, and distinction. A second suggestion had to do with the rich emotional core of life which is mediated by women and female figures, as an important supplement to the standard clichés—many of which are true in their limited, negative way—about the repressed, depressed, and dependent Middle Eastern women hidden in the crevices of a society of independent, aggressive men. To some extent, focussing on Zoroastrian women is unfair, because the clichés attribute the repression to Islamic culture; and Zoroastrian women, by all accounts, are freer than Muslim women. I have dealt with this objection elsewhere, pointing to tablecloth feasts (*sofrehs*), women's preachments (*rauzehs*), the positive images of Muhammad's daughter, Fatima, and especially of her daughter, Zainab, the symbolism of calculating divination through mothers, the attribution of managing emotions to women, and the potentials (albeit rarely realized) of participation in public life, as long as modesty is observed.[24]

Finally, as I have indicated, there is a relatively obvious hidden agenda here. Social science is not merely descriptive; its descriptions are often assimilated into the self-conceptions and projects of social actors. To stress the cultural importance of women and female symbols can also help foster women's emancipation, and with it male emancipation towards a richer use of our intellectual, physical, and emotional potentials. And to acknowledge the commonalities in religious development may help reduce the debilitating hostilities of religious differentiation. In sum, our descriptions of popular traditions and culture in Iran ought to be directed to be sensitive in three dimensions: culturally, sociologically, and historically.

NOTES

1. Gholem Husain Sa'idi, "Ahl-e Hava" [People of the Air], trans. K. Safa-Isfahani, unpublished manuscript, 1976.

2. Zar cults in Cairo, Ethiopia, and Mecca have been described by a number of authors. See, for example, C. S. Hurgronje, *Mekka in the Latter Part of the Nineteenth Century* (Leiden, Netherlands: E. J. Brill, 1931); C. S. Gordon, "The Zar and the Bhut," *Man* 24 (1929):153; C. Nelson, "Self, Spirit Possession and World View: An Illustration from Egypt," *International Journal of Social Psychiatry* 17 (1971):194–209; A. Okasha, "A Cultural Psychiatric Study of El-Zar in the U.A.R.," *British Journal of Psychiatry* 11 (1966); E. F. Torrey, "The Zar Cult in Ethiopia," *International Journal of Social Psychiatry* 13 (1967):216–23. A similar cult in Morocco has been described in detail by U. Crapanzano, *The Hamadsha: A Study in Moroccan Ethnopsychiatry* (Berkeley: University of California Press, 1973).

3. See note 1 above.

4. There are jinn on the plateau and diviners, but no elaborated cults of the zar form; they are rather used as individual paths of seeking "mental health" care (psychological comfort) or aid in decision making.

5. On *boneh*, see Javad Safinejad, *Boneh* (n.p., 1972); R. C. Alberts, "Social Structure and Cultural Change in an Iranian Village, doctoral dissertation, University

of Wisconsin, 1963; and W. Miller, "Hosseinabad: A Persian Village," *Middle East Journal* 18 (1964):483–98.

6. The water would be rotated in a cycle of so many days (*shaban-e ruz*). For example, in the village of Narsiabad-e Yazd there used to be a cycle of sixteen days, each day divided into 130 units (*jureh*), for a total of 2,080 shares. When deep wells were introduced, water was sold by the hour and volume calculated in *gafiz* (standardized at 1,000 sq. m.). Shareholders in the well received dividends according to the number of their shares. One such well had 34 shareholders, holding 2,080 shares, a number taken over from the old *jureh* system.

7. The general rate of endogamy for settled rural Persians is about one in three marriages. Land-holding gentry tend to have higher rates. See the statistics in M. Fischer, "Zoroastrian Iran: Between Myth and Praxis," doctoral dissertation, University of Chicago, 1973; and R. B. Livingston and M. Mahlouji, "Studies in Five Villages in the Province of Fars," *Pahlavi Medical Journal* 1 (1970):38–39.

8. In Iranian Zoroastrian tradition, *gahambars* were begun by Noshiravan Adel, in whose reign there were a series of droughts, earthquakes, and other natural calamities. In Parsi tradition, and in the Pahliva texts, *gahambars* are said to have been introduced by the culture hero, Jamshid, the fourth Peshdadian king, to commemorate the time at which elements of the universe were created: sky, water, earth, vegetation, animals, and man. Many Zoroastrian writers suspect this to be a late Semitic borrowing.

9. *Maidyojarem*, "mid-spring" harvest of winter wheat and barley; *Maidyoshem*, "mid-summer"; *Paiteshem*, "grain-bringing" or "harvest time" of summer crops; *Yathrem*, "home coming," sowing of winter crops; *Maidyarem*, "mid-year" dead season; *Hamspathdem*, "equal heat."

10. See Robert Dillon, "Carpet Capitalism and Craft Involution in Kirman, Iran," doctoral dissertation, Columbia University, 1976.

11. Mary Boyce, *Zoroastrian Stronghold* (Oxford: Oxford University Press, 1977), comments that these legends have no ethical content (p. 66). When I protested, she graciously encouraged me to write a paper. This paper is, therefore, a partial response to Boyce. See further Fischer, "Zoroastrian Iran," pp. 223–30.

12. See Fischer, "Zoroastrian Iran," pp. 223 ff.; Boyce, *Zoroastrian Stronghold*; and Michael Fischer, "On Changing the Concept and Position of Persian Women," in Lois Beck and Nikkie Keddie, eds., *Muslim Women in the Middle East* (Cambridge, Mass.: Harvard University Press, 1976) pp. 189–215.

13. For further suggestions along these lines see Crapanzano, *The Hamadsha*, ch. 11, and more particularly, Pierre Bourdìeu, *Outline of a Theory of Practice* (Cambridge: Cambridge University Press, 1977). Crapanzano's suggestion that illnesses are feminizations appears to be psychoanalytically derived, that is, from Western notions, and should therefore be treated with reserve. Bourdieu seems to be drawing much more upon Kabyle notions of wet/dry, swelling/flat, hot/cold, male/female. Furthermore, he shows how the uses of such oppositions are not simple taxonomies, but change with context. What can be established so far in the Persian materials is that women and the management of emotions go together. On a related subject, see Y. Lajevardi, "Luri Women: A Study of Nomadism and Sedentarization," B.A. Thesis, Harvard University, 1977, for a preliminary attempt to analyze folktales showing women as the problem solvers of difficult situations. The fact that there are many shrine stories about males— most of the minor stories' figures are male—indicates that the formulation of femininity and centrality is as yet rough. But it is the case that five of the six major shrines,

plus the *sofreh* shrines, are ruled by female spirits. Also, one's identity for purposes of fortune-telling and divination is always calculated through one's mother.

14. The six major shrines are Pir-e Banu, Pir-e Herisht, Pir-e Sabz (Chak Chak Kuh), Pir-e Narestuneh, Pir-e Naraki, and Seti Pir.

15. The figures involved are as follows: At Pir-e Banu, Pir-e Sabz, and Pir-e Herisht, the daughters of Yazdegird III: Banu, Hayat, Banu, and Gohar, respectively; at Seti Pir, a granddaughter, Mehrbanu, her mother, and a priest, Dastur Kerobad; at Naraki, the wife or daughter-in-law of the governor of Pars, Naz Banu; and at Narestaneh, Ardeshir, son of Yazdegird. There are three other shrines in or near Yazd, and two near Kirman, which fit in this series. They represent respectively two sons and a daughter of Yazdegird, a governor, and a lady of the court who was also the sister of this governor.

16. There are at least six such shrines around Ardekan-e Yazd, two near Yazd, and four on the border between Yazd province and Fars.

17. These days are named in the Zoroastrian calendar, respectively, Bahman, Mehr, Bahram, and Ashdad.

18. See, for example, the description of a stratified town in Yeman in Abdalla Bujra, *The Politics of Stratification* (Oxford: Oxford University Press, 1971); and the use of Shi'ite passion plays in a Lebanese village in E. Peters, "Aspects of Rank and Status among Muslims in a Lebanese Village," in J. Pitt-Rivers, ed., *Mediterranean Countryman* (The Hague: Mouton, 1963).

19. To become a member of the village ruling council, one must be of *jasht* rank. To become a *jasht* one must give 21 feasts over three years (averaging one each six or seven weeks), eleven for the entire community and ten for other *jasht*. Theoretically, anyone may become a *jasht*, but in fact one can only do it if one controls an extended family and large flocks. There is a rank above *jasht*, that of *mir*, which requires three huge annual feasts.

By contrast, rich Yazdi merchants and professionals tend not to participate in the village rituals, though they may paternalistically try to sponsor them. This does not hold as much for the pilgrimages to Pir-e Sabz, but among the urban Parsis in the nineteenth century this differentiation was even sharper (see Fischer, "Zoroastrian Iran." But this is an urban-rural differentiation which may well eventually also occur among Nuristanis.

20. Mary Boyce, "Bibi Shahbanu and the Lady of Pars," *BSOAS* 30 (1967):30–44.

21. Boyce, "Bibi Shahbanu," p. 31. She notes the example in the hillside shrine to Khwāja Khedr near the city of Kermanshah.

22. It is a small room dug out of the rock with a ledge in back on which lamps are lit, and a small wooden door opening into a room roughly hewn out of the rock and covered with soot. Aside from the Qur'an and prayer beads on the main room floor and the wish-ribbons tied onto the little wood door, and the absence of a fire, there would be nothing to distinguish it from a fire temple. People run their hands in the soot of the little interior room for good luck.

23. Mary Boyce, "Zoroastrianism," in C. J. Bleeker and G. Widengren, eds., *Historia Religionum* (Leiden, Netherlands: E. J. Brill, 1971), 2:211.

24. See Fischer, "On Changing the Concept and Position of Persian Women."

8

The Mecca Pilgrimage in the Formation of Islam in Modern Egypt

Juan Eduardo Campo

Treatments of Islam in the modern era have commonly shown a propensity for totalization.[1] Orientalist discourses have tended to reduce the variety of Islamic institutions, cultures, peoples, histories, and texts to a single unity—that of the Other. Engendered by nineteenth-century colonialism, this set of discourses has functioned ideologically to establish modern European and North American (hereafter "Euroamerican") civilizational identity of and to legitimate the domination of the Muslim Other. The contours of this process have been described in a number of publications that have appeared in recent years.[2]

Though Orientalist totalizations no longer dominate the study of Islam and Muslim peoples, they still hold an appeal in the media and in some governmental circles. A recent example of this appears in the copy used to promote sales of Oxford University Press's new paperback edition of Bernard Lewis' *The Assassins*: "Particularly insightful in light of the recent rise of Muslim fundamentalism, the readable, factual account of the group that lent its name to politically motivated murder, places recent events in historical perspective and sheds new light on the fanatic mind." Such statements portray Islamic religion in grossly negative terms, and attribute a unity to it that transcends time, if not place.

Modern Muslim "insider" discourses tend to totalize Islam too, but usually in extremely positive terms. They stress its unwavering God-centeredness, the miraculous nature of the Qur'an, and the sacred history of revelation, which culminates in the idealized figure of the Prophet Muhammad. One well-known contemporary apologetic work, written for English-speaking Muslims and non-Muslims, states:

There is only one true religion coming from the one and the Same God, to deal with the outstanding human problems of all times. This religion is ISLAM. . . . So Islam has been and will continue to be, the true universal religion of God, because God is One and Changeless, and because human nature and major human needs are fundamentally the same, irrespective of time and place, of race and age, and of any other considerations.[3]

Such statements reflect a bold assertiveness that has roots in the recent colonial past of African and Asian peoples, and in Muslim experiences with the ideologies and practices of the modern nation-state. Indeed, the shortcomings and failures of national governments in the Muslim world have only enhanced the desire shared by many Muslims to look to the perduring features of their religious beliefs and practices for solutions to the problems of modernity.

Pilgrimage, the Hajj to Mecca, has been a prominent feature of Islam since the time of the Prophet Muhammad in the seventh century C.E. It is one of the "pillars" of religion, required by God of all who are able, according to the Qur'an. Basically, the Hajj is a complex of ritual practices that occurs annually during the twelfth month of the Muslim lunar calendar. It brings Muslims from wherever they live to a sacred place in western Arabia, their ontological center of the world: the Ka'ba in Mecca, God's Sacred House, and the holy precincts that emcompass it.

The Hajj, like Islam itself, has been an object of totalizing discourses among non-Muslim and Muslim writers alike. Mainline Orientalist scholarship has interpreted it as a survival of primitive pre-Islamic religions.[4] Anthropologists, most notably Victor Turner, explain it as a ritual that fosters feelings of communal solidarity in a large-scale agriculturally based society.[5] Lately, Middle East specialists and commentators have stressed its spiritual, as opposed to its political, significance for the majority of Muslims.[6]

Refractions of these interpretations can be found in Muslim discourses on the Hajj. Religious scholars through the centuries have discussed the Hajj in regard to its divine origins and place in the history of prophecy, from Adam to Ibrahim (Abraham) to Muhammad. Jurisconsults have concerned themselves with systematically summarizing the rules of pilgrimage, setting guidelines for judging whether a pilgrimage is acceptable, and what penalties should be assigned for infractions. Mystics have interpreted the Hajj as an allegory for the resurrection of the dead and the assemblage of all humankind for the final judgment, or as the journey of the soul from the lower world of the passions to obtain a beatific vision of God.

Among the most widespread interpretations advanced by Muslim writers today is that the Hajj is an occasion wherein Muslims efface their individual differences so as to experience a shared corporate identity with others who believe in the one God in the holiest place on earth.

Hajj demonstrates the real and practical unity and brotherhood of mankind. Pilgrims belonging to hundreds of countries and communities, languages and colors, flock to one center through a thousand and one routes. They remove their national dress and everybody without a single exception puts on unstitched cloth called *Ihram*. It consists of nothing more than two sheets of cloth and a pair of slippers. . . . In this way, the differences of nationalities and races and colors are obliterated and a universal group of God-worshipers is constituted. The assembling at one place of people drawn from all the nationalities of the world, and that with remarkable unity of heart and purpose, identity of thought, harmony of feeling, pure sentiments, sacred objects and chaste deeds is, in fact, such a great boon as has not been granted to mankind by any agency other than Islam.[7]

This kind of interpretation receives strong support from the rulers of Saudi Arabia, who have the weighty responsibility of governing the pilgrimage sites. They find it an effective foil against Muslim revolutionaries like Ayatollah Khomeini, who, in proclaiming that "all of Islam is politics," follow a "Hajj philosophy" that calls on Muslims to seize the occasion to solve their problems, to overthrow corrupt regimes, and fight against the enemies of Islam.

No matter what the particular slant of the interpreter, both Muslims and non-Muslims have structured their discourses, with few exceptions, around the journey to Mecca and the rituals performed *there*. I argue for a different analytical approach—one which examines the Hajj as conceived and realized *away* from Mecca, in the milieu of pilgrim homelands. There is a difference between the place where the Hajj rites occur and the places where the meanings of the place and its rites are construed. Muslims, after all, go to Mecca with preconceptions formed within their native cultures. When they return home, they eventually make sense of their pilgrimage experiences in relation to indigenous forms of religious discourse. Sometimes, as evidenced by patterns in modern Islamic revival and reform movements, the return from the holy land leads to radical revaluations of religious ideas, practices, cultural values, and even of the social order. For most pilgrims and their supporters, however, Hajj experiences are assimilated to modes of religiosity and social discourses prevailing in their countries of origin.

In order to develop my thesis more fully, I shall classify and describe the varieties of discourse about the Hajj found in modern Egypt, a nation which usually leads other Arab countries in the number of pilgrims it sends to Mecca each year, with the exception of Yemen and Saudi Arabia itself. My strategy is to counteract the urge for totalization by drawing attention to *discontinuities and differences* among Egyptian Muslim discourses about the Hajj.

Taken together, these discourses constitute an important component of the "formation" of Islam in Egypt. That is to say, they are part of a *localized* pattern of Islamic belief and practice, analogous to the concept of formation employed in geological science. Moreover, just as the processes that create a geological formation are dynamic, so are the processes that have created Islam in Egypt. It has been subject to forces of erosion, transformation, and the interruption of the old by the new. Thus, discerning the discontinuities among Hajj discourses in Egypt helps with mapping the contours of Egyptian Islam, and it holds the promise of obtaining a glimpse at the emergence of new strata of religious discourse and action.

There are three distinct kinds of Hajj discourse in Egypt today: that of the state, that of Muslim oppositional groups, and that of the populace in urban working class (*baladi*) neighborhoods and in the countryside. *Governmental statements* are disseminated to the Egyptian public primarily through the semiofficial press, the broadcast media, and sermons in governmental mosques. They become operational through an intricate state security apparatus that regulates Egyptian pilgrims from the time they apply for their visas until they return from Saudi Arabia and go through customs at the airport or dockside. *Oppositional statements* occur both in legal and clandestine publications issued by leading Muslim activist groups seeking to transform the sociopolitical order into a purely Islamic one. Oppositional statements can, but do not necessarily, lead to antigovernmental conspiracies and actions. *Popular Hajj discourse* lacks the support of the organizational superstructures that produce governmental and oppositional discourses. It is predominantly oral; it is conveyed in songs, ritual formulae, colloquial expressions, personal narratives, and folk art. It is operationalized primarily in festivities connected with the departure and arrival of pilgrims.

THE HAJJ OF THE NATIONAL GOVERNMENT: DISCIPLINE AND REWARD

The regimes that have governed Islamic Egypt have had a centuries-old involvement with the pilgrimage to Mecca.[8] Fatimid, Ayyubid, Mamluk, and Ottoman rulers recognized the importance of supporting the Hajj and the holy shrines of Mecca, not only with an eye to their image in the wider Islamic world, but also as a way to win the loyalty of their local subjects. Rulers provided quantities of food and supplies for pilgrims in the Hejaz, and they funded building projects there. Above all, beginning in the thirteenth century, they organized the annual caravan of soldiers and pilgrims around the figurehead of the *mahmal*, an elaborately decorated camel-borne palanquin. This palanquin, which was seen as a symbol of the sultan's power, was paraded through the streets of Cairo to a public square next to the governmental palace, then proceeded with the Hajj caravan out of the city along the Egyptian Hajj road all the way to Mecca. When the caravan returned, it was led once again through the city, and people rushed to touch it in order to gain some of the blessing power it was believed to carry back from the Hejaz, the holy land of Islam.[9]

In 1926 the forces of 'Abd al-'Aziz Ibn Saud gained control of Mecca and Medina. The new Arabian dynasty and its supporters, who promoted a militant platform of Islamic reform known as Wahhabism, immediately moved to ban the

Egyptian *mahmal*. They regarded it both as a reprehensible un-Islamic practice and as a symbol of Egyptian claims to sovereignty over the Hejaz.[10] *Mahmal* processions continued to be celebrated inside Egypt itself until the 1950s, but the Egyptian government had to relinquish attempts to exercise dominion over the Hajj rites and the Arabian holy places, recognizing Saudi sovereignty instead. With respect to promoting and supervising the participation of Egyptians in the Hajj, however, the Egyptian government still predominates.

To obtain an impression of the scope of Egyptian involvement in the Hajj, it is useful to consider patterns reflected in Hajj statistics (see Table 8.1). During the era of 'Abd al-Nasir (1952–70), there was a marked overall increase in pilgrims in comparison with pre–World War II figures. As a result of Egypt's defeat in war with Israel, however, only about half as many pilgrims traveled each year in the late 1960s as did in 1966. The Sadat era (1970–81) witnessed the most dramatic increases in Egyptian Hajj participation: about 672 percent. This was the result of a combination of factors, the major ones being a cessation of hostilities with Israel, a "return to Islam" in Egyptian domestic politics, economic prosperity in both Egypt and Saudi Arabia, and improved air service between the two countries.

In the 1980s, Mecca received the largest influx of pilgrims it had ever seen from all over the world. About two of every thousand Muslims went there each year for the Hajj.[11] Between 1981 and 1985, the number of Egyptian pilgrims increased by 56 percent, which meant that their proportion of participation (about three of every thousand Egyptian Muslims) exceeded that of the Muslim world at large. Egypt has consistently ranked among the top twenty Muslim nations (out of forty) with respect to total Hajj participation. Between 1985 and 1986 there was a noticeable decrease (about 24 percent) in Egyptian pilgrims, but this paralleled a drop in total Hajj participation (about 20 percent). Saudi security measures taken to counteract demonstrations and coup attempts during the Hajj, concern for the safety of the pilgrims, and massive construction projects in Mecca and Medina are the main factors responsible for the decrease in overall Hajj participation in the late 1980s. Nevertheless, as of 1990, the annual number of Egyptian pilgrims is still greater than it was prior to 1981. Arab socialism (or Nasirism), the establishment of a secularistic national government based on European prototypes, and the encouragement of foreign investment and private enterprise in the late 1970s and 1980s have clearly not curtailed Egyptian involvement in the Hajj. Indeed, they may have even bolstered it directly and indirectly.

Formerly, pilgrims departed from Egypt as part of a caravan protected by the sultan's troops, led by the sultan's representative (*amir al-hajj*), and administered by a small corps of functionaries. Now, pilgrims leave in groups by plane and boat. Their movements are carefully controlled by an elaborate array of governmental bureaus and procedures in Egypt and Saudi Arabia, instead of by a traditional configuration of authority centered on a single ruler. Paradoxically, the chief bureau for managing the Hajj in Egypt is the Ministry of the Interior. This agency has the authority to issue passports, but its foremost functions are to

Table 1
Egyptian Participation in the Hajj, 1927–90[a]

Year	Egyptian Pilgrams	Total from All Countries[b] (in millions)
1927	14,099	0.12
1933	1,625	0.04
1966	19,495	
1967	10,005	
1968	7,134	
1969	12,413	
1970	10,875	
1971	11,490	1.10
1972	29,171	1.04
1973	39,606	1.20
1973[c]	36,452	1.15
1974	89,617	1.50
1975	51,230	1.55
1976	28,045	1.40
1977	30,951	1.60
1978	41,828	1.80
1979	48,297	2.10
1980	66,106	1.90
1981	83,907	1.90
1982	98,408	2.00
1983	121,178	2.50
1984	133,071	
1985	130,872	2.00
1986	100,000	
1987	100,000	1.60
1988	70,000	1.00
1989	100,000	1.75
[1990][d]	[100,000]	[1.75]

[a]The figures in this table have been culled from several different sources. The principal ones are David Edwin Long, *The Hajj Today: A Survey of the Contemporary Mecca Pilgrimage* (Albany: State University of New York Press, 1979), Appendix A; the Ministry of Finance and National Economy, Kingdom of Saudi Arabia, *Statistical Yearbook* (Riyadh: Central Department of Statistics, 1970–85); and Fouad al-Farsy, *Saudi Arabia: A Case Study in Development*, rev. ed. (London: Kegan Paul International, 1986), pp. 32–35. Other sources include Richard Nyrop, ed., *Saudi Arabia: A Country Study*, 4th ed. (Washington, D.C.: U.S. Government Printing Office, 1984), P. 114; Robert Lacey, *The Kingdom: Arabia and the House of Sa'ud* (New York: Avon books, 1983), p. 228. The 1986–89 figures are based on official Egyptian and Saudi Estimates quoted in the Egyptian press: *Uktubar* (Cairo), August 2, 1987, p. 21; *al-Ahram* (Cairo), July 18, 1988, p. 8; ibid., July 22, 1988, p. 16; ibid., July 19, 1989, p. 8; *al-Liwa' al-islami* (Cairo), June 29, 1989, p. 1.

[b]The figures in this column are approximate, mostly obtained from al-Farsy and Egyptian press articles listed in the previous note. Totals include pilgrims from abroad and from within Saudi Arabia.

[c]The Hajj season, which occurs once each year on the Muslim lunar calendar, fell twice on the Western solar calendar in 1973: the 1393 A.H. Hajj was celebrated in early January, and the 1394 A.H. Hajj in late December.

[d]The 1990 Hajj had just occurred when this chapter went to press. The figure cited is my own estimate, based on the assumption that the same factors which diminished the size of the 1989 Hajj will also be in effect in 1990. In 1987, before the Saudis took measures to curtail Hajj traffic, a reliable Saudi source predicted that 134,000 Egyptians would participate in the 1990 Hajj; *Uktubar* (Cairo), 2 August 1987, p. 21.

guard the country's internal security and operate its prisons. All pilgrims leaving Egypt are monitored by departments of this ministry.

The modern systemization of Egyptian Hajj travel began at the end of the nineteenth century. A review of official procedures followed in the 1980s quickly shows how governmental technologies of power and surveillance have enmeshed themselves with the desires of individual Egyptian Muslims to fulfill a religious obligation. For example, the government divides pilgrims into three groups: pilgrims selected by a government-run lottery, pilgrims organized by voluntary cooperatives (*jam'iyyat*), and pilgrims who contract with private-sector travel agencies.[12] All expenses must be paid for in advance to prevent indigent pilgrims from resorting to Egyptian or Saudi authorities to pay for the return journey, and from remaining in Saudi Arabia to look for work. Beginning in Ramadan (about two and one-half months before the Hajj), pilgrims make their payments to their respective agencies; lottery pilgrims do so at local police stations. All must also undergo medical examinations and obtain the necessary vaccinations during this time. Through offices of the Interior Ministry, one month later, the Egyptian Security Directorate issues special Hajj passports containing all the forms and visas required by Saudi authorities. As a result of reforms initiated in 1989, these passports have been color-coded to correspond to the three pilgrim classifications (lottery—brown, co-op—gray, travel agency—green); they can be used only once; and they are valid for a maximum of thirty days. The centralization of these procedures helps Egyptian authorities carefully monitor pilgrim traffic, and makes it easier for them to adhere to the Saudi rule that prevents individuals from joining the Hajj more than once every three years.[13]

While pilgrims prepare for their journey, the Interior Ministry sends Hajj committees to Mecca and Medina to meet with Saudi security and Ministry of Hajj and Endowments authorities, to arrange for pilgrim accommodations and transportation and inspect facilities. Concomitantly, according to press reports, Egyptian police inspectors monitor the activities of known counterfeiters and dubious travel agencies to prevent the escape of criminals in pilgrims' guise and exploitation of Egyptians arranging to perform the Hajj. In recent years, the government has taken stern measures against fraudulent Hajj travel agencies and co-ops, imposing heavy fines and forcing a number of them to close down.[14]

With Saudi consent, the Egyptian government establishes offices in Mecca, Medina, and Jeddah during the Hajj itself.[15] It thereby undertakes "special procedures for following-up and organizing the pilgrims." Officials also state that the government wants to "offer the greatest measure of comfort and care to the pilgrims of God's Sacred House." One of the most persistent problems faced by pilgrims in Mecca is getting lost in the crowd. To remedy this, they are organized into groups. Everyone must wear identity bracelets with the name of their town, provincial district, and personal registration number. Each Egyptian government (*muhafaza*) keeps a list of its pilgrims and their addresses, and sends copies to the official head of the Egyptian delegation, the lost and found centers in Mecca and Medina, "administrative agencies," and to Egyptian delegation offices in Jedda and Medina. Thus, in theory, when people lose their way, Saudi authorities can guide them to the nearest Egyptian office, which will then reunite them with their group.

Health is another major concern during the Hajj, since gatherings of hundreds of thousands of people increase the chances of contagion and place a severe burden upon public sanitation facilities. Also, since many of the pilgrims are elderly, they are in danger of succumbing to heat prostration or heart attack. Thus the Egyptian Ministry of Health assigns doctors to accompany pilgrims, supplies ambulances with first-aid supplies and air conditioned buses, and, starting in 1989, it has operated twenty-four-hour medical clinics for its citizens in the main pilgrimage areas.

Many Muslims go to Mecca without knowing how to perform the canonical Hajj rituals or what they signify. As a consequence, they rely on customs and interpretations from their own native cultures. In order to correct this situation, the Saudis require that each group of pilgrims must be led by a licensed ritual guide (*mutawwif*). Moreover, the Egyptian Ministry of Endowments, which normally operates and staffs the country's public mosques, recently decided to assign one preacher per 1,000 pilgrims to help assure consensus and mediate disagreements among participants about the Hajj.

Egyptians must submit to their government's institutions and regulations if they want to go to Mecca. But the state controls the Hajj as much through official discourse as by procedure. In fact, state Hajj discourse is more significant because it shapes the thoughts and sympathies of the public at large, not just the pilgrims. This discourse is conducted in the semiofficial mass media; that is, television, radio, newspapers such as *al-Ahram* and *al-Akhbar*, and weeklies such as *Uktubar* and *Akir sa'a*. It is also conveyed through sermons by religious authorities cooperating with the state, and through pro-government Islamic publications.

Under normal circumstances, the content of state discourse is rather predictable. Al-Azhar sheikhs, muftis, and Ministry of Endowments officials issue *fatwas* (legal rulings) on Hajj requirements and prohibitions, describe the virtues of the holy sites, and provide relevant details about the sacred histories of the sites. Correspondents and photo journalists report their experiences and impressions from Mecca, praise steps taken by the Saudis to accommodate the hundreds of thousands of pilgrims, and they describe elaborate Saudi building projects in the *haram* (sacred) areas of Mecca and Medina. Details concerning the number of pilgrims, modes of transportation, departure and arrival times are published regularly during the pilgrimage season. When the formal rites of the Hajj are being performed (the month Dhu al-Hijja 8–13), pictures of the Ka'ba surrounded by pilgrims, the Mas'a (Running Place), and the plain of 'Arafat appear in newspapers, magazines, and on the television screen. In general, the state wants its subjects to view the Hajj as an orderly spiritual event that it strongly condones.

The Egyptian government benefits most from its ritual discourse—not so much by directly participating in the formal Hajj rituals as it did formerly, but by serving as the chief medium for re-presenting the rituals to the wider

Egyptian public. Thus, while the Ministry of the Interior governs the movements of pilgrims, the government-controlled media shape public perception of the pilgrimage.

State Hajj discourse becomes more intense in response to events that shatter the images of unity, order, and sanctity that should normally pervade it. This occurred in 1979 when a messianic group attempted to seize Mecca's Sacred Mosque, in 1987 when more than 400 people were killed during demonstrations by Iranian and pro-Iranian pilgrims in Mecca,[16] and in 1989, when several bombs rocked Mecca during the Hajj season. After each incident, Egypt's media condemned the violence and what it called the politicization of a purely religious occasion by extremists. It praised the severe punitive measures taken by the Saudi government. Egyptian religious leaders quoted the Qur'an and prophetic traditions to support their government's position and rally public sympathy.

In response to these events and to growing Islamic militancy at home—most clearly evidenced by President Sadat's assassination in 1981—proponents of the government's views have called for campaigns to improve the awareness (*taw'iyya*, which also suggests the idea of warning) of those traveling to Mecca. Mahmoud Mahdi, chief editor of *al-Ahram*'s Friday religion section, and writer for the "*al-Iswa al-hasana*" column, has indicated that reports prepared annually by Egypt's Hajj delegations complain of widespread ignorance among the pilgrims of basic ritual actions. Says Mahdi, the government should:

hold meetings and discussions in all of the Republic's governorate, in addition to a radio and television campaign, to explain and simplify Hajj rules, and how they should be carried out. Indeed, improving the awareness of pilgrims *in their places of residence here in Egypt* is more beneficial than doing so when they arrive at the holy places.[17] (Emphasis added.)

Furthermore, Mahdi links his remarks to a proposal for opening public schools and religious camps in the summer to instill correct Islamic teachings among young people. He supports his idea by quoting President Husni Mubarak's declaration that "the lack of religion and intellectual extremism are among the most important issues requiring the meticulous attention of relevant ministries, organizations, and agencies—including the Ministries of Education, Higher Education and Culture, Endowments, and the Supreme Council of Youth and Sports." In effect, by joining the call for summer religious education with the recommendation to "improve the awareness" of pilgrims before they leave the country, the columnist is advocating a massive governmental campaign addressed to all Egyptians, young and old. This campaign, he concludes, has but one goal: "Correct knowledge of the rules of our true religion."

The occurrence of serious disturbances at the chief Muslim holy places during the Hajj season in recent years is clear-cut evidence that not all Muslims agree with the Egyptian and Saudi views of the Hajj. Moreover, the Egyptian government's decision to stress the apolitical meanings of the Hajj (which is in fact a roundabout way of politicizing them), the measures it has taken to educate pilgrims, and the mobilization of its internal security apparatus to supervise Hajj traffic, if taken together, signal that it is genuinely worried about how organized groups might use the Hajj to subvert it. What are these groups? How do they construe the Hajj? How can their participation in the Hajj threaten the status quo?

THE HAJJ OF MUSLIM OPPOSITION GROUPS

Muslim opposition groups (*al-jama' at al-islamiyya*) in Egypt agree that the present sociopolitical order is unacceptable and that it must be transformed to be in conformity with Islamic law, the Shari'a. Where they differ among themselves is how this transformation is to be achieved. Some advocate gradual change through legislation. Others seek to precipitate violent revolution. Still others adopt a survivalist strategy, preaching millenial emigration (*hijra*) of true believers to the countryside until the un-Islamic regime collapses from its own decadence.

Since religious opposition groups maintain that the only true Islamic society is one based on the Shari'a, they tend to place great weight on the correct performance of Islamic ritual duties. These are not only prescribed by divine law, they are also among the primary areas of traditional jurisprudence (*fiqh*). However, whereas three of the four ritual "pillars" (prayer, fasting, and alms-giving) can be practiced at relatively little cost, the Hajj is a duty that requires sizable expenditures of money, time, and effort in order to be fulfilled. These apparent impediments, together with the ironic fact that all pilgrims must leave and return under state supervision, make determining the importance of the Hajj practices and attitudes of opposition groups an especially intriguing area of study.

The foremost domestic opponent of the Egyptian national government in the twentieth century has been the Muslim Brotherhood. Hasan al-Banna (1906–49) founded the movement in 1928 to free Egypt of the British and their collaborators, and to establish an Islamic government. By 1950 the Brotherhood had tens of thousands of followers, mostly men and women from the lower-middle class living in the country's cities and towns.

In a commentary published in an issue of the Brotherhood's newspaper in 1937,[18] al-Banna says that Hajj perfects the other pillars of Islam when performed, but lessens them when it is neglected. God will grant great rewards to a Muslim for going on the pilgrimage to God's Sacred House, and conversely God will punish him severely if he is able to fulfill the duty but fails to do so. According to the hadiths, pilgrims will obtain forgiveness for their sins, but Muslims who neglect the duty are to be considered disbelievers; their reward will be hell. Al-Banna exhorts Muslims who have the desire but not the means to go to the holy land to accompany the pilgrims in heart and spirit, whereupon God may regard them with the same favor as other pilgrims.

Al-Banna's essay represents pilgrimage as a means for perfecting Muslim religiosity. It cites a proof text from the Qur'an, which states, "Today I have perfected your religion for you. I have completed my grace for you, and have chosen Islam to be your religion" (5 *Ma'ida* 3). To underscore his point, al-Banna mentions that this verse was originally revealed to the Prophet Muhammad during the Hajj itself.[19] Thus, although his was not a particularly innovative interpretation of the Hajj, as the founder of the Brotherhood he nonetheless reaffirmed its place in the movement's doctrines. In fact, this helped sustain the Brotherhood during the years of tribulation it was to suffer after al-Banna's assassination at the hands of government agents in 1949.

The foremost ideologist of the Muslim Brotherhood after al-Banna was Sayyid Qutb (1903–66). While imprisoned between 1954 and 1964, he wrote a highly esteemed commentary on the Qur'an: *In the Shadow of the Qur'an*. There, discussing the Hajj, Qutb stressed its communal importance, like other commentators before him. He saw the pilgrimage as a "season of commerce and worship" in sacred places, where the faithful can discover their true origins and experience the presence of spirits of the prophets Ibrahim and Muhammad, together with members of their holy families and noble companions. As an international Muslim conference, Hajj attracts all believers to their ontological center, the *gibla* towards which they face. At Mecca,

(they) find their banner to which they return—the banner of the single faith in the shade of which ethnic, racial, and national differences disappear. They find their once forgotten power—the power of the collectivity, unity, and mutual bonding of millions. (The power) which no one could have opposed so long as it returned to its single banner, the banner of faith and monotheism which cannot be overcome.[20]

Zaynab al-Ghazali, the leading woman of the Egyptian Islamist movement, revived Qutb's ideas about the Hajj in 1980.[21] Writing in a more favorable climate than was Qutb, she explicitly urged pilgrims to take advantage of the Hajj to exchange information with Muslim brethren about "events, problems, crises, and needs, and to work on removing the barriers and obstacles" that prevented the reestablishment of the "government (*dawla*) of the Qur'an." She hoped that the beginning of the fifteenth century A.H. that year would bring with it the revival of "the greatest *umma*."

Qutb's and al-Ghazali's understandings of the Hajj must be seen as integral to the critique leveled by the Brotherhood and their offshoot organizations against modern national governments, including the Egyptian one. For them, the only true nation is the nation of Islam, so the Hajj ought to be seen as both a symbol of this *umma*, and an important instrument for bringing it back into existence.

During the 1950s, when Egypt's fledgling revolutionary regime decided to eliminate the Muslim Brotherhood by force and subterfuge for its own protection, some Brotherhood members found asylum in Arabia, where there was a growing Saudi opposition to Nasirist doctrines and influence in the region.[22] The expatriates organized cells in the holy cities of Mecca and Medina and took advantage of the Hajj to recruit members and hold meetings with Egyptian sympathizers. They received increased support from the Saudis themselves. Thus, while its membership was being eradicated in Egypt, the movement succeeded in promoting the establishment of the Islamic University in Medina (1961), which replicated the religious curriculum of al-Azhar University in Egypt, but was free of that school's Nasirist fetters.[23] There is strong evidence that the Brotherhood's attempts to reorganize its opposition to 'Abd al-Nasir's regime in Egypt during the mid-1960s were based on contacts between group members and sympathizers made during the Hajj.[24]

When President al-Sadat allowed them back in the seventies to strengthen his position against the Egyptian left, the Brotherhood and new Islamic activist groups (especially university-based groups affiliated with the General Union of Egyptian Students) used government subsidies and income from members employed in the Gulf to finance trips to Mecca. The brother of Khalid al-Islambuli, a leader in the *Jihad* group responsible for al-Sadat's assassination, was able to make two pilgrimages to Mecca while still a student at Asyut University.[25] I think it unlikely that he was able to meet the expenses for making the Hajj (from $1,500 to $2,500 per trip at that time) using his own resources.

In 1979, when Al-Sadat's government attempted to rein oppositional student religious groups, it banned the student union and froze its assets, thus limiting funds that could be used to subsidize pilgrimage expenses (among other things). The fact that a relatively large number of the foreigners directly and indirectly linked with the 1979 seizure of the Grand Mosque were Egyptians may well have made state intervention even more urgent.[26] In recent years, with increasing government regulation, there appears to have been a decline in the size of Hajj contingents sponsored by Egyptian religious organizations. In 1987 there were 40,000 pilgrims sponsored by cooperative societies; in 1988 there were only 20,000.[27] We need more accurate information about how religious groups organize trips to Mecca, and about how they come to terms with the powerful government Hajj apparatus, before we pursue studying the oppositional aspects of the Hajj in Egypt further, however.

THE HAJJ OF THE POPULACE

The greatest number of Egyptians—and here I mean the urban working (*baladi*) class and those living in rural areas—have tended to conceive of pilgrimage as a journey for acquiring divine blessing (*baraka*), the forgiveness of sins, and protection from misfortune. For them, it is an integration of normative religious beliefs and practices with the veneration of holy men and women, and with the highest values of domestic life. Common pilgrims bring honor to their families as well as gain community esteem and high status in the eyes of friends and neighbors when they accomplish the Hajj.

Popular attitudes about the Hajj are expressed during the celebrations of the departure and arrival of the pilgrims. These occasions bear striking similarity to Muslim saints'-day observances (*mulid-s*), with feasting, Qur'an recitation, and the chanting of pious songs about the Prophet Muhammad. People greet returning pilgrims with the exclamation "A Hajj properly performed, and sins forgiven!" In exchange, pilgrims are expected to distribute souvenirs of their journey to family and well-wishers, much as saints are expected to answer the petitions of their devotees with different sorts of blessing. Popular understandings are also evidenced in the striking murals drawn on the façades of pilgrim homes in their absence. I have discussed this phenomenon in detail elsewhere,[28] but here let me provide you with some brief remarks about them.

Egyptian Hajj murals are composed of two types of elements: formulaic epigraphs and iconic figures. The contents of the epigraphs include Qur'anic verses, hadiths, ritual expressions, and idioms from everyday speech about the following subjects: (1) God, (2) Muhammad, (3) Pilgrimage and Holy Places (Mecca and Medina), (4) Divine Blessing, and (5) Victory over Adversity. The iconic figures, which give evidence to a practice that runs counter to the aniconic tendency of normative Sunni Islam, represent: (1) Aspects of the Hajj and the Hejaz, (2) General Islamic religious motifs, (3) Features of Egyptian cultural life, (4) Trees, plants, and animals, and (5) Arabesque designs and talismanic figures. Sometimes occurring individually, but often in combination, these elements contribute to the visible transformation of pilgrim homes into shrines, sharing metamorphic identity with sacred areas of Mecca and Medina, and also with paradise.

Where do such murals occur? They are most likely to be found in Upper Egypt, especially in the vicinity of Qena, Luxor, and parts of the Fayum. They can also be found in *baladi* neighborhoods of the larger cities; especially in sections of Cairo, Giza, and Suez City.

It is also worth noting that some of the murals stress apotropaic symbols to deflect evil, instead of those for attracting God's blessing. Pictures of eyes, scorpions, lions, snakes, and hand prints occur, as do expressions such as "O Lord, your protection!" (*Ya rabb, satrak!*) and portions of the last two chapters of the Qur'an. Such elements can be explained in terms of the fear felt in some households that, because of their enhanced status, they are more susceptible to the dangers of envy and the evil eye.

Hajj motifs also occur in women's possession/healing cults (*zar-s*) and tattoo art. *Zar* amulets include images of the *mahmal*, mosques, camels, birds, scorpions, snakes, fish, flowers, palms and trees, stars, crescent moons, hands, eyes, soldiers, and mermaids—just like the Hajj murals. Participants in *zar* rituals sing to *zar* spirits such as Baba Amir al-Hajj, and to the pilgrim spirit al-Makkawiyya, who is invoked in these terms:

O lady of the pilgrimage!
Welcome Madame!

My lady! How outstanding—
Pilgrimage to the Hejaz!
You saw the Prophet.
You beheld the lights.
You saw the (Prophet's) room,
With it the Running Place (between Safa and Marwa),
And Mount 'Arafat.
The Arabs came to us,
Making the desired pilgrimage.
The pilgrims circumambulated.
We struck Satan
With pebbles.
They beheld Mecca,
They perfumed it
With musk and ambergris.
O men of God!
O you who acknowledge God's oneness!
O people of the house!
Repentance is sought!
That which is sought from God.
(Sultan) Ruma Najdi, my master,
Loosen the bonds,
For I am sick. . . . [29]

From Hajj murals to the *zar* cult to tattoos, the desire for material and spiritual prosperity, comfort, and security in home and body carries this type of pilgrimage discourse to a more enduring and intimate degree than the discourses of government and activist groups. In this way the pilgrimage becomes a reality even for the majority of Egyptian Muslims who are not able to make their way to the Hejaz physically.

CONCLUSION

In the current formation of Islam in Egypt, the government sees religion largely as a means for securing public order and legitimacy. The ruling elites would probably like to see their country move towards secularization—which does not entail the absence of religion, but its relegation to the status of private faith and civic symbol system. By dominating pilgrimage discourse and controlling who participates in the Hajj, the government is able openly to refute accusations of being un-Islamic, while simultaneously maintaining surveillance over sources of religious opposition.

On the other hand, religious opposition groups call their own members, and the public at large, to consider what for them is a higher order of law, order, and community—one that transcends any single nation-state. While submitting to the state is a short-term compromise, they remain poised to strike when the state shows signs of weakness or experiences reversals in its foreign and domestic affairs. For them, the secular state can sometimes serve as a useful means of attaining a religious end—the true *umma*, where divine law rules. For them, the Hajj can serve both as a means for reestablishing an Islamic state, and for planning the fall of governments that stand in their way.

Meanwhile, the populace at large must weigh whether to remain with the status quo, or change their orientation in favor of supporting religious opposition groups. Ironically, if it chooses the latter course of action, it will have to surrender many of its dearest beliefs and practices concerning the Hajj. This is because activist groups condemn the Hajj murals, *zar-s*, and talismans as harmful innovations that have adulterated the pristine Islam followed by the first generation of Muslims under the leadership of the Prophet Muhammad. On the other hand, despite calls for a government campaign for "improving awareness" of proper pilgrimage practices, the present regime seems inclined to allow premodern religious practices greater latitude as long as they do not conflict with its own interests. Nevertheless, we should bear in mind that in the end it is the government which dominates the apparatus of pilgrimage and its discourse in Egypt. The general populace and members of religious opposition groups are regularly reminded of this fact.

NOTES

1. An early version of this chapter was delivered at the 1987 meeting of the Middle East Studies Association in Baltimore. I am grateful to the Cultural Mission of the Saudi Arabian Embassy in Washington, D.C., for providing me with publications and data about the Hajj, and to the National Council on U.S.-Arab Relations for sponsoring my visit to Saudi Arabia in January 1990 as a Joseph J. Malone Faculty Fellow.

2. See, for instance, Edward Said, *Orientalism* (New York: Random House, 1978); idem, *Covering Islam: How the Media and the Experts Determine How We See the Rest of the World* (New York: Random House, 1981); Malcolm H. Kerr, ed., *Islamic Studies: A Tradition and Its Problems* (Malibu, Cal.: Undena Publications, 1980); Asaf Hussain, Robert Olson, Jamil Qureshi, eds., *Orientalism, Islam, and Islamists* (Battleboro, Vt.: Amana Books, 1984); Maxime Rodinson, *Europe and the Mystique of Islam*, trans. R. Veinus (Seattle: University of Washington Press, 1987); Henry Laurens, *Les origines intellectuelles de l'expédition d'Egypte: L'Orientalisme islamisant en France (1698–1798)* (Istanbul: Editions Isis, 1987). There is a growing body of literature on Orientalism in Arabic; for example, Nagib al-'Aqiqi, *al-Mustashriqun*, 3 vols. (Cairo: Dar al-Ma'arif, 1980–81).

3. Hammudah Abdalati, *Islam in Focus* (Indianapolis: American Trust Publications, 1975), p. 30. Of course, similar statements can be culled from countless books and periodicals published in Muslim countries.

4. The chief works of this nature are Julius Wellhausen, *Reste arabischen Heidentums*, 3d ed. (Berlin: Walter de Gruyter, 1927), pp. 68–101; and Snouck Hurgronje, *Het Mekkaansche Feest* (Leiden, Netherlands: E. J. Brill, 1880); and *Encyclopaedia of Islam*, s.v. "Hadjdj," by A. J. Wensinck.

5. Victor Turner, "The Center Out There: Pilgrim's Goal," *History of Religions* 12 (1973):191–230.

6. This claim is made especially on behalf of Sunni Muslims, while the Iranian Shi'a are accused of being the only ones to politicize it. For example, Robin Wright states, "For the Sunni, the pilgrimage was strictly religious, the ultimate personal homage to God. . . . " *Sacred Rage: The Wrath of Militant Islam* (New York: Simon and Schuster, 1986), p. 168.

7. Ibrahim Husain, *Handbook of Hajj* (Indianapolis: Islamic Teaching Center, 1977), pp. 21–22. See also Ibrahim Ismail Nawwab, "The Hajj: An Appreciation," *Aramco World Magazine* 25 (1974):13.

8. See Jacques Jomier, *Le mahmal et la caravane égyptienne des pèlerins de la Mecque (XIIIe–XX siècles)* (Cairo: Institut Français d'Archéologie Orientale, 1953); and Abdullah 'Ankawi, "The Pilgrimage to Mecca in Mamluk Times," *Arabian Studies* 1 (1974):116–66.

9. Jomier, *Le mahmal*, p. 207. Syria and Yemen also sent *mahmal-s* to Mecca, but Egypt followed this practice most consistently through the centuries.

10. The Saudis had not forgotten that Egyptian forces had crushed their attempt to dominate the holy sites and much of the rest of the Arabian Peninsula early in the nineteenth century.

11. Malise Ruthven, *Islam in the World* (Oxford: Oxford University Press, 1984), p. 25.

12. Of the 100,000 Egyptians who participated in the 1987 Hajj, 40,000 were selected by government-run lottery, 40,000 were members of co-ops, and 20,000 made arrangements through private travel companies. In 1988 the numbers were 30,000, 20,000, and 10,000 for each category respectively. Pilgrimage by lottery is least expensive (1989: $3,580 to $5,600), excluding plane or boat fare. Travel agency pilgrimage is the most expensive (1987: $5,425 to $21,700). See *Akhir sa'a* (Cairo), July 22, 1987, p. 58; and *al-Ahram* (Cairo), June 17, 1988, p. 15; June 30, 1988, p. 8; April 20, 1989, p. 1.

13. *Al-Ahram*, April 20, 1989, pp. 1, 12; May 9, 1989, p. 8.

14. *Akhir sa'a*, July 22, 1987, p. 58; *Al-Ahram*, May 23, 1988, p. 8; June 28, 1988, p. 3.

15. I have obtained details on Egyptian Hajj operations in Saudi Arabia from *Akhir sa'a*, July 22, 1987, p. 58; and *al-Ahram* June 17, 1988, p. 15; June 9, 1989, p. 5; and June 16, 1989, p. 5.

16. Pro-Iranian sources assert that there were more than 500 deaths; see, for instance, Zafar Bangash, *The Makkah Massacre and Future of the Haramain* (London: The Open Press Limited, 1988), p. 22.

17. Mahmud Mahdi, *"al-Iswa al-hasana: taw'iyyat al-shabab wa'l-hujjaj,"* *al-Ahram*, August 17, 1984, p. 15. See also the notice of meetings held by the Ministry of Endowments for just this purpose, which appeared in *al-Ahram* on July 27, 1984, p. 15.

18. Reprinted under the title *"al-Hajj wa'l-'umra fil'l-islam,"* in *al-Da'wa* (Cairo), October 1980, pp. 14–15.

19. Ibid., p. 14. Banna quotes a canonical hadith in which the Hajj is ranked third after faith and *jihad* as the most preferable task for Muslims.

20. From Sayyid Qutb, *Fi zilal al-Qur'an*, commentary to Sura 22 (*Hajj*), verse 26; reprinted in *al-Da'wa*, October 1980, p. 37.

21. Zaynab al-Ghazali, *"al-Hajj wa'l-'awda,"* *al-Da'wa*, October 1980, p. 33.

22. On Egyptian-Saudi relations at this time, see Nadav Safran, *Saudi Arabia: The Ceaseless Quest for Security* (Cambridge, Mass.: Harvard University Press, 1985), ch. 4.

23. *Encyclopaedia of Islam*, 2d ed., s.v., "al-Madina, the Modern City," by R. B. Winder.

24. Sami Gawhar, *al-Mawta yatakallamun*, 2d ed. (Cairo: al-Maktab al-Misri al-Hadith, 1977), pp. 186–90. It appears that Egyptian government intelligence learned of these contacts and manipulated events in order to suppress the movement once again in 1965–66. As a consequence, Sayyid Qutb and other leaders were executed for conspiring against the state. Zaynab al-Ghazali was imprisoned.

25. Hamied N. Ansari, "The Islamic Militants in Egyptian Politics," *International Journal of Middle East Studies* 16 (1984):135.

26. Ten of the sixty-three participants executed by the Saudis were Egyptians. About fifty other Egyptians were detained by Saudi authorities (at the time there were a quarter of a million Egyptians working in Saudi Arabia); some detainees died in prison, others were not released until years later. There was also indirect Egyptian influence: the Saudi leaders of the rebel group had previously studied with Shaykh 'Abd al-'Aziz ibn Baz, rector of the Islamic University in Medina (a center for the Muslim Brotherhood). Initially, the Saudi and Egyptian press tried to blame the incident on the Muslim Brotherhood, which drew denials from the group's leadership. The Brotherhood publicly supported the Saudi government and condemned the seizure of the mosque in its official magazine *al-Da'wa* (Cairo, January 1980).

See further James Buchan, "The Return of the Ikhwan 1979," in David Holden and Richard Johns, *The House of Saud: The Rise and Rule of the Most Powerful Dynasty in the Arab World* (New York: Holt, Rinehart and Winston, 1982), ch. 25; and Joseph A. Kechichian, "The Role of the Ulama in the Politics of an Islamic State: The Case of Saudi Arabia," *International Journal of Middle East Studies* 18 (1986):58–60. Egyptian involvement is best documented in a polemical book issued by the Organization of Islamic Revolution in the Arabian Peninsula: Fahd al-Qahtani, *Zilzal Juhayman fi Makka* (London: al-Safa Publishing, 1986), appendixes 7, 8.

27. Exactly how many of these were members of religious groups is difficult to determine, because government statistics group religious and nonreligious Hajj cooperative societies together.

28. See Juan E. Campo, "Shrines and Talismans: Domestic Islam in the Pilgrimage Paintings of Egypt," *Journal of the American Academy of Religion* 55 (1987):285–305; and idem., *The Other Side of Paradise: Explorations into the Religious Meanings of Domestic Space in Islam* (Columbia: University of South Carolina Press, 1991), ch. 6.

29. Enno Littmann, "Arabische Geisterbeschwörungen aus Agypten," *Sammlung orientalische Arbeiten* (Leipzig: Otto Harrassowitz, 1950), 19:27–29, 107–9. The English translation is mine, based on Littmann's transliteration.

Sacred Geography in Islam

Annemarie Schimmel

"Whithersoever you turn, there is the Face of God" (Sura 2/115). Thus says the Qur'an, and the conviction that God is not restricted to a single place but is *hādir nāzir*, "present and watching" everywhere, and that mankind feels his presence wherever it may be, has permeated the Muslims' attitude to sacred space. One has also to remember that the Qur'an states: "We have shown them Our signs in the horizons, *āfāq*, and in themselves" (Sura 41/53), thus alerting them to the presence of Divine signs both in the created space and time and in the depths of their souls.

And yet there are spaces which are singled out for their religious significance, the most important one being the sacred precincts of the Kaaba in Mecca. The Kaaba, built according to Islamic tradition by Ibrahim (Abraham) and his son Isma'il (Ishmael), was determined as the *gibla*, the place to which the believers were to turn when performing their ritual prayers five times a day; the direction toward which they should meditate, and, not least, toward which their faces in the grave should be turned. To be sure, in the beginning of Muhammad's preaching the sacred *gibla* was Jerusalem, called always *al-quds* or *bayt al-muqaddas*, "the sacred house," where he performed the prayer along with the previous prophets during his miraculous night journey, *mi'rājīsrā*. Later, however, at a critical point in Muslim history, when the Prophet was in Medina, the direction of prayer was changed to Mecca, which was regarded as the ancestral home of the worship of the One and Unique God as revered by Abraham—the God who had never left mankind without guidance from the days of Adam, the first prophet.

The sacred space around the Kaaba, the *haram*, and its surroundings became, as is natural, both the material and spiritual center of Islam, and the Indo-Muslim philosopher-poet Muhammad Iqbal (1877–1938) expressed the attitude of the Muslims as true witnesses of *tauhid* (the acknowledgment that there is only one God) by writing in his Persian poem "Asrār-i-khudī" ("The Secrets of the Self"):

> One God, one direction of prayer, one Prophet, one Book . . . [1]

The one direction of prayer around which the people of the world are placed, as it were, in concentric circles has been and still is the most visible sign of the unity of the Muslims; it is, so to speak, the spacialization of their belief in one, and only one, God.

It is easy to see how this concept of the Kaaba as the earthly center of life determined Muslim piety. One has to remember that a number of pious Muslim scholars in our day have tried to figure out how to determine the *gibla* in our space age—what does an astronaut do to find the proper direction when flying outside of the earthly coordinates? The mystical belief that the Kaaba is situated exactly opposite the heavenly Kaaba and forms, as it were, the point on which the world axis rests may help those who try to solve this problem.

Determining the direction of the *gibla* was indeed one of the important problems which confronted medieval Muslim mathematicians and astronomers, as every mosque has to face exactly the *gibla*. Therefore, numerous legends, especially in the Indo-Pakistani subcontinent, are connected with saintly people who, discovering that a mosque had a somewhat faulty orientation, performed a miracle to set the prayer niche, *mihrāb*, right. However, it seems that the direction was not everywhere perfectly correct, as one can see in a number of Near Eastern mosques which slightly deviate from the ideal *gibla*. One then often tried to remedy the situation by building a gateway or special entrance which, taking an angle from the street and the front of nearby houses, leads to the mosque, so that neither the direction of the street nor the orientation of the *mihrāb* are disturbed. The best-known case is that of the Masjid-i Shah in Isfahan.

The pilgrimage to the sacred place of Mecca has inspired numberless poets in the Muslim world, and the farther their countries were from the ideal center of the universe, the more eloquent did they wax in singing of their longing for Mecca, the place where the Divine Beloved dwelt; they also never tired of describing the hardships on the road to the Kaaba. The model for such descriptions of the journey to the "center" could easily be found in pre-Islamic and early Arabic poetry in which the poet describes his journey on his fleet steed or his strong camel into the presence of his patron, or another person worthy of his praise. Numerous are the longing and ardent poems in which poets like the Persian Khāqāni (d. 1199) or, three centuries later, Maulānā Jāmī of Herat (d. 1492) speak of the great experience of coming into the presence of the Kaaba which, in some medieval poetry, appears to the writers like the longed-for bride, covered with a black, gold-embroidered veil. In mystical love poetry, then, the house of the beloved becomes equal to the Kaaba, for, as Divine beauty may manifest itself through the medium of an earthly beloved, his or her dwelling place can easily be regarded as the "Kaaba of the lovers." The poets might then claim no longer to pray in the direction of Mecca but, as many Persian and Indo-Persian poets wrote from the early thirteenth century onward:

We have directed our *gibla* toward the direction of the one with his cap awry![2]

This latter expression is derived from an alleged saying of the Prophet; "I saw my Lord in the most beautiful form, with his cap awry." Although the majority of pious Muslims did not accept this tradition, it became a cornerstone of mystical love theories, as they permeated later lyrical poetry, as the eighteenth-century Urdu poet Mir Taqī Mīr sings:

Rose and mirror and sun and moon—What are they?
Wherever we looked, there was always Thy face.

On the other hand, one may think of the special feeling of the person performing the ritual prayer; directing his whole heart toward the Divine Presence manifested in the Kaaba, he also feels that the Prophet and Gabriel are at his right hand, hell to his left, and the Angel of death behind him. As a contemporary Egyptian Sufi expressed it: in prayer and in *dhikr*, "remembrance of God," one is between heaven and hell, between time and eternity.[3]

The experience of the pilgrimage, the way into the sacred space out of the profane, was often spiritualized by the mystics of Islam, the Sufis, who frequently connected it with the experience the Prophet had during his nightly journey into the immediate Divine presence.[4] This heavenly journey formed not only an important ingredient of poetry and miniature painting but, even more importantly, served the Muslims as a model of their ascent during the ritual prayer, or their "Pilgrim's Progress." In this connection one has to think of the numerous poems and prose pieces that deal with the Sufis' quest for the sacred place, a place which is, to be sure, beyond human description and which can, at the best, be called the *lā-mākān*, "No Place," or in Persian *nā-kujā-ābād*, "Nowhere-Town." When describing their journey and its hardships, they speak of the torments their bodies have to undergo so that the thorns in the desert will look like rose bushes because the lovers' torn hearts and livers are withering on them. And the hardest struggle is the pilgrim's constant attempt to subdue his stubborn camel or his restive horse, embodiments of his sensual lusts and of his *nafs*, his "lower soul." This struggle between the animal, which does not understand the beauty of the beloved's spiritual presence and longs for grazing land or for its offspring, forms a special genre in Islamic poetry.[5] In the regional languages of Pakistan, for instance in Sindhi, the adventures of the soul on her (for the soul is feminine!) journey are described in great detail, transforming the rugged landscape of Balochistan into a country of the soul.[6]

The topic of the sacred place, Mecca, and the pilgrimage may also be treated differently. In our century it was Muhammad Iqbal who places the Arabian homeland of Islam once more in the center of his philosophical poetry—one must remember that for centuries the Indian Muslims had always the choice between relating themselves and their cultural heritage to Mecca, to Arabia in general, and feeling more at home in the Indian tradition. Not surprisingly, the "Arabic" qualities of the Prophet Muhammad are highlighted in many Indo-Muslim writings and poems, and Qudsi's (d. 1645) poem, beginning with the line "O Muhammad, Meccan, Medinan, Arab lord!", is sung to this day in religious meetings.[7]

As for Iqbal, the very title of his first collection of Urdu poems, *Bāng-i darā*, "The Sound of the Caravan Bell," points to his preference: he felt like the bell at the foot of the Prophet's camel in the caravan which leads the souls back into the central sanctuary of Mecca after they had lost their way in the fragrant rose gardens of Iran or the glittering streets of Europe. For, as Iqbal points out in another poem:

> When the gazelle fled from the sanctuary of Mecca,
> It became the prey of the hunter.[8]

As hunting and killing is forbidden in the sacred precincts, the Muslims can live safely as long as they cling to the *haram*, undisturbed like the gazelles and the pigeons, but as soon as they leave the *haram* they are vulnerable and can easily fall prey to fatal foreign influences.

Reading such verses, one has also to keep in mind that Mecca was not only the central place for pilgrimage and a symbol of the unity of the Muslims but also an important gathering place for scholars, thinkers, and Sufis who often spent many years there—so much so that some of them were given the honorific title *Jār Allāh*, "God's neighbor" (such as Zamakhsharī, the famous commentator on the Qur'an, d. 1146). Many of the mystics were blessed with visions in Mecca—the most famous example is the leading theosophist Ibn 'Arabi (1165–1240) who, coming from Spain, received the inspiration for his magnum opus *al-Futūhāt al-makkiyya* (The Meccan Openings) during his stay in the sacred place. Furthermore, it is a recurring event in Islamic history that scholars who had come from the border areas of Islamic civilization, like India, Indonesia, or West and North Africa, and lived for some time in Mecca often returned home to inaugurate a radical reform movement. Having been blessed with the experience of pure, pristine Islam, unsullied by foreign influence, they felt they had to share their experience of a "higher" Islam with their coreligionists who, as it seemed to them, were deeply entangled in sinful syncretistic, nay outright "pagan," practices and belief.

But it was not only Mecca, the undisputed sacred center of the Muslim world, that attracted the Muslim's veneration. At a rather early point in history one speaks of the *haramān* (genitive *haramayn*), the two sanctuaries, namely Mecca and Medina, the city where the Prophet had migrated and where he is buried in a place called the *rauda* (garden). Medina gained more and more importance as the veneration of the Prophet grew. The great Egyptian Sufi poet Ibn al-Fārid (d. 1235) found that

> When the anguish of pain settles on my soul, the aroma
> Of fresh herbs from the Hijaz is my balm . . .

But as far as one can see, a special genre of poetry written to express people's longing for Medina was introduced by the Egyptian poet Ibn Daqīq al-'Id (d. 1302). Understandably, the greater the distance of the poets' homeland from Medina, the more tender became the poems that were submitted to the beloved Prophet. As in profane poetry the zephyr is asked to bring the lovers' greetings to the beloved's house, thus the morning breeze is often invoked to bring the sighs of the pious to the last resting place of Muhammad which one hoped to visit one day to recite the special prayers that should be uttered in his presence. For poets in Turkey and in the subcontinent, in West Africa and Central Asia agreed:

> More beautiful than all flowers are the flowers of Medina!

The angels make their prayer beads from the kernels of Medina's dates, as the great Persian poet Jāmī (d. 1492) claims in a most artistic poem, and many a writer wanted to pour out his heart's joy and sorrows before the Prophet.[9] An eighteenth-century poet in the Indus Valley sings:

> (Refrain) In the luminous Medina—could I be there, always there!
> Could I say with all the pilgrims
>   blessings for the intercessor
> In the luminous Medina—
> Could I tell some little matter
>   of my heart to him, our leader . . .
> In the luminous Medina—

and seems to echo Yunus Emre's verse written in thirteenth-century Anatolia:

> If my Lord would kindly grant it
> I would go there, weeping, weeping,
> And Muhammad in Medina
> I would see there, weeping, weeping . . .

And even a Hindu author in our century, Kaifi, has joined the ranks of those who dream of a visit to this longed-for place,

How should the visit not be a heavenly journey?
The luminous dust of his *Rauda* is highest Paradise!

because the light of the Prophet has given Medina the epithet "The Radiant," *al-munawwara*.[10] Despite the Wahhabi reaction to the veneration of tombs, even that of the Prophet, and the aversion of the Saudi authorities to all too outspoken expressions of love in the *Rauda*, the feeling of being overwhelmed by the presence of the one who was sent as "Mercy for the worlds" (Sura 21/107) finds its outlet even today in poems from Egypt and India, such as the progressive writer al-Faiturī's verse:

Over the Prophet's bones every speck of dust
Is a pillar of light,
Standing from the dome of his tomb
to the dome of the skies . . .

It is therefore not astonishing that a good number of collections of poetry—especially Urdu poetry—has been published under titles like *Madīnē kā sadaga* (Spiritual Alms for Medina), and Iqbal himself called his last collection of poetry, which was published only posthumously, *Armaghān-i Hejaz* (The Gift of the Hejaz), because here he expresses his longing for the birthplace of Islam (as a historical fact) and spiritual homeland of the Muslim in moving verses:

Old as I am, I'm going to Medina
to sing my song there, full of love and joy,
Just like a bird who, in the desert night
Spreads out his wings when thinking of his nest.

But again, the role of Medina too could be seen in a different light. The city to which the Prophet emigrated in 622 (which forms the basis of the Islamic calendar) is also the place where he appeared not only as the God-intoxicated prophet but as a successful statesman. Iqbal has emphasized the fact that the Prophet's hegira and his death in a place that was not his hometown may be a subtle hint to divert one's interest from narrow nationalism; "to leave one's homeland is the *sunna* [practice] of our Prophet."[11] The fact that the refugees from India to Pakistan after partition in 1947 called themselves *muhājir*, "those who participate in the hegira," the emigration from a non-Muslim country into the areas of Islam (*dār al-islām*), shows how deeply they still feel the importance of the Prophet's action.

For the Shia community, on the other hand, not only these two sacred places of Islam are venerable but also those where members of the Prophet's family had died or been martyred. The most important site is Kerbela in Iraq, where Husayn

Ibn 'Alī, the grandson of the Prophet and third imām of the Shia, was killed on 10 Muharram (October) 680. Besides, Kāzimiyya near Baghdad and the cities of Qum and Mashhad in Iran are surrounded by special sanctity, and nonbelievers are generally not allowed inside, as is the case in Mecca and Medina. An entire genre of literature centers around Kerbela—a name ingeniously derived by early writers from *karr* (grief) and *balā* (affliction). These are the *marthiyas*, developed out of brief poems into lengthy descriptions of each and every event during the terrible battle between the descendents of the Prophet and the representatives of the government. That the descriptions of the sacred earth of Kerbela often correspond rather to the environment of the poets—that is, nineteenth-century northern India, especially Lucknow—is as natural as the depictions in European art of Bethlehem and Golgotha in an Italian or Flemish setting. But Kerbela was also materially present in the lives of many pious Shi'ite Muslims: small tablets made of the clay of this site were placed on the ground or prayer rug during ritual prayer so that the forehead might touch them, and dust from Kerbela was often brought to religious buildings especially in India to sacralize a mosque or a mausoleum (thus in Hyderabad and Bjapur).

In this connection one may also think of the veneration shown to the tombs of Muslim saints, men and women alike, to whom sometimes hundreds of thousands of people wander to be blessed, at the saint's death anniversary, by participating in prayer, communal meals, and religious music.

Despite this strong feeling of the sacred presence in places like Mecca, Medina, and Kerbela or similar locations, the Muslims have also continued to emphasize, on a certain level, the ancient "orientation" in its traditional meaning: *ex oriente lux*. Although the highest Divine Presence is compared to a light "neither Eastern nor Western" (in Sura 24/35), yet the East retained some of its traditional symbolism. Even in countries east of Mecca, where the praying Muslim turns his face towards the West (such as India or Indonesia), the "spiritual" direction is still the East. It is certainly no accident that in certain trends of Indo-Muslim mystical poetry the term *pūrab* (East) means the area of illumination. Thus, when the Sindhi mystical poet Shāh 'Abdul Latīf (d. 1752) describes how the yogis (who, in this poem, symbolize the perfect "men of God") travel to the ancient sacred cave of Hinglāj, situated west of the Indus Valley in the mountains of Makran, he still speaks of them as "wandering eastward."[12] It seems also that the linguistic term *Pūrabī* (eastern) designates not only the dialect spoken east of Delhi but, at least in certain cases, "a secret mystical language."

The "orientation" in the classical sense of the word is often connected with Yemen, the country at the right side, *Arabia felix*. A word attributed to the Prophet of Islam says, "I feel the breath of the Merciful coming to me from Yemen," because, so it is told, in that country lived a pious shepherd, Uways al-Qaranī, who became a Muslim without ever meeting the Prophet. (Later, the "breath of the Merciful" was identified with the creative Divine breath.) Besides, Yemen was also connected with high religious experience by virtue of being the home of the Queen of Sheba (although this aspect is mentioned only rarely in mystical lore). It was also the place where the best '*aqīq* (carnelian) was found—and carnelian is considered to possess a special sacred power and is often used for signet rings and protective amulets bearing religious formulas. Yemen was further connected, in astronomical reckoning, with the star *Suhayl* (Canopus), which played an important role in navigation and therefore became a symbol of the guiding Divine light in the parlance of the Sufis.

Yemen, the favorite country in the East, is contrasted with the "western exile," located usually in Kairouan. In medieval Sufism, one finds the ancient gnostic idea that the soul, originating in the luminous land of Yemen, is exiled and then, after many adventures, imprisoned in a dark well in the farthest West: in Persian poetry Kairouan can therefore be combined with a wrong etymology, with the word *gīe* (tar) to emphasize its ugly, pitch-black quality. This story of the "occidental exile," *al-ghurbat al-gharbiyya*, has been elaborated most beautifully by Suhrawardī, the "Master of Illumination," who was executed in Aleppo in 1191 because his daring attempts to create a mystico-philosophical system in which both the Greek and the Zoroastrian spiritual heritages were integrated into the Islamic worldview seemed too dangerous for unimaginative theologians. Suhrawardī's whole system, as it was brilliantly interpreted in our time by Henry Corbin, centers around the increasing illumination of the soul and its return from the "western exile" to its sacred home in Yemen.[13] Illuminative wisdom is therefore called *al-hikmat al-yamaniyya* (Yemenite wisdom), while intellectual knowledge appears as *al-hikmat al-yūn'ñiyya* (Greek wisdom). It is still not fully known how the concept of the "spiritual Yemen" appeared during the Renaissance in the mystical philosophy of the Rosicrucians, and the concept of the East as the home of "the highest romantic feeling" ("Im Orient Müssen wir das höchste Romantische suchen," as F. von Schlegel remarked) sparked off the interest of Germans and following them other Europeans in Oriental cultures during the heyday of the romantic movement. Without knowing Suhrawardī's Eastern philosophy of Illumination, *ishraq*, the representatives of this trend seem to have followed his guidelines.

However, there is yet another way of orientation, a way known to Suhrawardī and those who follow him. This is the vertical orientation, toward the polar star, the Pole. In his thought-provoking book *L'Homme de lumière dans le soufisme iranien*, Henry Corbin has shown that truly mystical orientation tends not towards the horizontal but towards the vertical axis, pointing to the spiritual heights whence the soul had come down.[14] Not in vain is the highest representative of the esoteric knowledge of a certain time called *qutb* (the Pole, Axis), and the members of the hierarchy of saints around him are arranged like the parts of a cosmic tent, most importantly the four *autād* (tent pegs), whose duty is to supervise the four corners of the universe. The way of the soul, once it begins its ascent from the bottom of the well in Kairouan, leads through seven stages, the seven spheres, until the final point is reached. That is the Mount Qāf, which surrounds the world, the "emerald mountain" which exudes its own light, the home of the mythical bird 'Anqā or Sīmurgh to whom the pilgrimage of the individual soul-bird leads. This pilgrimage has been described most beautifully in Farīdaddin 'Attār's (d. 1220) Persian epic *Mantiq uttayr*, "The Birds' Conversation." This work tells of the seven valleys through which the soul-like birds wander until they reach Mount Qāf to discover that they, being thirty birds, *sī murgh*, are themselves the *Simurgh*. To reach the end of the way, the summit of the emerald mountain which lies behind the sphere of darkness (that of Saturn, the "black" planet) and of the "black-out" of any sensual experience in the experience of *fana* (annihilation; German *Entwerden*) means to have surpassed the material spheres and attained the eighth zone, where only light reigns. It is "the celestial earth of Hūrqakyā," as Suhrawardī calls it. This eighth zone, *kishwar*, is indeed, as mystical numerology and cosmology claim, the zone of eternal bliss, eight being the number of perfection connected with paradise. (The Islamic paradise has therefore eight gates, while hell has only seven.)

The poets, especially those in the Persianate areas (Iran, Turkey, Muslim India), have described this journey into the heavenly heights in numerous images, often taking the Prophet's heavenly journey as their model. The Prophet is called "the caravan leader" on this way home, and Maulānā Rūmī, the great Persian-writing mystical poet (1207–73) never tired of calling his friends to join him in the upward journey.

> We have come from the heights, and go back to the heights. . . .
> O mountain of our [material] existence, don't bar our way—
> We are going to the Mount Oāf and the 'Anqā![15]

The return of the soul-bird captured by the crooked old woman "World" to his royal owner's palace was one of the traditional ways of describing the heavenly journey of the soul.

But the mystics had not only these poetical images of the world; rather, some of them developed whole maps of the spiritual localities. They showed where, in descending order, the *'alam al-jabarūt*, the world of Divine Power, the *alam al-malakut*, the angelic world, and the *'alam an-nāsūt*, the world of the humans, were located and knew also an intermediate sphere, the *'alam al-mithāl, mundus imaginalis*, in which the material is spiritualized, the spiritual materialized. Just as the realms of the spiritual world up to the all-surrounding Divine Throne are sketched (for example in the *Marifetname* of the eighteenth-century Turkish Sufi Ibrahim Haqqi Ezerumlu), so also some Muslims have not hesitated (even in our time) to draw maps showing the localities in Hell.[16]

One look into Islamic poetry, especially from the eastern part of the Muslim world, shows that there was also a kind of poetical geography in which certain cities or countries were mentioned time and again because they had crystallized, so to speak, into religious-poetical symbols. Thus, the Turkish inhabitants of Central Asia were generally regarded as the embodiment of beauty owing to their moon-like, round faces and fair complexion, and thus Turkistan, Khata, Khitay,

Chigil, and a number of other Central Asian places occur frequently in lyrical verse although their locality was probably not exactly known to the poets—they were simply "the cities of the beloved." While Turkistan and related areas were always filled with a positive content, *Hindūstān*, India, on the other hand, was a term for "blackness," for in the Middle Ages Hindus were considered black, lowly people contrasting with the radiant, overpowering beauty of the Turks. Thus, Rūmī can speak of the "Turkistan of Heaven" and "Hindustan of matter," of the Hindustan "Night" which is conquered by the Turk "Day," and so on. And 300 years later, when numerous poets migrated from Iran to India to find better living conditions, Nazīrī (d. 1612) wrote:

> Leave your misfortune ("black fortune") at home, Nazīrī,
> For nobody ever brought a black Hindu as a present to Hindustan!

The contrast between the Turkish, "spiritual" land of the beloved and Hindustan, the material world, permeated classical Persian poetry to such an extent that even poets living in the Indian subcontinent used it almost without realizing its implications.[17]

There is, however, one other application of the term *Hindustan* in Persian, which is attested first in the early twelfth century and has remained a normal expression to this day: "The elephant saw India in his dream." It means that someone remembers suddenly his place of origin and, like the captive elephant, tears his shackles and runs towards his home, leaving his present place behind, to rejoin those to whom he belongs. In the Middle Ages this term was often used for the soul which, captured in the world of matter, suddenly remembers her spiritual home and begins the journey home.

The previous connotation of Hindustan as a dangerous, dark area was shifted, in the sixteenth century, to another area. After the first Portuguese attacks on the Indian west coast, the poets of the Moghul Empire and those in the provinces would sometimes speak of *Firangistān*, the country of the Franks (Europeans), as an attractive, colorful, but utterly dangerous place where the lover (that is, the Muslim) could be captured and imprisoned. It is, basically, nothing but a modernization of the old concept of the "occidental exile," filled with fresh spirit as a result of political changes.

Rivers too played a certain role in the mystical geography of Islam. There is in the first place the River Nile, known from the Qur'an as the river mysteriously changed by the stroke of Moses when he led the Children of Israel into freedom; its waters turned to blood, and Pharaoh died in the waves. The transformation of the river into blood made it a good symbol for the tears of blood which the unhappy lover sheds. Another river that appears very frequently is the Tigris on which the capital of the mighty Abbasid Empire was situated (the Euphrates is barely found!). And it is remarkable that even poets in India in later centuries still complain of their tears flowing like the Tigris, while rivers much closer to them, like the Indus or Ganges, occur only in topical verse. Another river "of tears" is the Jayhūn, Oxus, once the border of the Islamic areas, while the River Mūliyān near Bukhara has gained its fame in poetry only thanks to the verses in which Rūdakī incited the ruler to return to his homeland after spending a long time in the Samarqand area.[18] But Mūliyān has never become a "spiritual" symbol.

However, the concept of "river" was of much greater importance for Muslim thought than the names of single rivers which, as poetry tells us, would end in the greatest ocean, identified in Persian poetry with the *Bahr-i 'Ummān*, the Gulf of Oman. The river as such had been used as a symbol of Prophetic activity as early as in the works of the tenth-century Shi'ite theologian Kūlīnī, and to this day the Sufis feel that in the mystical chain of initiation the great shaykhs are "tributaries leading to the mainstream in the Prophet."[19] The image was used by Goethe in his famous German poem "Mahomets Gesang" of 1772, and Iqbal wrote a free Persian version of this poem in his *Payām-i Mashriq* (Message of the East), a collection of Persian poetry published in 1923. The mystics had discovered in the image of the river a fitting symbol for the spiritual way of the soul: they had seen themselves rushing like torrents through the world, and once more Rūmī is the most eloquent spokesman of this feeling.

> Prostrating ourselves we go toward the ocean like a torrent,
> Then, on the face of the ocean, we go on handclapping
> (or: "like foam," the word *kaf* meaning both "hand" and "foam").[20]

The ocean is the all-encompassing Divine being, into which the rivers and the raindrops return and lose their identity. But the ocean can also be the unfathomable Ocean of the soul, in which the seeker finally discovers the Divine whom he has sought in vain outside in the world—after all, the Qur'an states that God is closer to man "than his jugular vein" (Sura 50/16). And the mystical singer in Bengal will praise the Prophet, not as the poet in Turkey or Egypt will do, as the caravan leader, but as the helmsman of the boat of life without whom he cannot cross the mighty waves.

Sacred geography in Islam thus is determined by different coordinates: the sanctuary of Mecca and, in general, the "two sanctuaries" of the Hejaz; the pole to which the soul will ascend; and the ocean in which the spirit may find its final goal. All three concepts are used by mystical poets indiscriminately, and their spiritual flights carry the listener from ocean to desert, from the polar star to the radiant fields of Yemen. For all of them know that they try to confine the *lā makān*, the No-Place and Nowhere, of the Divine, into material coordinates and have therefore to use, at the best, weak shadows of the places they have visited in the spirit, paradoxes which try to explain the mystery of the emerald mountain behind the luminous black of confusion.

But it should also be pointed out that Muhammad Iqbal, the philosopher-poet in modern Islam, who revived the ancient symbolism and infused a new dynamism into Islam, has used for himself two terms that point to his role in the whole area of "sacred geography"; as he is the caravan bell leading the caravan to the center of the earth, the Kaaba, and so in his poetical account of the heavenly journey, the Persian *Jāvīdnāma* (1932), he also calls himself *Zindarūd*, the "Living Stream."[21] As part and parcel of the prophetic spirit he tries to carry with him the brooks and rivulets, leading them with increasing strength to the paternal Ocean, which surrounds everything and yet is the center in which all love ends.

NOTES

1. Muhammad Iqbal, *Asrāri-i khudī* [*The Secrets of the Self*] (Lahore: n.p., 1915).

2. For this development, see Annemarie Schimmel, *Mystical Dimensions of Islam* (Chapel Hill: University of North Carolina Press, 1975), pp. 288 ff. For all following references to the work of Muslim poets, see Annemarie Schimmel, *And Muhammad is His Messenger* (Chapel Hill: University of North Carolina Press, 1985), pp. 188 ff., unless otherwise indicated.

3. See Earle H. Waugh, *The Munshidīn of Egypt* (Columbia: University of South Carolina Press, 1988), p. 75.

4. Schimmel, *And Muhammad Is His Messenger*, ch. 9.

5. For this imagery, see Annemarie Schimmel "Nur ein störrisches Pferd," in *Ex Orbe Religionum* (Leiden, Netherlands: E. J. Brill, 1972).

6. H. T. Sorley, *Shah 'Abdul Latif of Bhit* (Oxford: Oxford University Press, 1940); and Annemarie Schimmel, *Pain and Grace: A Study of Two Eighteenth-Century Indo-Muslim Mystical Poets* (Leiden, Netherlands: E. J. Brill, 1976), part II.

7. Qudsi's poem in S. M. Ikram, *Armaghān-i Pāk* (Karachi: n.p., 1951), p. 219.

8. Iqbal, *Asrār-i khudī*, line 83.

9. Maulānā 'Abdur Rahmān Jāmī, *Dīvān-i kāmil*, ed. Hāshim Rezā (Tehran: Bīrūz, 1962), pp. 68–69, poem no. 61.

10. A good example is Emel Esin, *Mecca the Blessed, Medina the Radiant* (New York: Crown Publishers, 1963).

11. Muhammad Iqbal, *Stray Reflections* (written 1910), ed. Javid Iqbal (Lahore: n.p., 1961). At approximately the same time, Iqbal wrote in his Urdu poem "Wataniyat" [Patriotism], in *Bāng-i darā* (Lahore: n.p., 1923): "the *sunna* [custom, institutionalized by the Prophet] is, to leave one's homeland."

12. Schimmel, *Pain and Grace*, part II, especially the description of the yogis in Shah 'Abdul Latīf's *Sur Ramakālī*.

13. See Henry Corbin, *Sohravardi d'Alep, Fondateur de la Doctrine Illuminative (ishrāq)* (Paris: n.p., 1939); Henry Corbin, ed., *Suhrawardi, Opera Metaphysica et Mystica*, 2 vols. (Istanbul: n.p., 1945; and Tehran-Paris: n.p., 1952); and Henry Corbin, trans., *L'Archange Empourpré* (Paris: n.p., 1976).

14. Henry Corbin, *L'Homme de lumière dans le soufisme iranien* (Paris: n.p., 1971); English translation by Nancy Pearson (Boulder: University of Colorado Press, 1978); German translation by Annemarie Schimmel (Munich: n.p., 1989).

15. Maulānā Jalāluddīn Rūmī, *Dīvān-i kabīr*, ed. Badī 'uzzamān Furūzānfar, 10 vols. (Teheran: Teheran University Press, 1957–), poem no. 1677.

16. A voluminous study of the geography of Hell was distributed to the participants of the International Congress for the History of Religion in Marburg in 1960. It had been elaborated by a retired Turkish general; and lately, a few more studies of this kind have appeared.

17. Annemarie Schimmel, "Turk and Hindu: A Poetical Image and Its Application to Historical Fact," in Speros Vryonis Jr., ed., *Islam and Cultural Change in the Middle Ages* (Wiesbaden: Harrassowitz, 1975).

18. The Mūliyān story is told in Nizāmī 'Arūdī, *Chahār Maqālq*, ed. M. Qazvini (Tehran: n.p., 1952), pp. 49 ff. See also Edward G. Browne's English translation, *Four Discourses* (London: Gibb Memorial Series, 1921).

19. Waugh, *Munshidīn of Egypt*, p. 85.

20. Rūmī, *Dīvān-i kabīr*, poem no. 1713.

21. Muhammad Iqbal, *Jāvīdnāma* (Lahore: n.p., 1932); English translation by Arthur J. Arberry (London: Allen and Unwin, 1960). There are also numerous other translations into European languages. See also Annemarie Schimmel, *Gabriel's Wing: A Study into the Religious Ideas of Sir Muhammad Iqbal* (Leiden, Netherlands: E. J. Brill, 1963).

Afterword: The Geographics of Religion in a Postmodern Environment

Jamie S. Scott and Paul Simpson-Housley

Paul Gauguin's canvas, *D'où venons-nous? Que sommes-nous? Où allons-nous?* is an apt aphorism for the state of humanistic studies in the academy.[1] Today's practitioners of received disciplines are conscious of their antecedents, and they protect the traditional boundaries of these disciplines. Over the past fifty years, the human sciences have pursued policies of increased specialization. Most institutions of higher education are splintered into distinct faculties and departments. A formalist ethos discourages conversation among specialists within these units, let alone among members of different units. It is not in the nature of bureaucratic administrations to encourage activities which might disturb the status quo. Such a conservative and isolationist mentality exacerbates differences of matter and method among the human sciences. Worse still, this mentality impedes conversation among scholars who are in fact often engaged in research upon a common topic from different methodological perspectives, or in projects involving the use of similar methodologies in the study of quite dissimilar cultural phenomena. Whatever the strengths of academic specialization, we are now more aware of its weaknesses. Though our energies instinctively safeguard our chosen methodologies and fields of study, we are less antagonistic towards advocates of alternative paradigms. If many of us have no precise vision of where we are, and are still less clear about future directions, at least we recognize that we must not simply reiterate the same tired patterns of the past.

At first glance, the diversity of method and matter displayed in the chapters in this collection give an impression of a discipline unsure of its identity, or of an editorial task performed with much too large a dash of liberality. But one should not confuse the random with a deliberate attempt to challenge the status quo in a given area of study from a variety of perspectives. There is neither space nor need to identify all points of contact and contrast among the topics and approaches represented in these chapters. Careful reading of these essays discovers a number of common themes and patterns. We will draw attention to a few of these comparisons and conflicts. But our main object is to point out that the study of Judaism, Christianity, and Islam exists within the wider environment of the academic study of religion, and that the study of religion takes place within the academy as a whole. Bearing these circles of influence in mind, we argue that scholars of religion must lose or find their places within a contemporary academic environment which not only encourages, but is defined by, a centrifugal, rather than a centripetal, sense of disciplinary identity. This centrifugal tendency takes a number of forms, but whatever the realm of scholarly discourse, the term "postmodernism" is invoked most often to describe the present mood of the academy. This mood characterizes the study of religion, in particular the study of Judaism, Christianity, and Islam, as surely as it characterizes other areas of scholarly enquiry. The interest shown by scholars of religion in what we are calling the "geographics" of these monotheistic traditions may be understood as part of the centrifugal tendency.[2]

POSTMODERNISM, WITTGENSTEIN, AND THE STUDY OF RELIGION

The variety of themes and methods demonstrated in the chapters in this volume is a direct result of the challenge posed by the geographics of Judaism, Christianity, and Islam to traditional approaches to the study of the Religions of the Book. Such challenges to received ways of thinking and doing in the academy are both symptomatic of and contributive to the broader cultural phenomenon of postmodernism. Postmodernism clearly has a relativizing effect upon the stable structure of the academy. Within the academy, postmodernism also has a relativizing effect upon the nature of humanist studies, under the rubric of which the disciplines of geography and religious studies are in many ways traditionally considered. For humanist studies, postmodernism contains what Hans-Georg Gadamer and other contemporary philosophers of interpretation call "prejudices."[3] Here, "prejudices" is intended nonprejudicially simply to mean anticipatory ideas. We may identify some of the anticipatory ideas informing postmodernism by dividing theoretical positions describable as postmodernist into two camps.[4] On the one hand, French thinkers like Jacques Derrida,

Michel Foucault, and Jacques Lacan mount a deconstructionist critique of modernism. This critique proclaims the death of the human subject. In North America this line of attack is carried forward in the work of figures such as Paul de Man, J. Hillis Miller, and Kenneth Burke. Derrida's philosophical agenda, Lacan's psychoanalytical work, Foucault's archaeologies of public and private discourse, and the work of their North American counterparts, may be understood as strategies of interpretation. Their stance is revolutionary; it is a radical form of Paul Ricœur's "hermeneutics of suspicion." On the other hand, German thinkers as various as Gadamer and Jürgen Habermas attempt different approaches to what Ricœur calls the "hermeneutics of recovery." Along with non-European figures as diverse as Ihab Hassan, Clifford Geertz, and Hilary Putnam, whatever their disagreements, Gadamer and Habermas concur with much of the deconstructionist critique of modernism, but look to the ability of practical reason to help us reconstruct our understanding of the roles of experience and language in the shaping of ideologies. In short, "the basic difference between deconstructionists and pragmatists may be construed as script versus speech, words written versus words uttered."[5] At the same time, however, it could be argued that the deconstructionist critique of modernism undermines even the pragmatist critique, since the latter assumes at least the desirabilty, even the possibility, of some sort of normative or authoritative interpretation of cultural phenomena. For the deconstructionists, "the truth one would know has always receded behind the formulations it makes possible, and therefore those formulations are always ignorant of themselves and incomplete."[6]

Both deconstructionist and pragmatist postmodernists, however, warn against modernism's epistemological confidence in the powers of human reason to discover essential truths and definitive meanings. As Richard Rorty has shown, the metaphor of the mind as mirror lies at the heart of modernism's rationalist confidence.[7] Such confidence is characterized by traditional philosophical concepts like substance, essence, identity, and truth. Never so naïve as to assume that we can escape completely from this lexicon of rationalist assertiveness, the postmodernist nonetheless argues that we may avoid the temptation to totalize culturally relative presuppositions into potentially tyrannical philosophical systems. How might we avoid this temptation? By deliberately cultivating an approach to cultural phenomena which is less a method than a strategy of interpretation. Deconstructionist hermeneutics of suspicion and pragmatist hermeneutics of recovery, for all their differences, may be understood as strategies of interpretation. Insofar as each of these strategies focuses less on what seems essential, and more on what seems of marginal significance to understanding a given cultural phenomenon, they challenge the very foundations of modernist thinking. In this respect, all postmodernist attacks on established ways of thinking share a concern for the issue of authority. At the heart of this concern lies a double-edged problem. On the one hand, we need to be able to use language to expose the ways in which language is abused to maintain the hegemony of privileged interests; and on the other hand, we need to be able to use language to reveal avenues of self-determination for those to whom the privileged have denied a voice. Assuming this connection between discourse and power, postmodernists stress the Janus-like quality of language. In all areas of cultural expression, we are urged to turn our attention away from what has been spoken or written and towards what has been obscured or left unsaid. If language itself is ambiguous, received conventions of interpretation, in terms both of matter and of method, hide as much as they reveal, and thus disvalue, as much as they privilege, certain objects of study and certain academic procedures and those who practice them. Like the contemporary academy, modernism collapses under the weight of its own rationalism into a collection of formally consistent, yet mutually exclusive discourses, each advancing an epistemological stance founded on its own explanation of the order of things.[8]

The resurgence of inter-, cross-, and multi-disciplinary studies in the academy indicates that to a large degree, scholars endorse these ideas. Rorty speaks of postmodernism in terms of "a conversation which presupposes no disciplinary matrix which unites the speakers, but where the hope of agreement is never lost so long as the conversation lasts."[9] True, there are dissenting voices. Thomas Short, for example, rails mightily against "diversity" and the "breaking of disciplines" as "two new assaults on the curriculum."[10] But a growing number of humanists now see the creative possibilities of blurring genres.[11] The neologism "geographics" expresses a particular instance of this turn away from established procedures in the study of geography and religion towards a more fully self-conscious, inter-, cross-, and multi-disciplinary strategy in the interpretation of Judaic, Christian, and Muslim self-understanding. But instead of invoking the support of deconstructionists and pragmatists, we would like to add another voice to the conversation. We would like to enlist the efforts of the later Ludwig Wittgenstein of the *Philosophical Investigations* to offer a methodological paradigm for the study of the role geographical phenomena have played in the life and letters of the Religions of the Book, and hence an interpretive matrix for understanding the varieties of matter and method exhibited in the essays which comprise this volume.[12]

The *Investigations* is a rich and multidimensional text, and there is not space here to go into the various debates surrounding the complex ideas Wittgenstein explores in it.[13] What is crucial, however, is the fact that the *Investigations* may be understood as representing a postmodernist rejection of modernism. Three concepts are of importance here: "forms of life," "language games," and "family resemblances." More specifically, the Wittgenstein of the *Investigations* may be understood as asserting that human existence—individual, societal, universal— consists of limitless variations of roles and functions. He calls these "forms of life." Each form of life embodies and is embodied in sets of communicative procedures, some explicitly formalized, others merely assumed because of habit, convention, or tradition. These sets of communicative procedures Wittgenstein calls "language games." When a religious person speaks of God as father, for example, he uses the word "father" according to a set of communicative procedures different from that obtaining when he addresses his male parent, and different again from that obtaining when he speaks of himself as the father of his children. It is nonsense or pathological jealousy to ascribe omniscience to myself with respect to the dating habits of my offspring, just as the communicative procedures of theology necessitate the falsehood of any statement literally referred to the divinity. In other words, the use of words determines their meaning, and the truth of a proposition depends upon rational criteria such as consensus of opinion and coherence within the rules of a given language game, rather than on any correspondence between a proposition and a state of affairs—a picture good for all times and places.

The Wittgensteinian postmodernist thus pursues a line not dissimilar in spirit from deconstructionist and pragmatist postmodernism. The relativism of the *Investigations* echoes the call of these other postmodernists for an end to foundationalist philosophy and a commitment to the free play of conversation. In order to facilitate this free play of conversation, the Wittgensteinian postmodernist draws upon the third concept crucial to an understanding of the *Investigations*— "family resemblances." "Family resemblances" mediate, as it were, the complex interrelationships among language games and forms of life. Without this concept, the Wittgensteinian paradigm is skewed. Wittgenstein's is an anti-foundationalist stance, but in a way it is not an absolutely relativistic analysis. If we think of the example of fatherhood once again, it is clear that certain common expectations attach to the use of the word "father" in each of the language games determining questions of meaning, truth, and rationality for the churchgoer and the child. To give an obvious instance, we both expect a divine father in heaven and a male parent to exhibit similar qualities of love and justice. Although the meaning of each of these terms will vary according to the communicative procedures defining the language game in which it is used, there are family resemblances amongst forms of life. In Wittgenstein's celebrated image, just as a thread may be a single entity made up of countless strands, one of which runs the whole length of the thread, so at any given time and in any given place we may talk of a pattern of meanings, some of which figured in previous times and places, and some of which will figure in subsequent times and places. "The strength of the thread does not reside in the fact that some one fibre funs through its whole length," Wittgenstein writes, "but in the overlapping of many fibres."[14]

If, then, we turn to the study of Judaism, Christianity, and Islam, this methodological paradigm is useful in two respects. Among other things, the Wittgensteinian postmodernist will be concerned with identifying family resemblances of matter and method within departments of religion about the ways in which geographical phenomena shape religious self-understanding. This concern has to do with the internal structure of the study of religion. The idea that the study of religion possesses an internal structure may be construed as a kind of shorthand for the many forms of life, each embodying and embodied in various language games, that make up the study of religion in a given time and place, even though definitions of internal structure will overlap and criss-cross from time to time and from place to place. As we noted at the beginning of the volume, the emphasis the Religions of the Book place on the temporal dimension of religious self-understanding has always offered occasions for historical analysis. In turn, historical analysis has led to philosophical and theological efforts to distill the significance of divine activity in history into conceptual frameworks resistant to or interpretive of the contingencies of history. This emphasis on thematic and methodological variations in the historical, philosophical, and theological study of the three monotheistic traditions has consigned concern with their spatial dimension to the margins of the academic enterprise. But as the chapters in this volume make clear, the God who acts in history makes his will known to particular people in particular places. The spatial dimension of religious self-understanding is as susceptible to sociological, political, and anthropological analysis as it is to historical, philosophical, and theological interpretation. Within departments of religion, family resemblances among the objects of study in the Judaic, Christian, and Muslim traditions thus draw practitioners of diverse methods into conversation.

Second, the Wittgensteinian paradigm provides a rationale for establishing conversations between historians, philosophers, theologians, sociologists, political scientists, and anthropologists at work in departments of religion, and scholars engaged in the interpretation of the cultural expressions of Judaism, Christianity, and Islam in other divisions of the academy. This concern has to do with the external relations of a department of religion. Among other things, the Wittgensteinian postmodernist will look for family resemblances of matter and method among the projects pursued in departments of religion and other divisions of the academy. Such a search will lead the scholar of religion to consider what sociologists, political scientists, and anthropologists in departments of sociology, political science, and anthropology have to say about the ways in which geographical phenomena shape Judaic, Christian, and Moslem self-understanding. The Wittgensteinian paradigm thus enables constructive conversations between those practicing the various subdisciplines within the study of religion and those pursuing related interests in other academic disciplines beyond the boundaries of departments of religion. The idea that the study of religion is inevitably related to other academic disciplines, such as human geography, each embodying and embodied in various language games, expresses the combined efforts of scholars of religion to defend their domain from outside interference from other forms of academic life, even though, once again, from time to time and from place to place the way this domain is defined, and therefore, what exactly needs defending from what, will overlap and criss-cross.

WITTGENSTEINIAN PEDAGOGY AND THE GEOGRAPHICS OF RELIGION

How might Wittgensteinian postmodernism work when it comes to the practical business of doing the geographics of religion? In such books as *An*

Examination of the Place of Reason in Ethics and *The Uses of Argument*, a disciple of Wittgenstein, Stephen Toulmin, elaborates on questions having to do with similarities and differences among academic disciplines and their relationship to human affairs beyond the confines of the academy.[15] Toulmin makes a critical distinction between the notion of understanding and such notions as meaning, truth, and rationality. The criteria for determining what is meaningful, true, and rational in a given discipline will vary according to the kind of question that this discipline addresses. " 'Reality,' " Toulmin writes, "in any particular mode of reasoning must be understood as 'what (for the purposes of argument) is relevant,' and 'mere appearance' as 'what (for these purposes) is irrelevant.' "[16] From discipline to discipline, these purposes will differ. The space of interest to the geographer of religion is in one sense mere appearance for the art historian, and mere appearance in another sense for the subatomic physicist. Thus the terms any given approach to human reality uses to adjudicate what is meaningful, true, and rational have what Toulmin elsewhere calls a "field-variant force" and "field-dependent standards."[17] The words "meaningful," "true," and "rational" constantly mean something, but the criteria prescribing their use vary according to the user's understanding of those terms themselves. What connects the various fields of analysis one with another is, for Toulmin, the contribution all make to our understanding of human existence. Every discipline in some way furthers our efforts so to apprehend the complexities of the human situation as to avoid the unpredictable and to prepare for the potentially perilous. Almost in the manner of classical humanism, the academy mediates between the powers of light and darkness, however perceived. There is always the risk that unthinkingly we will perpetuate the status quo, but Toulmin makes it clear that change is as necessary for the preservation of civility, however defined, as it is a sign of impending barbarity, however defined.

Keeping in mind these criteria, let us conclude with a look backwards at the chapters which comprise this volume. The three chapters which approach the literal role played by the geographical in the development of religious self-understanding adopt different methods. If Yossi Katz may be understood as a legal geographer of the relationship between Jewish law and settlement patterns, Ronald Bordessa works as a political geographer of the kinds of Finnish landscapes which result from Lutheran ideology. By contrast, Michael Fischer uses the methods of ethnography and anthropology to describe the interplay between Shi'ite Muslim and Zoroastrian perceptions of the Central Iranian Plateau. But despite these differences, we may identify overlapping patterns in the way Judaism, Christianity, and Islam influence forms of human occupancy. As Fischer shows, for example, the Central Iranian Plateau possesses an extreme climate. Muslim and Zoroastrian life takes on communal forms in response to these climatic conditions, and shrines are constructed for the benefit of the deity. Similarly, Bordessa describes the works of Lutheran Finns in a harsh environment. As a result of its geology and northern latitude, the Baltic shield imposes major restrictions on human efforts to enforce their will upon the land.

Nature, however, is seen as the work of God. Even towns such as Tapiola do not impinge upon its pristine state. Rocky outcrops and trees are preserved within urban areas. If, in Finland, Christian theological concerns elevate the importance of landscape, in nineteenth-century Palestine the framework of Judaic religious law dominates the patterns of settlement. Katz contends that synagogues, for instance, had to be built in the functional centers of neighborhoods. Cultural landscapes thus result when humans interact with the natural environment. Part of this human interaction is guided by theological principle. These endeavors are acted out on a terrain which may be harsh or benign in terms of potential settlement. But the resulting forms of human works, including religious works, reflect the dual influence of the land and other geographical aspects of culture.

The three essays focusing on what we have called the symbolic function of the geographical in the shaping of religious self-understanding also adopt different methods of analysis. Roger Friedland and Richard Hecht work as social and political historians of the struggle for control of the Temple Mount in Jerusalem, while Juan Campo uses political science to analyze the discursive practices of vying social groups in Muslim Egypt. By contrast, Ellen Ross presents herself as a feminist interpreter of the spatial dimensions of women's experience of the Divine in the Christian tradition. But despite these variations in method and topic, once again we can identify some sort of patterning in the ways Judaism, Christianity, and Islam induce political aspirations which affect the use of the human landscape. Friedland and Hecht, for instance, recount the political struggle between Jew and Palestinian for control of sacred precincts of the Temple Mount. Similarly, Campo discusses the political aims of disparate social groups competing for control of Egyptian participation in the Muslim pilgrimage to Mecca. If Friedland and Hecht and Campo are concerned with the overt political conflicts which develop over rival claims to sacred sites in Judaism and Islam, Ross's feminist revisioning reveals a history of covert political disenfranchisement in the Christian tradition. By focusing our attention on a variety of spatial manifestations of the Divine in the lives and letters of Christian women, Ross's essay may be understood as an attempt to empower women and to raise our awareness of the creative and innovative power of women in the Christian tradition. Political geography thus considers the role of nations and other communities in structuring geographical space and spatial images. The political process manifests itself in the landscape. This landscape includes monuments and other geographical features which symbolize moments or movements of significance in the development of religious traditions.

Likewise, the three chapters concerned with the role played by the geography of the prophetic and apocalyptic imagination in the shaping of religious self-understanding make use of different methods. While Martha Himmelfarb draws upon the techniques of literary hermeneutics to examine the spatial images of Judaic apocalyptic literature, Annemarie Schimmel may be seen as a literary historian locating the mystical poetry of Islam in its various geographical contexts. In a different vein, Leonard Thompson uses cartographic terminology as an exegetical tool for the interpretation of Revelation. Again, however, despite these variations in approach and field, we may perceive patterns of similarity among the ways in which the geographical imagination expresses itself in the prophetic and apocalyptic literature of Judaism, Christianity, and Islam. Thompson notes that journeys between spheres occur in Revelation. These spheres have places of crossing, and religious transformations occur at these points. In a similar way, Himmelfarb refers to journeys to otherworldly lands. In the Book of the Watchers, for instance, Enoch is taken on a trip to the ends of the earth, the purpose of which is to assert the wonders of God's creation. In addition, Schimmel argues that the Sufis connected pilgrimage with the nightly journey of the Prophet into the immediate divine presence. Schimmel also refers to Iqbal's poetical account of the heavenly journey, in which he calls himself the living stream. Similarly, Himmelfarb's description of Ezekiel's temple stream portrays a river which is so full of life that it causes the Dead Sea to teem with fish. In turn, Thompson points our attention to the river of life flowing through the new Jerusalem. Geographical terminology thus recurs in the metaphorical patterns of prophetic and apocalyptic literature of Judaism, Christianity, and Islam. These recurring images and motifs help to ground highly figurative landscapes in reality, and thus to give concrete reality to their speculative religious worlds.

Taken together, these chapters reveal that the current practice of many scholars of religion diverges from familiar ways of analyzing and interpreting the role of geography in the shaping of Judaic, Christian, and Muslim self-understanding. These chapters do not fall within the parameters of the traditional study of the Religions of the Book, which is to say, these essays are not what, by traditional lights, however defined, interpreters of Judaism, Christianity, and Islam should be doing. But the difference of these essays is their strength, insofar as they resist the tyrannical totalizing of any particular view of the study of religion into a system of subject matters and methods good for all times and all places. The true ideologues in the academy are not those who wish to push beyond the boundaries of what traditional academic ideology advocates, whether or not we construe that ideology in terms of some kind of social scientific program. The proliferation of subdisciplines in departments of religion reflects the inability of traditional academic ideology, whatever form it takes, to provide adequate communicative procedures for the various forms of life pursued by today's interpreters of the three monotheistic traditions. When books come from the publishers with titles like *The Shape of Sacred Space: Four Biblical Studies*, *Landscapes of the Sacred: Geography and Narrative in American Spirituality*, and *Iran: From Religious Dispute to Revolution*, it is clear that certain scholars of Judaism, Christianity, and Islam are straying from fields traditional academic ideology normally countenances into very strange domains indeed.[18] Does this mean that these scholars are not scholars of religion, and that what they do is not the proper study of religion? Of course not. Conversely, we now have a series, *Geographia Religionum*, the latest volume of which, *Pilgrimages in World Religions*, draws upon the empirical methods of physical geography, with their emphasis on statistical analysis and cartography.[19] Will a scholar investigating the topic of pilgrimage from an historical, philosophical, or theological perspective argue that this volume has nothing to do with the proper study of religion? Again, of course, not. Rather, the proper study of Judaism, Christianity, and Islam is what scholars of religion do—or rather, it seems, what they do not do—not what an outmoded pedagogical ideology imposes upon them. In turn, this transformation of matter and method in the study of the Religions of the Book means that outmoded pedagogical ideologies must—in both transitive and intransitive senses of the word—yield to a restructuring of the study of religion reflecting present practice and future promise.

More specifically, those concerned with the role of things geographical in the shaping of religious self-understanding have to decide not only in conversations among themselves, but in conversations with those in other disciplines, what, if anything, is distinctive in a given time and place about the various disciplinary forms of life and language games which comprise the study of religion. It will not do arbitrarily to privilege the sociological, the political, or the anthropological, any more than it will do to privilege the historical, the philosophical, or the theological. At the same time, however, we will find ourselves having to justify our moving in one direction rather than another. Often this sort of decision involves a distinction between practical criteria, having to do with issues of social utility, and theoretical criteria, having to do with issues of scholarly integrity. But such a distinction itself depends, in a manner reminiscent of Toulmin, as much on some sort of equivalence, as on some sort of distinction, between social utility and scholarly centrality in determining criteria for defining what is and what is not an appropriate concern for the study of religion.

CONCLUSION

In the traditions of the Western academy, humanist scholars have always liked to think of themselves as mediating between the powers of light and darkness, however perceived. Traditionally, the interplay among these powers has embodied and expressed variations in our perceptions about the metaphysical status of humanness, about humanist modes of knowing, about the humanities construed as a field of education, and about humanitarian values.[20] But if the postmodern environment is characterized by skeptical attitudes towards the metaphysical and epistemological traditions of humanistic studies, then human scientists must accept the challenge to redescribe their territory. As participants in the humanist enterprise, scholars of religion must also join in this process of redescription. Refusing firm foundations, the contemporary scholar of religion must find new ways to articulate major issues confronting the contemporary academy, especially such postmodernist issues as the anti-foundationalist fragmentation of knowledge, the hidden contrast between will and reason in our understanding of the human subject, and the infidelities of language and communication.[21]

It seems to us, both in terms of the formal definition of the geographics of religion and in terms of what scholars are actually doing in their analyses of the role of geographical phenomena in the development of religious self-understanding, that the question of social relevance lies at the heart of the fragmentation of the study of religion into a myriad of subdisciplines. In some ways, we do not wholeheartedly embrace postmodernist relativism. But if it is the case that a false dichotomy between social relevance and scholarly centrality is in different ways responsible for this fragmentation, perhaps that is because in practice scholars of religion understand their work in terms of its social relevance, however defined. Overtly or covertly, it is their criterion for adjudicating amongst subdisciplines what is and what is not properly the study of religion. Such a criterion enables them to determine which subdiscipline is likely to yield useful results in the description and explanation over time and space of the development of a particular religious tradition. The conditions predominating in any given field of study dictate which subdiscipline is more or less fruitful according to the criterion of social relevance.

Recognizing that the study of religion at once embodies and is embodied in some understanding of its social relevance helps us better to appreciate the external relations of the study of religion to other disciplines within the academy. In Wittgenstein's terms, to turn in a new way to the study of the geographics of Judaism, Christianity, and Islam is to discover fresh family resemblances among the study of religion and other areas of academic enquiry. The predominant tendency in the interpretation of Judaism, Christianity, and Islam has privileged the temporal dimension of these monotheistic traditions over against the spatial dimension. To concern oneself with the temporal dimension is to concern oneself with the way in which events shape religious self-understanding. But as we have seen, to concern oneself with the spatial dimension is to discover relatively unexplored territories in the literal, the symbolic, and the imaginative roles of geographical phenomena in the development of religious self-understanding. If we focus on the criterion of social relevance to determine the nature of the external relations of the study of religion to other academic disciplines, we see how the scholar of religion may feel just as at home in a department of geography as in a seminary or theological college. It will all depend upon the particular cultural object made the subject of description and explanation. Such considerations constitute the first steps towards a new paradigm of constructive conversation among the subdisciplines of the study of religion and between scholars of religion within departments of religion and those pursuing related interests in other academic divisions.

Change is as necessary for the preservation of civility, however defined, as it is a sign of impending barbarity, however defined. Or to put it another way, how what any scholar within religious studies does relates to what her colleagues are doing, and how what any one of these colleagues does relates to what scholars in other disciplines are doing, and to what goes on in the world beyond the Western Ivory Tower, may be seen in terms of the "splintering and

assembling in new ways" characterizing "the development of knowledge [which]
is the ongoing goal of academic research, in the humanities and in other areas
of study."[22] To paraphrase Francis Bacon, we must investigate new remedies, if
new evils are not to beset us because of time's innovations. The impossibility of
ever being on firm metaphysical and epistemological ground does not mean that
we may not conjure up medleys to meddle in metaphysical and epistemological
preconceptions. Being meddlers in matters of social relevance is not an unhappy
circumstance. Surely we do not need reminding that we are not omniscient, "and
were we indeed to become gods, no longer tethered to the local place within
which crises and troubles emerge, we would not feel the urgencies that impel
us forward."[23] By invoking the neologism "geographics" to refigure the study
of religion in terms of a rhetoric of social relevance, we are refusing to ignore
larger issues of political myopia and cultural chauvinism. At the same time, to
adopt Stanley Fish's adaptation of Alan Bloom's trope, we are recognizing that
the human mind "will always be closed, and the only question is whether we find
the form of closure it currently assumes answerable to our present urgencies."[24]
These first steps in the geographics of Judaism, Christianity, and Islam are of the
order of Gauguin's rejection of the prevailing aesthetic ideology of his day. That
we have arrived at a thoroughly decentralized understanding of what constitutes
the study of religion in the academy, in terms of both internal structure and of
external relations, seems to us not only inevitable, but exciting. In a suitably
postmodern paradox, the study of religion might thus become what theologians
used to claim as their domain—the *locus classicus* of the future of the academy.
But perhaps in this respect, as yet, "we are more advanced on the discursive
level than on the institutional."[25]

NOTES

1. The painting is certainly the most ambitious of Paul Gauguin's art and is a colossal
four meters in length.
2. Many of the remarks we make in this "Afterword" draw upon, expand, and apply
to the geographics of religion remarks made in our paper "Relativizing the Relativizers:
On the Postmodern Challenge to Human Geography," *Transactions, Institute of British
Geographers* N.S. 13 (1989):231–36.
3. See Hans-Georg Gadamer, *Truth and Method* (New York: Continuum, 1975).
4. This division of postmodernists follows Mireya Folch-Serra, "A Postmodern
Conversation," *Queen's Quarterly* 95 (1988):618–40.
5. Ibid., p. 619.
6. Stanley Fish, "Being Interdisciplinary Is So Very Hard to Do," *Profession* 89
(1989):17.
7. Richard Rorty, *Philosophy and the Mirror of Nature* (Princeton, N.J.: Princeton
University Press, 1979), p. 12.
8. Michael Dear, "The Postmodern Challenge: Reconstructing Human Geography,"
Transactions, Institute of British Geographers N.S. 13 (1988):1–12.

9. Rorty, *Philosophy and the Mirror of Nature*, p. 318.

10. Thomas Short, " 'Diversity' and 'Breaking the Disciplines': Two New Assaults on the Curriculum," *Academic Questions* 1 (1988):6–29.

11. Clifford Geertz, "Blurred Genres: The Refiguration of Social Thought," in Hazard Adams and Leroy Searle, eds., *Critical Theory since 1965* (Tallahassee: Florida State University Press, 1986), pp. 514–23.

12. At this point, let us hearken to the voices of Wittgenstein. We say "voices," because it is customary to speak of two Wittgensteins, an earlier and a later. Wittgenstein's early work, notably the *Tractatus Logico-Philosophicus* (London: Routledge & Kegan Paul, 1922), constitutes in both form and content one of the most succinct manifestos of modernist rationalist philosophizing. The *Tractatus* comprises seven propositions, the first six of which are elaborated upon in further propositions numbered in decimal form. Wittgenstein's guiding principle, based on the so-called New Logic of Bertrand Russell and Gottlob Frege, is to show how the truth or falsity of a complex proposition is a logical function of the truth or falsity of the simple propositions out of which it is composed. Language is reduced to symbolic relationships of the kind characterizing mathematical functions. Wittgenstein's point is to define the limits of language, and in particular of philosophy, and to establish the nature of the relationship between language and reality. Central to the whole enterprise is the idea that words have meaning when they correspond, on a one-to-one basis, to objects in the world. The more complex the state of affairs pictured, the more complex the proposition picturing it. None of this might seem significant were it not for the final proposition of the *Tractatus*: "What we cannot speak about we must pass over in silence." What must we pass over in silence? The picture theory of meaning disallows us from speaking with confidence about all questions of value—aesthetic, ethical, or religious—which are perforce matters of interpretation. Put another way, if Wittgenstein's early work epitomizes the modernist perspective, it also reveals the total bankruptcy of modernist rationalism when it comes to interpreting the ambiguities and nuances of life.

13. See Ludwig Wittgenstein, *Philosophical Investigation* (London: Macmillan, 1953).

14. Wittgenstein, *Philosophical Investigations*, p. 320. For an illuminating discussion of the role of Wittgenstein's imagery, including the image of the thread, in shaping our appropriation of his ideas, see W.J.T. Mitchell, "Wittgenstein's Imagery and What It Tells Us," *New Literary History* 19 (1988):361–70.

15. See Stephen Toulmin, *An Examination of the Place of Reason in Ethics* (Cambridge: Cambridge University Press, 1950); and *The Uses of Argument* (Chicago: Cambridge University Press, 1958).

16. Toulmin, *Examination*, p. 114.

17. Toulmin, *Uses of Argument*, p. 38.

18. See Robert L. Cohn, *The Shape of Sacred Space: Four Biblical Studies* (Chico, Calif · Scholars Press, 1981); Belden C. Lane, *Landscapes of the Sacred: Geography and Narrative in American Spirituality* (New York: Paulist Press, 1988); and Michael M. J. Fischer, *Iran: From Religious Dispute to Revolution* (Cambridge, Mass.: Harvard University Press, 1980).

19. See S. M. Bhardwaj and G. Rinschede, eds., *Pilgrimage in World Religions* (Berlin: Dietrich Reimer Verlag, 1988).

20. Anne Buttimer, "Geography, Humanism, and Global Concern," *Annals of the American Association of Geographers* 80 (1990):7.

21. Ibid., p. 20.

22. Barbara Hernstein Smith, "Presidential Address 1988: Limelight: Reflections on a Public Year," *Publications of the Modern Language Association* 104:3 (May 1989):290. The emphasis is in the original.

23. Fish, "Being Interdisciplinary," p. 21.

24. Ibid.

25. Dominick LaCapra, "On the Line: Between History and Criticism," *Profession* 89 (1989):5.

Selected Bibliography

Altmann, Alexander, ed. *Biblical Motifs: Origins and Transformations*. Cambridge: Harvard University Press, 1966.

Bachelard, Gaston. *La Poétique de l'espace*. Paris: Presses Universitaires de France, 1957.

Bhardwaj, S. M., and G. Rinschede, eds. *Pilgrimage in World Religions*. Berlin: Dietrich Reimer Verlag, 1988.

Brueggemann, Walter. *The Prophetic Imagination*. Philadelphia: Fortress Press, 1978.

———. *The Land: Place as Gift, Promise, and Challenge in Biblical Faith*. Philadelphia: Fortress Press, 1977.

Buttimer, Anne. "Geography, Humanism, and Global Concern." *Annals of the American Association of Geographers* 80 (1990): 1–36.

Butzer, Karl W., ed. *Dimensions of Human Geography*. Chicago: University of Chicago Department of Geography Research Papers, 1978.

Campo, Juan E. *The Other Side of Paradise: Explorations into the Religious Meanings of Domestic Space in Islam*. Columbia: University of South Carolina Press, 1990.

Clifford, Richard J. *The Cosmic Mountain in Canaan and the Old Testament*. Cambridge, Mass.: Harvard University Press, 1972.

Cohn, Robert L. *The Shape of Sacred Space: Four Biblical Studies*. Chico, Calif.: Scholars Press, 1981.

Collins, J. *Semeia 14: Apocalypse: The Morphology of a Genre.* Missoula, Mont.: Scholars Press, 1979.

Curry-Roper, Janel M. "Contemporary Christian Eschatologies and Their Relation to Environmental Stewardship." *Professional Geographer* 42 (1990): 157–69.

Davies, W. D. *The Gospel and the Land: Early Christianity and Jewish Territorial Doctrine.* Berkeley: University of California Press, 1974.

Deskins, D. R., et al. *Geographic Humanism: Analysis and Social Action.* Ann Arbor: University of Michigan Department of Geography Publications, 1977.

Dougherty, James. *The Fivesquare City: The City in the Religious Imagination.* Notre Dame, Ind.: University of Notre Dame Press, 1980.

Eliade, Mircea. *The Sacred and the Profane.* Trans. Willard R. Trask. New York: Harper and Row, 1961.

Fischer, Michael M. J. *Iran: From Religious Dispute to Revolution.* Cambridge, Mass.: Harvard University Press, 1980.

Himmelfarb, Martha. *Tours of Hell: An Apocalyptic Form in Jewish and Christian Literature.* Philadelphia: University of Pennsylvania Press, 1983.

Isaac, Erich. "Religion, Landscape and Space." *Landscape* 9 (1959): 14–18.

Janzen, W. "Geography of Faith: A Christian Perspective on the Meaning of Places." *Studies in Religion/Sciences Religieuses* 3 (1973): 166–82.

Kopf, Ulrich. "Kirchengeschichte und Geographie." *Zeitschrift für Theologie und Kirche* 77 (1980): 42–68.

Lane, Belden C. *Landscapes of the Sacred: Geography and Narrative in American Spirituality.* New York: Paulist Press, 1988.

Lincoln, Bruce. *Discourse and the Construction of Society: Comparative Studies of Myth, Ritual, and Classification.* New York and Oxford: Oxford University Press, 1989.

Long, David Edwin. *The Hajj Today: A Survey of the Contemporary Mecca Pilgrimage.* Albany: State University of New York Press, 1979.

McDannell, Colleen, and Bernard Lang. *Heaven: A History.* New Haven, Conn.: Yale University Press, 1988.

McNally, Dennis. *Sacred Space: An Aesthetic for the Liturgical Environment.* Bristol, U.K.: Wyndham Hall Press, 1985.

Meinig, D. W., ed. *The Interpretation of Ordinary Landscapes: Geographical Essays.* New York: Oxford University Press, 1979.

Mol, Hans. *Meaning and Place: An Introduction to the Social Scientific Study of Religion.* New York: Pilgrim Press, 1983.

Nash, Roderick Frazier. *The Rights of Nature: A History of Environmental Ethics.* Madison: University of Wisconsin Press, 1989.

Peters, F. E. *Jerusalem and Mecca.* New York: New York University Press, 1986.

Rahman, Fazlur. *Islam.* Chicago: University of Chicago Press, 1980.

———. *Major Themes of the Qur'an.* Minneapolis: Bibliotheca Islamica, 1980.

Schimmel, Annemarie. *And Muhammad Is His Messenger.* Chapel Hill: University of North Carolina Press, 1985.

———. *Mystical Dimensions of Islam.* Chapel Hill: University of North Carolina Press, 1975.

Scott, Jamie S., and Paul Simpson-Housley. "Relativizing the Relativizers: On the Postmodern Challenge to Human Geography." *Transactions, Institute of British Geographers* N.S. 14 (1989): 231–36.

Shiner, Larry E. "Sacred Space, Profane Space, Human Space." *Journal of the American Academy of Religion* 40 (1972): 425–36.

Smith, Jonathan Z. *To Take Place: Toward Theory in Ritual.* Chicago: University of Chicago Press, 1987.

———. *Map Is Not Territory: Studies in the History of Religions.* Leiden, Netherlands: E. J. Brill, 1978.

Sopher, David. *Geography of Religions.* Englewood Cliffs, N.J.: Prentice-Hall, 1967.

Tuan, Yi-Fu. *Space and Place: The Perspective of Experience.* Minneapolis: University of Minnesota Press, 1977.

———. *Topophilia: A Study of Environmental Perception, Attitudes, and Values.* Englewood Cliffs, N.J.: Prentice-Hall, 1974.

Turner, Harold W. *From Temple to Meeting House: The Phenomenology and Theology of Places of Worship.* The Hague: Mouton Publishers, 1979.

Turner, Victor. *Dramas, Fields, and Metaphors.* Ithaca, N.Y.: Cornell University Press, 1974.

Van der Leeuw, Gerardus. *Religion in Essence and Manifestation.* 2 vols. Gloucester, Mass.: Peter Smith, 1967.

Index

About the Contributors

RONALD BORDESSA teaches in the Department of Geography at Atkinson College, York University. He is co-author of *Wonderland through the Looking Glass: Culture and Planning in International Recreation.*

JUAN EDUARDO CAMPO teaches in the Department of Religious Studies, the University of California at Santa Barbara. He is working at present on a book, *The Other Sides of Paradise: Explorations into the Religious Meanings of Domestic Space in Islam.*

MICHAEL J. FISCHER teaches in the Department of Anthropology, Rice University, Houston. He has been a fellow of the Woodrow Wilson International Center for Scholars in Washington, and he is the author of *Iran: From Religious Dispute to Revolution.*

ROGER FRIEDLAND teaches in the Department of Sociology, the University of California at Santa Barbara. He is co-author, with Richard Hecht, of *To Rule Jerusalem* (forthcoming).

RICHARD D. HECHT teaches in the Department of Religious Studies, the University of California at Santa Barbara. He is co-author, with Roger Friedland, of *To Rule Jerusalem* (forthcoming).

MARTHA HIMMELFARB teaches in the Department of Religion, Princeton University. She is the author of *Tours of Hell: An Apocalyptic Form in Jewish and Christian Literature.*

YOSSI KATZ teaches in the Department of Geography, Bar-Ilan University. His most recent publication, "Principles in the Construction of Jewish Neighbourhoods Outside the Old City of Jerusalem in the Years 1860–1914," was published in *Mehkarim Bageografiyah Yishivit-Historit Shel Erets Israel.*

ELLEN ROSS teaches in the Department of Theology, Boston College. She is the author of several articles in the *Downside Review* and elsewhere on the role and status of women in the Christian tradition.

ANNEMARIE SCHIMMEL teaches in the History of Religion Department, Harvard University. She is the author of numerous books and articles on Islam, including *And Muhammad Is His Messenger* and *Mystical Dimensions of Islam.*

JAMIE S. SCOTT teaches in the Division of Humanities, York University. He is co-editor of *Cities of God: Faith, Politics and Pluralism in Judaism, Christianity and Islam.*

PAUL SIMPSON-HOUSLEY teaches in the Department of Religion, Lawrence College. *The Book of Revelation: Apocalypse and Empire* is his most recent book.

LEONARD L. THOMPSON teaches in the Department of Geography, York University. He is co-editor of *Geography and Literature: A Meeting of the Disciplines.*